The **Faker's Guide** to the **CLASSICS**

EVERYTHING YOU NEED TO KNOW ABOUT THE BOOKS YOU SHOULD HAVE READ (BUT DIDN'T)

Lyons Press is an imprint of Globe Pequot Press.

Text design: Sheryl Kober
Layout: Casey Shain
Project editor: Ellen Urban

Library of Congress Cataloging-in-Publication Data is available on file.

ISBN 978-0-7627-8540-7

Printed in the United States of America

10 9 8 7 6 5 4 3 2 1

Although the author and publisher have endeavored to ensure that the information provided herein is complete and accurate, they shall not be held responsible for loss or damage of any nature or negative reactions from people with broken satire and parody meters. Those should be taken for immediate repair to a shop that specializes in intelligence, irony, sarcasm, and subtlety. At-home performance can be improved by reducing your intake of sitcoms and reality TV.

I dedicate this to the one I love. When I find him, that is. Hey, Darcy, if things don't work out with Lizzie, gimme a call. How about you, Ladislaw? Anyone? (But not you, Humbert Humbert. You creep me out.)

Contents

INTRODUCTION

Spoiler Alert!
This book is one giant spoiler. Open it, and you *will* see details of what happens in each work, their endings laid out nice and neat like church clothes. But that's the genius of it, really. You're not in high school anymore, so why force yourself to maintain a reading list that would bore even hardcore lit majors to uncontrollable tears? Oh, Dostoyevsky, why must you torment us so? However, if you are in high school, do all of your assigned reading—even the really long and boring ones. It's good for you, like spinach and the dentist.

But that's where *The Faker's Guide to the Classics* comes in handy. Some of these texts are painfully dull on their own. Who wants to add to that by reading even drier and more boring synopses and discussion points? Let's be real. You don't have time for thousand-page tomes anymore. Even if you enjoy many of the classics, some just won't strike your fancy or even mildly interest you. For those books, a quick and dirty overview of the nitty-gritty is what you need. You've got the plot and ending right here. No need to wonder who exactly Doctor Zhivago is anymore . . . just flip to page 58. See? Easy peasy.

Please note: I am an avowed lover of the classics—or at least lots of them. The inspiration for this book struck in a moment of weakness when I wondered whether to read some of the great but endlessly depressing Russian novels. I wanted to know what they were about and how they ended, but I had no desire to read them. Even Wikipedia takes too long. Ten pages of summary to tell us that the brothers Karamazov all hate each other and their dad? Uh, no thanks. I wanted someone to tell me straight-up what happens without a lot of unnecessary details or obscure plot distractions. Tragically, as the author of this book, I've since had to read those Russian ~~bricks~~ masterpieces. I took some bullets for you. Don't let my agony go to waste. Strangely, some people actually enjoy Russian literature, but I am not of their number. Others don't like gothic novels or Victorian lit, which I devour whenever I can. As with all literature, it's a matter of taste. Some books just taste better than others. Nomnomnom . . . *<burp>*. Excuse me.

Disclaimer

The Faker's Guide to the Classics takes absolutely zero responsibility for any homework assignments or book reports that might lazily derive from this work, or the jaw-dropping grades that might ensue.

No-duh Statements

1. Yes, authors write fiction about events that happened a really long time ago. As in, years before the writers were little fetuses doing the backstroke in amniotic fluid. James Fenimore Cooper? Not alive during the time of *The Last of the Mohicans*. He was born in 1789, and *Mohicans* wasn't published until 1826, about seventy years after the story's events. A little bit of a time difference.

2. Historical fiction isn't history, which means you can't always believe a writer's creative and artistic version of historical events. Take, for instance, *The Crucible*. Oh, yes, the Salem witch trials happened, but there was no revenge plot from a jilted lover. Sorry to burst that bubble. Hey, even Arthur Miller admits that he ignored facts in favor of fiction: "A playwright has no debt of literalness to history." So you're saying that there aren't really dinosaurs in the center of the Earth? Great. I just put down a deposit on an all-inclusive Center of the Earth cruise.

If you were hoping to read some of the classics to help with a history test, *bzzzt!* You lose! So drop the notion that the classics present an accurate portrayal of people and events. Authors have to spice things up a bit, don't they? Toss in a few extramarital affairs, kill off some people who don't die until much later . . . it's all fair game.

3. Movies aren't usually a good representation of what's in the book. In fact, they frequently change enough material that they shouldn't really be described as "based upon the book" at all. It's more like: "The characters have the same names, and the events are somewhat similar,

but nothing else is even close." Or, if you like: "The director thought he could improve on a time-tested classic but only succeeded in making a total mess of it." If you were hoping to pass a literature class by watching the movie instead of the book, you're in a whole lotta hot water, bud. Most books-to-movies aren't even close.

Which reminds me: Thank you, Walt Disney, for massacring *The Jungle Book.* (page 119) Didn't even bother reading it, did you? (He really didn't, and he told the writers not to crack the binding on the book, either: "The first thing I want you to do is not to read it.")

Banning Is Fun!

Well, kids, it's time to dig out those dusty old doorstoppers and do some dull, dry reading before your English lit test in, oh, four hours. These books are *soooo* snooze-worthy it's a wonder anyone can sit through an entire novel without dying of boredom. I mean, it's astounding that people in the past read at all, right?

Heck no! Most of these boring old classics were incendiary in their day—and not just when some book banner tossed one on the fire. Get past the archaic language, and you'll find a treasure trove of naughtiness. Looking for a bit of sexytimes between the pages? Trot over to Canterbury, where the tales bubble with outrageous acts like tricking someone into kissing a bare derriere and scorching someone else's backside with a red-hot poker. *Yikes!*

For a splattering of violence, *Lord of the Flies* should hit the spot: rampage, murder, kids killing kids, society devolving into chaos. Why, it's almost like Golding was commenting on and condemning murder and war . . . nah. Any book that portrays violence must celebrate it, *non?* To make things more interesting, let's ban books for contradictory reasons. Say with Steinbeck's *Of Mice and Men,* which holds the dubious honor of being challenged by both the KKK *and* the group 100 Black United. Y'know, it takes talent to make *everyone* hate you. Bravo, Johnny boy!

1984 by George Orwell

Published: 1949
Category: novel (dystopian)
Banned for: irony. Oppressive governments ban a book satirizing oppressive governments? Oh, how it burns.

"BIG BROTHER IS WATCHING YOU."

So Big Brother is Hall and Oates? Huh.
That does explain a lot . . .

Let's talk Newspeak, people. What's that? Why, it's the dumbing down of the English language to control how people think. It's simple. We cut out complicated words and phrases like *independence* and *thinking for yourself* in favor of *yes* and *whatever you say.* Synonyms? Toss 'em. No more deciding between large, humongous, or gargantuan. Nope, now it's just morebig. Consider how grades will improve on spelling tests. Books like *The Faker's Guide to the Classics* aren't just great anymore, they're gooder. (Why does that word sound so familiar? Oh, right . . . because people say this all the freaking time. Wanna place your bets on when Newspeak will grace Webster's officially? I got five monies on 2015.) *Faker's* is gooder than that, even. Perhaps goodest?

And so we enter the blissful future of the year 1984. Wait, that can't be right. 1984 isn't the future. That was thirty years ago. Also 2 + 2 = 5? Um, Orwell isn't very good at math, is he? Anyway, after numerous wars, three superstates emerge: Oceania (USA, UK, and allies), Eastasia (China and co.), and Eurasia (USSR and Europe). In Oceania, The Party holds the power. ALL THE POWER. At its head stands Big Brother, the friendly neighborhood dictator sporting a cute little Hitler 'stache. Doesn't it just feel like family?

Big Brother can be a tad controlling, but it's all good. Really. Those telescreens tracking everyone's movement 24/7/365 allow the government to be like The Police (watching every breath you take, every move you make) to protect you from yourself, of course. Big Brother loves you goodest. They know when you're sleeping, and they know when you're awake. They especially know when you're being bad—so toe the line, and no one gets hurt.

Our protagonist, Winston Smith, works for ~~Wikipedia~~ the Ministry of Truth (Minitrue) rewriting history by changing news articles and creating *unpersons* by making people disappear from written record so they never existed. (How easy is it to disappear, say, the Kardashians?) Isn't that cheating? Not really because what *is* "truth"? And what *is* "is"? Trust the totalitarian government because they love you morest. Let us welcome our great mustachioed overlords.

A bit of a rebel, Winston writes in a diary about how much he hates Big Brother. Ooh, so dangerous. I bet he even litters. *<gasp>* Unfortunately, even thoughts can hurt you, and bad ones are execution-worthy. So Winston writes in the only spot in his entire apartment where the ~~CCTV~~ telescreens can't see him: the corner of his living room. Oh, yeah, such a bad boy.

Enter Julia. At first Winnie thinks she's with the enemy since she's part of the ultra-loyal Junior Anti-Sex League. (Quite a few men still consider that enemy behavior.) But she's just pretending to be a goodthink. Good one, Julia! They'll never see through that ruse. Soon our secret rebels have a secret love affair. They even arrange to meet each other alone, away from the prying eyes of Big Brother. ~~Scandalous!~~ Er, lessgood.

Their friend O'Brien, a fellow badthink and part of the rebellious Brotherhood, would never do anything to betray them—until he does. Obviously. He's actually a leader of the Thought Police, who have been watching Winston for years. O'Brien separates the couple and drags them off to Miniluv (Ministry of Love), where they torture him so he'll doublethink, which is kind of like believing that "War is peace. Freedom is slavery. Ignorance is strength."

After a bit more torture in dreaded Room 101, Winnie the Goo finally caves. All it takes is the threat of putting rats on his face, and he cries Big Brother. But now Winston is chugging the Kool-Aid. He runs into Julia a few months later, and they're both all, "We used to do the nasty, but the thought of touching you is pretty much disgusting. What were we thinking?"

Awkward.

George Orwell really knew how to tick off governments. He actually started out working for the government as a policeman in Burma. Later, he turned to less officially sanctioned activities like fighting Nationalists in the Spanish Civil War. You could say his interest in social reform and/or anarchy sounds oddly familiar, almost like he had a teacher with likeminded philosophies. Perhaps, oh, Aldous Huxley (page 23), who taught French while the young Eric Blair (Orwell's real name) was a schoolboy at Eton.

The Adventures of Huckleberry Finn by Mark Twain

Published: 1884
Category: novel (picaresque)
Banned for: the word "nigger," but some nice professor at Auburn kindly bowdlerized a version for us. Halle-*[effing]*-lujah! It takes *forever* to cut out all those offensive words using safety scissors. Stupid rounded tips.

"Tom told me what his plan was, and I see in a minute it was worth fifteen of mine for style, and would make Jim just as free a man as mine would, and maybe get us all killed besides. So I was satisfied, and said we would waltz in on it."

So true, Huck. Nothing is worth doing unless there's imminent danger and it's done with style.

Here's what you missed in our last episode, *The Adventures of Tom Sawyer:* Huck's BFF, Tom Sawyer, lives to get in trouble, but this time trouble means luck when they find some robbers' super-secret stash of gold! Huck can't use any of his Benjamins, though, because killjoy grownups chuck it in the bank to keep it from his drunk, good-for-nothing Pap. Now on with the show.

Huck hates bathing and getting all prissied up like a sissy-boy by the Widow Douglas, who took him in, but he needs a good cover story for anything that happens after he joins Tom Sawyer's new gang of robbers. Gold in the bank just ain't enough bling, yo.

While they're plotting their steal-y fun, Pap staggers into town to snatch Huck's ill-gotten gains. Lucky for Hucky, a new judge also comes to town. Old white dude not only knows how the world works, he can fix things—ALL THE THINGS. Including Huck's pappy. This can only end well. Judge tries to put Pap through rehab, but the drunk says, "No, no, no." Apparently daddy thinks he's fine. (He won't go go go. . . .) When Pap inevitably washes out, he kidnaps his kid and holds him ransom. Can you say daddy issues?

What's a devilishly smart boy to do when a mean drunk ties him up and leaves him alone in a secluded cabin? Fake his own death, of course. Huck slaughters a pig and slathers blood all over the place, obviously improving the décor—though Huck might have thought about making it look like dear old dad chopped up his kid then tossed him in the river. Or sticking the pig's head on a spike and worshipping it, but who does that anymore? (See page 132.)

Huck hightails it to an island in the Mississippi River so he can watch the neighbors search for his body. But Huck isn't alone. *Dun dun dunnnn!* Whatever will he do?

Not much when he realizes it's just Widow Douglas's escaped slave, Jim. Silly slave, freedom's for whites. Jim's a ~~good guy~~ decent slave, but what a terrible, awful thing he's done by running away. Staging your own death and framing your dad for murder is one thing, but helping an escaped slave? That's just wrong. If they can get Jim down the ol' Miss to where it meets the Ohio River, Jim can chug north to the free states. So they sail downriver—except they kinda miss their turn. Someone really ought to put up a sign.

When a steamboat crashes their little raft, it's every man for himself. Huck ends up with the Grangerfords, some nice country folk with a friendly blood feud against a neighboring clan. When the vendetta erupts into full-on war, survey says: Get out fast, kid! Well, whaddaya know? Jim shows up just then with their repaired raft. Such convenient timing.

They pick up some ~~con artist~~ aristocrat hitch-boaters, and the shysters get themselves and our adventurers in hot water when they pretend to be the uncles of some particularly wealthy girls who were just orphaned. But then the real relatives show up, and hijinks ensue. They all escape, but the con men then sell Jim to some farmers. *What?* They can't sell Jim; he's a huma—

Dammit, Jim's a slave, not a human being. But surprise, surprise, the people who buy Jim are actually Tom Sawyer's aunt and uncle. What a co-inky dink. They confuse Huck for the real Tom Sawyer, though. Convenient again since Huck knows a thing or two about his bestie. When Tom shows up a few days later, Huck debriefs him on the fun: Huck is Tom, and Tom gets to be his own brother, Sid. Poor Jim's still in chains, though, so the boys plot an overly complicated escape for their friend. The plan succeeds (sort of), but Tom gets shot in the leg. Instead of bolting for freedom like a sane person would do, Jim helps Tom and ends up back in chains . . .

. . . until the next day when Tom reveals that the Widow Douglas has died. Sad. Except not really because she freed Jim in her will. Which Tom knew the whole time, but he was just playin'. No harm done, right? Also, as long as we're making overly convenient yet poorly timed disclosures, turns out Jim found Huck's Pap dead earlier but neglected to tell Huck. Which is . . . considerate? Huck decides he's done with being "sivilized," so he's heading out West.

Mark Twain (a.k.a. Samuel Clemens) made a whole bunch of moolah off his über-successful *Adventures* series—and then lost it all plus plenty more on bad investments. No wonder he became such a curmudgeonly old coot.

The Aeneid by Virgil

Published: 19 BC
Category: epic poem

> *"Roman, remember by your strength to rule*
> *Earth's peoples—for your arts are to be these:*
> *To pacify, to impose the rule of law,*
> *To spare the conquered, battle down the proud."*

Huh. I didn't realize that beating them into submission was part of "sparing" the conquered. I must be using the wrong Latin dictionary.

So the mean Greeks destroyed Troy over a girl because men are idiots. What else is new? But seriously, if you want to know what happens to the Greeks after the ~~Condom~~ Trojan War, go ask Odysseus (page 162). They might have had it just a *tad* worse than the Trojans, considering that Odysseus is the only one of his gang that made it home alive. So what are the Trojans supposed to do after being decimated by a giant carousel animal? Tuck tail and hide. Well, that and found Rome, which will conquer Greece and the rest of the known world. Might take a few centuries, but payback's a beeyotch, innit?

Aeneas gathers the beleaguered survivors of Troy and sets out to find a new home. After chatting with the Oracle of Apollo, they sail for their ancient homeland: Crete. But then they get there and—oops, wrong homeland. Everyone back in the boats! We meant Italy. Yes, we're sure this time. Don't worry, guys. Aeneas will get us there safely. But we should probably stop for supplies on this nice little island. Please ignore the ominous black clouds. So the men get out to hunt and collect water. It's all going just ducky until—hey, look at those funny birds. Wow. They are butt ugly and smell bad. Wait, those aren't birds, they're ~~Latin teachers~~ harpies! RUN!

Great. The crazy bird ladies ate all the food the men caught. Now the Trojans will go hungry, and not just because the reigning mean girl cursed them all with hunger. Once they set sail again, the gods start meddling. Fortunately, Aeneas's mommy, the MILF Venus, is watching out for him. But then Juno tells the wind god to blow them—off course, you perv. They end up in Carthage.

The goddesses come to a truce: They'll let Aeneas stay for a bit in the company of the ~~singer~~ queen, Dido. She's kinda hot, so they get their duet on.

Aeneas: I can handle this gig for a bit, but, lover, I gotta book it at some point, so don't go falling in love with me.

Dido: *(crosses fingers)* Yeah, right. Like I'd ever love a jerk like you. So what color do you think would be best for the draperies in the ~~baby's~~ currently unoccupied room over there?

Everything's going great for a while, but then the other gods—who, let me remind you, are immortal—start getting impatient. So Jupiter sends his bike messenger, Mercury.

Mercury: *(poke poke)* Aeneas, wake up. We need to talk.

Aeneas: Five more minutes.

Mercury: I said, get. up. *NOW*. You've had your fun, but it's time to go, son. Don't worry about Dido. ~~Eminem will sample one of her songs and launch her career.~~ She'll be fine.

Except she wasn't. By this point, she's wondering why she got out of bed at all. Her twu wuv is gone. Aeneas was kind enough to leave his sword with her, though, so she takes it, plus all the other crap he never hung up or folded and put away, and builds up a huge pyre. Uh oh. This isn't looking good.

Dido: Aeneas, I hate you! But not really because I love you!

OK, so maybe she was a little bonkers. Back at sea, Aeneas *et al.* get blown off course to Sicily. They'd made a pit stop there before and received a nice welcome, so when they disembark this time, the women set them on fire. I mean, yeah, the men keep getting lost and won't listen when you try to backseat steer the ship, but fire?

The gods really want their Romulan city, though, so Jupiter dispatches a nice rainstorm to extinguish the fires. They lose four ships, so Aeneas lets anyone who wants to stay behind. *Ciao!* But guess what, suckas. This time they actually make it to Italy! Only took them seven years. Odysseus still has three years to go (page 162). Chump.

They make sure things are good with the new neighbors first this time, and, to make extra double sure, Aeneas takes a trip to the Underworld where he chats with some old friends. They tell him how cool his city will be in a few centuries and all the great stuff Romans will do. Blah blah blah. While he's down there, he sees Dido. But she doesn't want to see him. Awkward. Dude, she *just* committed suicide because you abandoned her. Give her some space. A century or two might help.

Other than getting the stink-eye from an angry ex, things are going well. You know what that means. Here comes Juno, right on cue, to stir up trouble. Seriously, lady, what's your deal? It's the usual suspects: grudges from the Trojan War and early-onset anger that Rome will stomp on all her favorite cities. Yadda yadda. She incites the Latinos to start war, always a good card to play when going for the jackpot. Too bad for Juno, though, because her team loses, and—

The End, er, *beginning* of the Roman Empire. Ta da!

The Roman poet **Virgil** was a bit of a perfectionist. Unfortunately he didn't live long enough to perfect *The Aeneid*. So, when he told people to burn the manuscript after his death because he hadn't finished it, they ignored him.

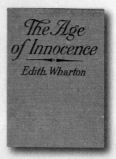

The Age of Innocence
by Edith Wharton

Published: 1920
Category: novel (serialized)

"I'm sick of the hypocrisy that would bury alive a woman of her age if her husband prefers to live with

harlots. . . . Women ought to be free—as free as we are,' he declared, making a discovery of which he was too irritated to measure the terrific consequences."

Noble, but only a woman could put those words into a man's mouth.

Newland Archer, a wealthy young lawyer, is engaged to nice girl May Welland. Ah, too cute—young love and all that barf—and they're both pretty happy about it. Sounds like the perfect match among Gilded Age New York society, doesn't it?

Not for long! May's cousin Countess Ellen Olenska arrives in New York, freshly separated from her philandering husband, a Polish count, and, boy, is she scandalous. *Va va voom!* She wears revealing clothes and behaves far too informally for polite society. (Not the ankles!) Plus, people are whispering rumors of affairs.

Archer, like any red-blooded man, finds the countess intriguing because (a) she isn't boring and (b) she's rather carefree, which sounds like the same thing but (c) is a lot more fun. Trouble is, he gets tired of hanging around his dull but proper fiancée. May is exactly what society dictates a woman should be: agreeable, demure, polite, and pretty much sans opinion or any sense of self. When an engaging and lively woman enters the picture, Archer doesn't stand a chance.

The Welland family tries to bring Ellen back to the starchy fold by dragging her along to social engagements—because that always works—where of course she scandalizes everyone. A woman who thinks for herself? I never! Ellen decides that she wants to divorce the count. Archer's all for it—except not. Choices, choices: support a friend, cave to the in-laws, have an affair?

All of a sudden it hits him: He loves Ellen. You don't say. So, smart cookie, he runs away from temptation to, um, Florida to join May and her parents and cajole them into moving the wedding forward. ~~Because I'm totally in love with your cousin~~. No reason. Also a smart cookie, May suspects something's up, but Archer swears he's in love with just her. Aw, so sweet. *Big fat liar*, but sweet. When he goes back to New York, he tells Ellen that, nope, he really loves her. *Oh Archie.*

So Newland and May marry because he'll totally forget about temptation waiting in the wings once she puts a ring on it. When they get back from their honeymoon, Archie settles into being a husband . . . and feels fondness only for Ellen. Sure, uh huh. When he runs into her again—*whoosh!*—the passion returns with a vengeance because the guy's a friggin' magpie. *Shiny!* Turns out the two-timing count asked Ellen to come back, but she said nothin' doin'. Just as she and Archie decide to get it on, Ellen announces she's returning to Europe. Archie finds out why after a farewell party May throws for cousin Ellen: May is preggers, which she told her dear cousin a few weeks before. May might be dull and boring, but she's no fool.

Years pass, and the couple has three kids. Then May dies of pneumonia. Archie and his sons plan a trip to Europe, which includes visiting the countess. *Oooh?* May is dead, after all. But Archer sends the boys without him, happy to dwell on memories of the past. She's not so shiny anymore, probably old and gross. With cankles. Memories retain youth better than any wrinkle cream on the market, ladies. Trust me.

Edith Wharton's parents, George and Lucretia Jones, threw the coolest parties and built the bestest houses. They're also the original Joneses of keeping up with the Joneses, so little Edie knew a thing or two about kowtowing to boring old New York society. Take that, suckas.

Alice's Adventures in Wonderland by Lewis Carroll

Published: 1865
Category: novel (children's)
Banned for: talking animals—cute except in China (ironically) where Alice and her animal friends were banned. Perhaps someone should mention that to Napoleon (page 13).

"If you drink much from a bottle marked 'poison' it is almost certain to disagree with you, sooner or later."

And so we begin the long and cherished literary tradition of heroines too stupid to live. Thanks, Lutwidge. Thanks a lot.

Young Alice is dozing as her sister reads to her—*yawn*—when, out of nowhere, a talking white rabbit runs past. Her first thought? *I should follow that unnatural creature to see where it goes.* So she follows it straight down a rabbit hole. *Wheee!*

She finally hits ~~rock~~ bottom in a hallway with a Barbie-size door at the end, plus a table with a key, and some odd food and drink labeled EAT ME and DRINK ME. Which she does because drinking unknown liquids from strange containers is never a bad idea.

She drinks then shrinks (sound familiar, guys?) only to realize that she forgot to grab the key. *D'oh!* Now she has to eat some weird cake, which embiggens her. But then she realizes that she drank all the small juice, so no more shrinky dinky. What's a dumb blonde with an eating disorder and dependency issues to do? She starts to bawl, and ends up shrinking, only to be swept away in an ocean of her own tears. Don't you hate when that happens? So embarrassing.

She finds her way ashore, where she runs into the White Rabbit again. [Insert your own innuendo/drug reference here.] At his house, she finds more strange food and drink. Somebody has addiction issues, so of course she gobbles them up. This time, though, when she drinks, she grows gargantuan, which bites. Can't even trust food to do one thing and drink another. What kind of crazypants world is this?

One with large chain-smoking insects, apparently. She meets the Caterpillar, who is smoking a ~~bong~~ hookah while lounging on a large mushroom. They have a semantics argument, which bugs the bug, so off he storms. But not before telling her to do 'shrooms. Dumb blonde still hasn't learned her lesson, so she nibbles the magic mushroom and shrinks again. Then she spins it around and takes a bite from the other side to make herself big again. Poly dysmorphia, anyone?

Next she meets a kitteh that speaks in riddles and has body parts that randomly disappear. Totally normal. After messing with her scrambled-egg brains for a bit, the Cheshire Cat directs her to the Mad Hatter's place for a tea party. Every little girl's favorite activity, right? Kitteh evaporates into a floating grin as he informs Alice that everyone in Wonderland—including her—is mad.

You don't say.

Alice continues to the home of the less-than-sane Mad Hatter. Apparently, pissing off Time is not the best idea, as Hatter and friends discovered when they became stuck in perpetual teatime. They're an even crazier lot—possible!—so she heads back to the forest, where she finds a door leading to the hallway where she started. Now that she's mastered the binge-purge process, she finally passes through the mini door . . .

. . . into a garden where the Queen of Hearts is ~~cheating at~~ playing croquet with a flamingo mallet and a hedgehog ball (not that kind of ball, perv). The Cheshire Cat pops back in for a chat with Alice, who complains about the queen. Probably not a good idea if you want to keep your head, Alice dear. The queen wants to behead basically her entire kingdom. Keeps things entertaining—and awash in her favorite color. Matters get even more ridiculous when the Knave of Hearts goes on trial for stealing the queen's tarts. Stacked deck, anyone?

Then Alice wakes up next to her sister, who is still reading aloud.

Yep, it was all a dream. Total copout, but take solace in knowing that little Alice is seriously going to need a real "shrink" if any of this is coming from her own psyche. Oh, and just say no, kids—except to Johnson & Johnson and Bristol-Myers Squibb. Always do what the nice doctor says.

Lewis Carroll (a.k.a. Charles Lutwidge Dodgson) liked kids more than grownups. *Like,* liked them. But no one who knew him worried much about his fascination with young children, especially girls. The series of photographs he took of them *au naturel* just explored and documented childhood innocence. Nothing sinister here, folks. Move along.

Animal Farm by George Orwell

Published: 1945
Category: novel (dystopian)
Banned for: politics . . . with bonus points for being banned in the entire Eastern Bloc. Bet you didn't see that one coming.

"Four legs good, two legs bad." Then later: "Four legs good, two legs better."

Oh, Napoleon, you're so great at the whole propaganda thing. Have you ever thought of going into politics?

This little piggie lived in the barnyard, this little piggie was chased off the farm, this little piggie became pork chops, this little piggie got drunk, and this little piggie demanded, "Kill the traitors!" until everyone else was dead. What do you mean, it's not that kind of fairy story?

The ancient boar Old Major calls a meeting among the animals of Manor Farm. He tells them, "Mr. Jones, your lazy, drunken farmer, is like a parasite, as are all who walk on two legs!" He strikes up the cry of revolution! Then he buys the farm—metaphorically, that is—three days later. He was old. What do you expect?

Two young pigs—Snowball and Napoleon—see their chance, and they take control of the revolt, putting themselves in positions of power. They take Old Major's ideas and turn them into a full-blown philosophy, complete with commandments and ~~Marxism~~ maxims. The Seven Commandments of Animalism:

1. Whatever goes upon two legs is an enemy.
2. Whatever goes upon four legs, or has wings, is a friend.
3. No animal shall wear clothes.
4. No animal shall sleep in a bed.
5. No animal shall drink alcohol.
6. No animal shall kill any other animal.
7. All animals are equal.

Snowball and Napoleon lead the charge to evict Jones and his flunkies, who flee the onslaught of angry farm animals. (Honestly, if a brood of angry chickens were after me, I'd run too. Those things are vicious.)

At first, things go great. There's plenty of food, the animals are happy, and a few of them actually learn how to read. (How could this possibly go wrong?) When Farmer Jones returns to take back the farm, the animals drive him off, victorious in the Battle of Cowshed. Nothing can stop these animals from prospering.

Except, perhaps, corrupt leaders. *Sigh.* The power-hungry piggies soon squabble over leadership, which ends poorly for Snowball, who is driven from the farm. *Run, porker! Run!* Turns out Napoleon had been training puppies in stealth to become his secret police. *Uh oh.*

So how do you successfully assume leadership and rally the troops when bad things happen? Blame the other guy, which is what Napoleon does. The situation worsens, though, when Napoleon moves to cleanse ~~Russia~~ the farm of any Snowball supporters, instructing his pooches to make lunch of any animal who harbors Snowball sympathies. The dogs eat well, I can tell you. *Mmmm . . . bacon.*

Napoleon also recruits the golden-tongued Squealer to serve as minister of propaganda, putting a pretty little spin on everything he does, which soon includes taking privileges from the worker animals and giving them to the pigs. Since Napoleon can do whatever he likes, he starts "adjusting" the commandments.

4. No animal shall sleep in a bed *with sheets.*

5. No animal shall drink alcohol *to excess.*

6. No animal shall kill any other animal *without cause.*

Then one of the neighboring farmers attacks, and the animals successfully rout another hostile takeover. *Take that, you dirty human!* When Napoleon's most devoted supporter, the carthorse Boxer, is injured in the battle, Napoleon sends him to a glue factory. Napoleon *says* it's an animal hospital; poor Boxer didn't make it through surgery. Yeah. Surgery. Only if they were planning to glue him back together. HA!

Fast forward a few years. The pigs are living in the farmhouse, getting drunk all the time. Since they've broken pretty much every commandment, they ditched all but one, adjusted accordingly:

1. All animals are equal, but some animals are more equal than others.

These little piggies aren't flying, but they are wearing clothes and strutting around like hot stuff. They carry whips, and now they even walk on two legs. <gasp> The pigs have the neighboring farmers over for a dinner party at Animal House, where they announce an alliance between porcine and homosapine brothers. Napoleon gets special props for having the hardest working but least fed worker animals in the whole country. *Hooray?*

Several of the animals eavesdrop on the party, and for the first time (yeah, right) notice that the pigs' faces are becoming so human that they can't tell which is which anymore. Why, it's almost like they're *becoming* ~~communists~~ human!

George Orwell wasn't *actually* a communist; he was a socialist, which really isn't the same thing. But people love to oversimplify, so Orwell must have been a Big Bad Commie! Let's ignore that he hated Stalin for corrupting the ideals of socialism and that this whole book is one big critique of Russian communism. Democracy good, communism bad! (We'll also ignore the fact that the grand ol' US of A isn't really a democracy, but a democratic republic. Oversimplification rules!)

Anna Karenina by Leo Tolstoy

Published: 1877
Category: novel (serialized)
Banned for: being Russian. The Nazis burned Tolstoy's books because they didn't like him or his pacifism. But they didn't like anyone, so . . . eh.

"Happy families are all alike; every unhappy family is unhappy in its own way."

And has its own reality show. I'm looking at you, Kardashians.

Everything's going great at the Oblonsky house.

Dolly finds out that her beloved hubby, Stiva, has been boinking the kids' governess. When all hell breaks loose, they call in Stiva's sister Anna to calm everyone down. There's no ironic foreshadowing here that ~~Keira Kn~~ Anna is going to screw everything up in the future by having an affair. None whatsoever. She reconciles the couple and keeps them from getting a divorce. Let's see where that non-foreshadowing takes us, shall we?

Levin has the hots for Dolly's younger sister, Kitty, but when he asks her to marry him, she says no deal. She's hot on a sexy officer in the army named Count Vronsky, who's like whatevs, but then he meets Anna at this fancy ball, and it's instalove times a bajillion. Kitty who?

V follows Anna when she goes home to St. Petersburg to her husband and child. Because that's always a good idea. Anna figures the over-the-top flirting was just a temporary crush, but Vronsky's all gung ho for some extramarital sexytimes.

Heartbroken, Kitty falls ill. Seriously? What's up with women getting sick and almost dying because the guys they like don't like them anymore. Yes, Marianne, I'm talking to you, too (page 205). Ladies, it's called coping; all it requires is a big box of tissues, over-sized sweats, a tub of ice cream, a large batch of chocolate chip cookie dough (oven optional), and a bottle of wine. Have a weekend-long crying jag, and then *ding!* You're ready to get back to your life sans jerkwad. Eating all that might make a girl sick, but not to the point of *dying* over a bad breakup.

Or, you know, option B, which Kitty is smart enough to take: time at a spa. She returns from Germany a new woman. Not really, but at least she's over that Vronsky ass now. Levin's none too happy at getting jilted, nor does he want to stick around to be the rebound guy, so he says thanks but no thanks and heads back to his house in the countryside.

Meanwhile, it's getting a bit spicy between Anna and Vronsky, which Anna's poor hubby, Karenin, kinda notices. When he confronts Anna about it, she uses Evasive Maneuver #1: Deny the accusation, then bristle at the insult to your integrity. That holds him off for a bit, but Karenin isn't stupid. He asks again later. This time, she confesses and admits that, yeah, she's totally noodling with Vronsky . . . and she's kinda pregnant with his kid. Oh boy.

Understandably upset, Karenin won't give her a divorce and makes her keep up the "happy, smiley, everything's great!" act for a while. Vronsky's more interested in his career than her, which puts Anna in the middle of a crap sammich.

Kitty and Levin run into each other at a party, and they're finally both at a point where they can have a relationship. They're so in lurve that they get married. Then Levin realizes what marriage really means: so long, freedom of bachelorhood; hello, smothering wife.

Anna, meanwhile, is about to have Vronsky's baby . . . and it's not going well. They all think she's dying, so when she begs for Karenin's forgiveness, he says, "Of course. I don't want your angry ghost chasing me." Then she survives. Er, nevermind. But he still feels good about being the bigger person, so he tells her she can have the divorce. She, however, hates that he's being nice to her—and actually meaning it—so she refuses the divorce out of spite. Way to cut off your own nose, sweetie.

Vronsky and Anna jet off to Italy for a few months on a romantic honeymoon. When they get back, Anna goes to see her son, even though Karenin says no. She's upset because she loves her son, so of course that means she must love her daughter less. Your math's a bit off there, Anna. It is possible to love both kids at once. She heads out to the opera with a relative. Seriously bad move, which Vronsky tries to explain, but she ignores him. When she's snubbed and openly mocked for being an adulteress and Vronsky is still accepted by society, she gets bitter and jealous of loverboy. Because V breaking up her marriage is all Anna's fault. I thought we'd see you around here somewhere, double standard.

It's all downhill from there. First her marriage failed, and now her affair is failing because Vronsky is getting frustrated with her clinginess. Nothing left to do but throw herself under a train. *<splat>*

That's . . . unfortunate. Vronsky heads off for war. Kitty has a son, though Levin isn't sure what he thinks of the red, wrinkly newborn. As an FYI, Levy, kids all look like a wrinkly Elmer Fudd the first few days after they're born. Anyway, he's still not sure until a big storm comes up and Kitty and son get stuck outside. Levin's frantic while he searches, then finds out that they got home while he was playing maniac-search-and-rescue solo—which makes him realize that he does like his kid. Well that's nice, a parent loving his child. It's not like that happens every day all over the world. But whatevs.

Count **Leo Tolstoy** had tons of money, but he didn't roll like that. Later in life, he got religion—and then got rid of everything else. He was eighty-two when he ditched all his stuff, including his family, to search for greater spirituality, which he'd only been thinking of doing for decades. He died a few days later. Huh. Is that like passing some kind of test, so he got a direct flight to heaven? I wouldn't mind a layover, just so long as the airline doesn't lose my luggage. So annoying.

The Awakening by Kate Chopin

Published: 1899
Category: novella
Banned for: immorality, sex, violence, and faulty lifeguarding.

"I would give up the unessential; I would give my money, I would give my life for my children; but I wouldn't give myself."

How about a puppy then? They're really cute and very loving. No? Who'd like to go for a swim instead?

It's summer, which means months-long vacay! For the Victorian upper crust of Creole society, that means living it up on Grand Isle off the Louisiana coast. Pass the sunscreen and malaria nets, please.

Edna Pontellier is bored with life. Let's face it, women during that era didn't have much in the way of intellectual stimulation or business to keep them occupied. What, no *Young and the Restless?* OK then, how about some romance novels? None of those either? This housewife thing bites. So what is there for Edna to do? Contemplate her life. A lot. And we all know what thinking does to a woman—it makes her *dangerous!* I mean, honestly, how are you supposed to keep her happily chained to the parlor or kitchen if she has thoughts? Such independence must be quashed. *Immediately.*

Even though she's vacationing with hubby Robert and their two young sons, her thoughts start to churning, and soon enough she's seeking an outlet for all her pent-up sexual energy. Her hubby doesn't exactly inspire passion, so she, um, simmers for a bit.

Edna: Now, where'd I pack my v—oh, hey kids. Having fun on the beach? Why don't we just toddle on back out there so mommy can have some mommy alone time.

Meanwhile, Edna is making friends with other guests at the pension. Madame Ratignolle is the ideal stay-at-home mom, who devotes her entire life to her husband and children.

Madame Rat: Craft time, everyone! Today we're using macaroni and pipe cleaners. So much fun!

Then there's Mademoiselle Reisz, a fierce pianist who tells it like it is. Which often puts her at odds with genteel New Orleans society, where hospitality comes first, and sweet words and a brilliant smile wrap double-edged insults. Hoo boy! Sign me up!

Edna meets Robert Lebrun, the dashing son of the woman who runs the pension. This sexy slice of southern hunk makes a habit each summer of flirting openly and outrageously with one married woman staying at the pension—always understood to be harmless, since the hubby and kids are usually around.

Robert: Hey kids, I'm Uncle Bobby. Don't worry, I'm only joking when I make public sexual overtures to your mommy. Heh, heh.

That is, until he sets his sights on Edna. Natch. Flirtation becomes fancy, which leads to infatuation, and finally love. So Robert decides that he must run off to Mexico. Without Edna. Okaaay. He has to make his fortune, obviously, because what woman would abandon a wealthy hubby to ~~play with the pool boy~~ marry the not-rich love of her life? With Bobby gone, Edna has a big sad. Then summer's over, so Edna and the fam return to New Orleans, where hubby once again dives into business and ignores her completely. Yes, my friends, this is the kind of loving, devoted marriage that a woman fights to keep ~~away from~~.

Life is *bo-oring*, so Edna starts painting again. Just a hobby, though. Women can't actually be *artists* and make a living by selling their work. That kind of thing is for the poor and the crazies. Soon enough she earns what she needs to move out and rent her own itty-bitty apartment. A married woman, leaving her husband and living on her own? Whatever will the neighbors think? (Put the opera glasses down and spill!)

Edna embraces her newly discovered sexuality—*now what do I do with the whip?*—so she has an affair with a notorious womanizer. Her heart, though, never strays from Robert—the lover, not the husband, if you're keeping tabs. Aww, tender. So when she runs into Bobby unexpectedly while visiting ~~Lady Gaga~~ Madame Reisz, she's a tad upset. EDNA SMASH.

Edna: Oh. So you're back. Thanks for letting me know. Oh wait, YOU DIDN'T.

Robert: Well, uh, you're sorta married, and, um, I'm trying to be a good boy.

Edna: *Lame.* Come here, you. *(launches herself at him)*

Robert *(gasps for breath)*: So I kinda actually love you, but I was really trying to be good.

Edna: I'll show you what I do to good boys . . .

Later, Edna heads over to see the very pregnant Madame Rat, who's about ready to pop. Not only does Edna have to help deliver the kid, she ends up getting an earful, too.

Edna: Breathe. Just breathe.

Rat: *(groans)* Think of your children!

Edna: Push!

Rat: Having a mother who is an adulteress *(pants)* and divorcée *(grunts)* would ruin their chances in life.

Edna: *(tries not to strangle Madame Rat until after the baby is out)* Why don't you push some more? Isn't this so much fun?

Rat: How will they ever find respectable girls to marry? *(screams)* They're certainly not getting any of mine.

Edna: *(gets stabby)* Here, let me cut that umbilical cord for you.

For the first time, Edna considers how her behavior might affect her boys. Conclusion: teh oops. Of course it's *totally* better for her boys to have a dead mother than one who is aware of her sexuality, so Edna goes back to Grand Isle for a little swim. Don't forget your floaties! Except she wades into the ocean and drowns. *Wah waaah.*

For some strange reason, you might get the feeling that Edna was a bit autobiographical. Something about **Kate Chopin** being widowed at thirty-two and raising six kids by herself. What reason could she possibly have for wanting to discover herself and live life on her own terms (read: enjoy teh sex)? Nah, couldn't be . . .

Beowulf
by Anglo-Saxon Poet Man

Published: AD 700, give or take a century
Category: epic poem
Banned for: not being Nazi friendly. Yeah, they hated pretty much everything.

> *"Beowulf got ready,*
> *donned his war-gear, indifferent to death;*
> *his mighty, hand-forged, fine-webbed mail*
> *would soon meet with the menace underwater."*

He wore metal armor to fight underwater? Beowulf's got brawn, but those muscles certainly didn't extend to his brain.

King Hrogarth of Denmark knows how to throw a kegger. He builds himself a fab new mead hall called Heorot, and the place is *hot*. They get their freak on so hard that the neighbors get pissed about the noise. Pissed as in angry, not drunk or, um . . . OK, never mind.

Unfortunately the perturbed neighbor is the demon Grendel, who lives in the marshes nearby. Instead of calling the police like a normal demon, he terrorizes everyone with lots of killing and mayhem every night for the next few years. Because one night just isn't enough. When cocky Geatish warrior Beowulf hears about the demon problem, he offers to help. His dad and 'Garth were buds, and Wulfy's dad still owes him one. He's totally got their back, yo.

Here's an idea: why don't they just STOP THROWING PARTIES. Definitely not, because that would be the obvious—and easiest—solution. Nope, they need a big strong man to take out the neighbors. Don't even get me started on the demon's lair. No curb appeal whatsoever. It's bringing down the whole neighborhood.

So the fun-loving Danes throw a party (natch) for the dude who's gonna kick the demon's butt, which just pisses Grendel off even more. Can't a demon get any peace and quiet around here? Bummed about not getting an invite—again—Grendel shows up with mayhem in mind, but Wulfy tears the demon's arm off. Ooh, that's gonna leave a mark.

Grendel runs home to cry to mama . . . and die. Which makes mama angry. Never make a mama swamp witch angry. She heads over to Heorot and goes all mama demon on the drunk Danes. So now Beowulf has to fight her as well and dives into her swampy underwater lair. #notametaphor. How well armed is he? He got himself a sword made specifically for a *giant* to use—not including the arm that he, ahem, borrowed from Grendel. They wrestle and he beheads her. #reallynotametaphor. After he drops off the head and picks up his loot, Beo heads back home, where he gives most of the treasure he earned from killing the demons to his king. You're kidding, right? King didn't do squat, and he still gets all the gold? That sucks.

Years later, the king and then his son die, leaving Beowulf to become king. So he gets all the treasure back eventually. Better late than never? Anyway, Wulfy is a good ol' king for fifty years. Then when Beowulf is getting a bit old for his britches, a sneaky little thief tries to steal treasure from a dragon; inadvisable, as dragons are generally protective of their booty. Angry dragon unleashes his dragony agony on the Geats.

Wulfy knows he's about to kick the big wooden bucket, so he takes off to fight the big bad dragon—and defeats it. Hooray! Except dragon chomped Wulfy's neck, and he dies. Boohiss. The Geats burn Beowulf's body on a funeral pyre then bury what's left in a massive barrow with globs of treasure and a nice view of the sea.

Although some **Anglo-Saxon Poet Man** finally wrote down the story around AD 700, people had been talking about Beowulf for years. The story took place two hundred years earlier in Denmark, before Saxons invaded England and converted the natives to Christianity. Nobody really cared about it until some dusty old scholar named J. R. R. Tolkien wrote a paper on it. Apparently the poem inspired him to write his own epic stories. They're a little obscure, though, so you might not have heard of *The Lord of the Rings*.

Brave New World by Aldous Huxley

Published: 1932
Category: novel (dystopian)
Banned for: the sexy fun times, accompanied by plenty of illicit drug use, and without a hint of morals. Yep, sounds like fun, so it was obviously banned.

"The world's stable now. People are happy; they get what they want, and they never want what they can't get. . . . And if anything should go wrong, there's soma."

Emotions suck. I'd much rather sink into a warm tub with plenty of soma and bath salts. Er . . .

Since our lives are only so long, I'll abbreviate the ridiculously complicated first chapter. Ready? The year is AD 2540; in their calendar, 632 AF (After Ford). Yes, Henry Ford, who invented the assembly line and got the world rolling. Ford's socio-mechanical engineering proved so amazing—*efficiency! streamlining! eliminating jobs!* Sound familiar?—that he is revered like a god.

Mankind has "progressed" to the point at which people are born in bottles. Fetuses are sorted into castes: Alphas ($E=mc^2$) to Epsilons (can't tie shoes). Anything lower than Alpha is given chemicals to stunt its growth. Charming. Add in sleep-teaching, and you have one totaliated society.

The World State governs this "utopia" with a firm but depraved hand. All the sex you want, with anyone—and no guilt! *Um, yes, please.* No more icky childbirth? *Yay!* No more traumatic families? *Yay?* Best of all, anytime you feel a smidge gloomy, pop a soma pill and take a ride on the hallucination express. Just make sure you're a good consumer by buying new stuff and tossing out the slightly used to keep the economy strong. Ain't life grand?

Now to the plot: Bernard, a loner, hates his boss, Thomas Tomakin, who threatens to send him to Iceland if he doesn't start having promiscuous sex like normal people. Um, OK. Bernard likes Lenina, the resident hottie, so he asks her out. (I really hope she doesn't get her looks from Uncle Vladimir, no matter how well preserved he is.) Bernard doesn't impress her terribly much, but they have sex anyway. (If you've got an itch . . . just sayin'.) But Bernard is jealous that she still sleeps with other guys. Go fig.

Trying to impress Lenina, Bernie takes her on vacation to the Savage Reservation in Nuevo Mexico. Families? *Quel horreur.* There they find Linda, who was . . . dun dun *dunnn* . . . boss Thomas's date to the Rez twenty years ago. She got lost, and Tom took off. Even worse: She was pregnant! Oh noes. Then *ding!* goes the light bulb over Bernard's head—he can finally take sweet revenge on boss-daddy Tom. *Bwahaha!* So Linda and her son, John, trot back to London for a lovely family reunion, which goes something like this:

John the Savage: Daddy!

Papa Thomas: *(eyes bug out)* Uhhhhh . . .

Linda: You abandoned me, and I HAD A BABY!

Papa Thomas: Nooooo! *(runs)*

Ashamed at having a son, Tommy boy resigns from his prestigious job overseeing the bottle babies, even though he was really good at making them. *(Badum ching!)*

The Savage becomes the coolest new plaything in the "civilized" world. Bernie follows John like a puppy, wanting to be popular, too. Not so much. When Linda dies of a soma overdose, John cries, which freaks everyone out and they riot. They're not big into emoting.

John likes Lenina but hates that she sleeps around and loves her some soma (which means "body" in Greek, not to be confused with Soylent Green, which means "people" in Charlton Heston). When a soma-infused crowd gets its orgy on outside John's not-so-secret lair, Lenina convinces him to join. Yay, orgy! Boo, crushing guilt the next morning. So instead of popping some soma to forget like a normal person, John the Savage hangs himself. Sadness.

Moral of the story? All sex and drugs with no responsibility make humanity pointless. Supposedly.

Aldous Huxley was big into the psychedelics, man. Especially LSD. And perhaps the free love, as he was a good friend to D. H. Lawrence (page 121) and his Bloomsbury crowd. That surely didn't have any influence on Huxley's writing. Of course not.

The Brothers Karamazov by Fyodor Dostoyevsky

Published: 1880
Category: novel (serialized)
Banned for: not being the right kind of socialist. Man, those Commies just don't like it when people don't agree with them—even when they kind of do.

> *"'I love mankind,' he said, 'but I do surprise myself: the more I love mankind in general, the less I love people in particular.'"*

So. True. As anyone who has ever _____ would know. [Fill in the blank with your favorite least-favorite activity! Example: As anyone who has ever gotten to second base with a TSA agent would know.]

Fyodor Karamazov is a—hold on. Did the author name one of the characters after himself? A drunken louse and accomplished womanizer hated by pretty much everyone he knows? OK, just wanted to check. From two marriages, Fyodor has three boys, and supposedly another son from that time he seduced the village idiot. He forces the last boy to work as his servant and never acknowledges him as a son. Man, you're messed up, and we haven't even gotten to the part where you fight with your son over the same woman.

None of the boys grew up with their pop, and their mothers were all dead, so they were dumped on various relatives. 'S all good, though, because not having to deal with kids gave Fyodor more time for drunken orgies. Sweet!

Dmitri is oldest, and his mom left him an inheritance before she died. When he goes to collect it from Papa after he's all growed up, his old man lies so he can keep it all for himself. Naturally. So they're fighting and pretty soon feuding. That's when the two middle brothers intervene. Ivan is a philosopher. Doesn't help, though, because neither Dmitri nor Fyodor will listen to reason. Then acoylte Alyosha offers to have his elder at the monastery play mediator. This sounds like an excellent plan: a glutton, a fornicator, and an atheist walk into a monastery . . . er, sounds more like a joke.

Fyodor is a big fan of the jokes, so he makes sure to tell plenty of crude ones to the monks, just to make them feel all (un)comfortable. Thanks, dad. After Dmitri arrives late, they launch into a screaming match. Turns out, more than cash is up for grabs: Both father and son are in love with Grushenka. Er . . . Dmitri abandons—and steals 3,000 rubles from—his fiancée for Grushenka, while daddy says he'll pay Grush to be his mistress. Classy, boys. Classy.

The illegit son, Smerdyakov is an . . . *odd* fellow. He likes to discuss philosophy with Ivan mostly because he likes the idea that there is no good or bad in the world, which means no morality or guilt. Yay?

With this set of players, looks like we're going to have us some fun! Dmitri decides that Alyosha should break off Dmitri's engagement to Katerina for him. *(*cough*coward*cough*)* If that isn't fun enough, Al then breaks up a fight between papa and son, which ends with Dmitri throwing dear ol' dad to the ground and threatening to kill him.

The next day, Alyosha stops by Katerina's to do Dmitri's dirty work. Hey, Ivan's already here. Wait a second. Ivan's in love with Katerina, who's engaged to marry Dmitri, who's blowing her off for a skank? So that means . . . *(does the math)* . . . Ivan and Katerina can totally hook up. Yay! Or maybe not, since everything's such a mess that neither will admit their feelings. Yeah, bad timing.

Dmitri's not having luck borrowing money to pay Katerina back the cash he stole to pay for his orgy with Grush. It's almost like people are worried that he'll bolt with their cash and have a huge party somewhere. Upset, he stops by Grushenka's place, but she's not there. He figures she's off banging daddy Fyodor and takes off for dad's crib. Neither pops nor Grush are home, so he beats up one of his dad's old servants instead. Gotta put that energy somewhere, right? He goes back to Grush's place, but she's run off with a former lover who abandoned her like forever ago. Dmitri decides that the only option left is suicide. Because that solves everything.

He figures he should see Grushenka one last time before offing himself. In other words, he wants her to talk him out of it and tell him she loves him forever and ever. Our smart boy then goes to the store in clothes covered in the servant's blood and a wad of cash in hand to buy some wine and nibbles. Not. Suspicious. At all. He finds Grush and her lover, and she realizes that she really loves Dmitri. Yeah, that's it. Has nothing to do with Dmitri being covered in blood. They lock the other guy in a closet so Dmitri and Grush can plan their wedding. Because this is the perfect time for that. Then the police bust down the door and haul Dmitri off for the murder of his father.

What? Fyodor is dead? Yup—and with blood all over Dmitri, things aren't looking good. Ivan later speaks with Smerdy about their dad's death.

Ivan: I hate to tell you, but Fyodor is dead.

Smerd: Yeah, I know. I killed him.

Ivan (*bug-eyed*): Say *what?*

Smerd: 'Member all those times we talked about good and evil not existing? Figured killing the frakker was OK. So really, it's your fault for telling me stuff like that.

And Smerdy goes off to hang himself.

During the murder trial, things go a little batshit. Ivan yells from the witness stand that he's guilty, but then Katerina pulls out a letter from Dmitri saying he's afraid he might eventually murder his father. Because that's not incriminating at all and something you totally want to ~~post on Facebook~~ write down for posterity. What next, Dmitri? Are you going to put the noose around your own neck, too?

Despite all the evidence, most people believe that Dmitri's innocent. But the jury of peasants goes all vigilante and finds him guilty anyway. Possibly because he looks guilty as sin for *some* kind of crime (which he is). So Dmitri's off to the slammer before being exiled to Siberia. Pack a warm coat, sweetie.

Katerina drags Ivan back to her house, where she plans to help him back to the land of the sane. In the end, she and Dmitri apologize and forgive each other, so there's that. She does arrange for Dmitri to escape and flee with Grushenka to America. You are much too generous, lady. Alyosha gives some lovey-dovey speech about appreciating the little moments, yadda yadda. At least someone in that family turned out normal.

Lots of famous people *loved* **Fyodor Dostoyevsky**'s work, including super-fun party guy Sigmund Freud, who said *The Brothers Karamazov* was the best book *evar* and liked to analyze it for Oedipal themes. But he didn't stop there. Oh no, Freud jumped into an analysis of Dosty's guilt over his papa's death. Because, you see, he obviously wanted his dad out of the way so he could put the moves on mom. Obviously.

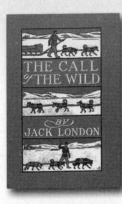

The Call of the Wild
by Jack London

Published: 1903
Category: novel (serialized)
Banned for: being a bit too "radical" for European dictators. Seems neither Mussolini nor Hitler was fond of London's book, though the Nazis were kind enough to invite it to a book-burning party.

> *"The domesticated generations fell from him. In vague ways he remembered back to the youth of the breed, to the time the wild dogs ranged in packs through the primeval forest and killed their meat as they ran it down."*

I'm with you, Buck. Hunting my own food and killing it with my bare teeth is so much better than the deli counter.
Reject the posers.

Buck the dog is living the good life on his owner's estate in sunny California. He's chillin' out, maxin' and relaxin' all cool, sitting in the sunshine by the side of the pool, when one of the gardeners, who was up to no good, dognapped poor Buck from his neighborhood.

So Buck finds himself sold to dog traders who beat him into submission and then send him to his final destination: Canada. *Not Canadia!* He'll really be chilling now . . . in the subzeros of the Klondike, where it gets so cold the snot freezes inside your nostrils. Lovely.

The dog traders ship him and some other poochies north to gold diggers in search of more shiny stuff. California's mined out, but Canada's got new territories for money-grubbers who want the Midas touch. The only problem? Whole lotta snow. Like, mountains of the stuff. Hence the need for über-strong dogs—like Buck—to pull sleds. When they arrive, a pack of huskies greets them by killing one of the new dogs. Toto, you're not in Cali anymore. Welcome to the Klondike, kid. Keep your nose down, do as you're told, and you might live.

Shaken by the gruesome howdy-do, Buck vows not to end up like shiska-dog. That Buck, he's a survivor. He gonna make it, keep on survivin'. It helps that French-Canadian mailmen buy him. They're a good pair of hosers, lo. Buck becomes part of a sled team that roams the country delivering mail. Ah, when mail delivery was a noble profession and didn't require men with knobbly knees to wear silly shorts.

He settles in to pack life, except for the whole rivalry thing. He doesn't get along too well with the pack leader. Jerk. They get in one little fight—to the death. I'll let you guess who wins, considering we're only halfway into the book.

With Buck's leadership, the pack makes record time. Life ain't bad—until the dog team gets handed off to another mailman who's not so good with dogs. Life in the Great White North has sent the guy a bit postal: He's a mean one, that Canuck. He's a crooked, dirty jockey, making them pull loads that are way too heavy and beating them relentlessly.

When they finish that run, the mail guy sells the puttered-out pooches to a trio of American gold diggers searching for a jackpot. Not surprisingly, the arrogant gringos know less than nothing about dog sleds and bitter Canadian winters. Not good, eh.

Their new overlords overload the sled and make it worse by not bringing enough of the foods. So everyone's pretty much cranky, starving, and dying. Only five of the original fourteen dogs make it to straggle into the camp of John Thornton. He's rough around the edges, but Thornton knows aboot the countryside and dogs. He warns the money-grubbers that the ice is too thin, but they ignore him. Typical Americans, pretending they know better than everyone else. Hosers. Buck knows something ain't right, so he stays put. As lead dog, that means all the other dogs stay put, too. The Yanks don't take that too kindly and beat little Buck.

Thornton cuts Buck loose and tells the fools to leave. They take off, boiling mad, until the ice cracks and all of them—dogs, sled, people—

plunge into the icy water. No need to worry about drowning, though; the cold will get them long before that. *(Cue the theme song from* Titanic.*)*

So Buck has a new master, and they become bestest buds. Then Buck begins to hear the siren song of the wild calling him (less like Celine Dion and a lot more like Shakira, trust me). Jaunts into the wilderness grow longer, and visits to Thornton shorter. Buck returns a final time to find John murdered by Yeehat Indians. *Oh no they didn't.* No one messes with Buck's human, which he shows them in an almighty slaughter. Then he takes over a wolf pack and does it doggie style with the lady wolves. Now ~~feared~~ known as the Ghost Dog by the pesky Yeehat, he returns each year to the spot where Thornton died. *Arooo!*

Jack London was a gold prospector up in the bitterly cold Klondike? Get outta town! But don't worry about those accusations of plagiarism. I mean, yeah, he used that other guy's book as a "source" and even thanked him for it later—what's the big deal? Everyone totally remembers that guy, right?

The Canterbury Tales
by Geoffrey Chaucer

Published: 1390s
Category: poem (and some prose)
Banned for: fart jokes and humping

> *"Thus swyved was this carpenteris wyf,*
> *For al his kepyng and his jalousye;*
> *And Absolon hath kist hir nether ye;*
> *And Nicholas is scalded in the towte.*
> *This tale is doon, and God save al the rowte!"*

*Can you believe that some high school teachers make their
students read this crap in Middle Earth English? jk! lolz 2 funny*

ROADTRIP! This is gonna be epic. It should only take, oh, four or
five days to travel from London to Canterbury, then back again. Don't
bother bringing your iPod, though, because the pilgrims are going to
tell stories to keep themselves entertained during the long commute.
Who wants to sing "Man Mai Longe Liues Wene"? No takers?

The narrator and his merry band of twenty-nine pilgrims travel en
masse to see Saint Thomas à Becket's shrine in Canterbury Cathedral.
It's a pious occasion, so they make a bet: Whoever tells the best story
wins dinner. Perhaps they should have clarified what kind of stories,
because most of them take a turn for the crapper. Unlike the toilet,
bathroom humor's nothing new. People have been sniggering at poop
jokes since the beginning of time.

We don't have time for all twenty-nine, so here are the four tales
you need to know.

Knight's Tale

Two friends want to marry the same girl. She wants neither, but they
don't care. Typical. They fight, so Theseus, duke of Athens, tells them to
duke it out in a tournament like men. Palamon prays to Venus to win
Emily; Arcite prays to Mars to help him win the fight, which is all that
matters; and Emily prays to Diana to stay single, but if she can't have that
at least let the guy who actually loves her win. (Yes, even though they're
in Greece, they're praying to Roman gods. Good catch. Now shush.)

Love conquers all, so Arcite wins the tournament—but then his
horse crushes and kills him, so Palamon gets Emily by default, and
Emily gets the guy who loved her more. So she almost got what she
wanted. Yay?

Miller's Tale

It shouldn't surprise you to learn that the Miller is totally sloshed, so
when it's the next guy's turn, he cuts in line.

Miller: Hey guys. Guys. My turn. It's the best story ever, guys. You're gonna love it.

Host: Ugh. Whatevs. Just get on with it.

Miller: Wait, what was I saying? *(hiccup)* Oh yeah—

So this carpenter John isn't the brightest candle in the chandelier, if you know what I'm sayin'. His wife, Alison, is hot, but she thinks her hubby's an idiot. Because he is. They have a renter named Nicholas. Some dirt-poor college kid, which means he's always horny. He and Alison plan to do the nasty, but they gotta distract the hubs first. They convince John that the Second Flood is coming. You know, Noah and all that stuff. Anyway, that night they climb into three huge tubs suspended from the rafters in the barn so that they'll float away safe and sound. I know, right?

Once the carpenter falls asleep, the other two skedaddle to the bedroom for some sexytimes. But Alison's, like, *really* hot, so this paper pusher named Absolon's in love with her too. He comes to the window and asks for a kiss. She's already being sneaky, so why stop now? She goes to the window and sticks her butt right in his face. He's got his eyes closed—such a romantic—so he can't tell that he's actually kissing her porthole . . . until she and Nick bust a gut laughing. Mortified, he runs off, but when he comes back a few minutes later he's got himself a hot poker and a cunning plan. This time when he calls for a kiss, Nick takes a turn at the window and rips a whopping huge fart. Nasty, dude. Absolon takes his revenge by shoving the poker right up Nick's back door.

Nick's butt is on fire—literally—so he screams for water. Which wakes up John, who thinks the flood has started, so he cuts the rope holding his tub. Down he goes and breaks his dim-witted arm. Bahahahaha!

Host: Uh, thanks for that. . . . *Next!*

Pardoner's Tale

Three friends at a pub decide it's their duty to find Death and avenge everyone who ever died. Smart. They wouldn't have been drinking, by chance, when they came up with their brilliant plan? An old man tells them they can find Death at the foot of an old oak tree. They stumble over and find a leprechaun's worth of gold coins. *Cha-ching!* They decide to sleep there till morning, so one of them goes off to get wine. Because more alcohol is always a good plan. While he's gone, the two guys plot to stab him when he gets back and split the gold between them. When the wine guy returns, they stab him dead, then get the party going by cracking open the bottle of wine—which the dead guy had poisoned to kill the other two and take all the gold himself. So that's how the three men found death at the foot of the tree. *Ba-dum-ching!*

Wife of Bath's Tale

There once was a gallant knight in the time of King Arthur. OK, there were *lots* of knights—stickler—but this one's on trial for raping a woman. Wait, what? Knights are the good guys. Sure, Lance put the moves on the queen and got Arthur killed because of it, but that is so romantic.

Arthur's about to have the knight executed when Guinevere steps in.

Guin: Imma let you finish, but why don't I take care of this one.

Art: Yes, dear.

Guin *(to the knight):* Answer this correctly, and you go free: What do women really want?

Knight: *(blank stare)* Women have wants?

Guin: *(pretends she didn't hear)* You've got a year to find the answer or it's off with your head.

For the next year, Sir Rapey asks around, but every woman wants something different. Jeez, it's like they all have individual wants and needs. How infuriating! Time's nearly up, and he's got nothing, so he's a little desperate. Then an ugly old crone shows up right on time to give him the answer—if he marries her.

Hmmm. Lose your head or marry *that.* Tough call. He finally agrees, so he's off to the throne room with his answer: Women want to rule over their husbands.

Ding ding ding! We have a winner. You live—and marry the ugly hag. Yay? They get married, and that night the crone asks if he wants a wife who's beautiful but a floozy, or ugly and faithful.

Knight: Whatever you want, dear.

Ding ding ding! Correct again! He turns around and . . . she's beautiful. Of course. She couldn't be, oh, sort of cute but not hot, right? So close, Wife of Bath. You were *this close* to getting feminism right. Ah, well, bonus points for being centuries ahead of your time.

Those were some pretty amazing stories, amirite? Now, I know you're dying to know who won because the competition was so, um, fierce. Drumroll, please . . . and the winner is . . . no one.

What the what? Someone probably did win, but we have no idea who because *someone* lost part of the manuscript. I'm not naming names, but apparently several versions of the book are floating around, many with whole chunks missing and tales stuck in a different order. This contest sucks. Switching the channel back to *Jeopardy!* I don't care if they do have their questions and answers bass-ackwards.

That **Geoffrey Chaucer** was such a card. He wanted to write poetry, but not in French, the official language of the English court. (Hate to break it to you, kids, but for several centuries, the peeps who ruled England were actually French. Even Richard the Lionheart was a froggie.) Nor did Chaucer write in Latin, which the Church used. He wrote in the vulgar tongue—English—which only the common people spoke. Poetry for commoners? *Hahaha!* Now that's funny.

Catch-22 by Joseph Heller

Published: 1961
Category: novel
Banned for: language because war is filled with nothing but sunshine, roses, and adorable kittens that chase laser pointers. But, hey, life is grand, and students should only know about good things, right?

*All he had to do was ask; and as soon as he did, he would no longer be
crazy and would have to fly more missions. Orr would be crazy to fly
more missions and sane if he didn't, but if he was sane he would have to
fly them. If he flew them he was crazy and didn't have to; but if he didn't
want to he was sane and had to.*

*I'll say. Actually, I'm totally confused, but I think that's the point.
Maybe? If I were insane, would I understand? Or just sane
pretending to be insane.*

Explaining this book is super fun because the text doesn't flow
chronologically or even sequentially. It's a free association free-for-
all! There *is* method to Heller's madness, madness being the key
word here.

All John Yossarian wants is to stay alive. Is that too much to ask? If
you're a bombardier with the US Air Force stationed on the island of
Pianosa in Italy at the end of World War II, then yes. So he tries every
way imaginable to get out of flying more bombing missions. The insan-
ity argument doesn't work. According to Catch-22, only a sane man
would say he's insane to get out of flying missions. So mental health
problems are out. Next up: physical health problems.

Yossarian: *(fake coughs)* I'm sick, Doc. I think I'm dying.

Doc: What is it this time?

Yoss: My liver. It hurts.

Doc: Whatever. Get on the table.

Wouldn't it be easier just to fly his required missions so he can
get home sooner? Well, yes—if the mission quota didn't keep going
up without explanation. And if the officers didn't send them into
increasingly dangerous combat situations to get perfect snapshots of
the big *kaboom!* as they drop their bombs on the people below. Oh,
look. So pretty. That, and our boy Yoss is a bit paranoid. When he
talks with an officer about how the world is trying to kill him, the guy
gives him a pat lecture about loyalty and fighting for your country.
But Yoss does have a point: A bunch of people are *shooting at him*,

trying to kill him. If that's not the world out to get you, it's pretty friggin' close.

So what exactly *is* Catch-22? It's illogical circular thinking so complicated that most people give up trying to understand it and live within the paradox instead. Smart move, ~~Big Brother~~. Sorry, wrong book (page 1). Still, it's the perfect way to keep insignificant peons doing what you want. Plus, the military *looooves* rules, and soldiers can't sass back or ask questions. *Perfetto.* It's also illegal to read Catch-22, as it states in the text of—

Hey, wait a second. If we can't *read* it, how do we know you're telling the truth? "Just because" is not a valid answer.

Yoss finally realizes the obvious: There is no Catch-22, but their superiors say there is, so the inferiors believe them, which means it exists in their minds. Since it doesn't actually exist, there's no way to repeal or undo it. That's the biggest load of crap I've ever heard. Which is why it's brilliant.

Yoss is plagued by what happened to his friend Snowdon, who died in his arms during an earlier mission. Which is also when Yoss stopped caring about the war and started figuring out a way to stay alive. No loyalties here—but with officers like theirs, who *would* be loyal?

Fed up after another friend dies, Yoss wanders Rome, happily sightseeing while rape, murder, and other nasty stuff occur as he passes by. He gets caught for going AWOL, and his superiors offer him a way out: If you say we're totally awesome and you think our policies are the bestest ever, we'll send you home with an honorable discharge. Either that, or you're getting court-martialed. Yoss chooses (c) none of the above, and he escapes to neutral Sweden. Take that, suckas.

Joseph Heller served as a bombardier in Italy during World War II. Funnily enough, he actually liked all his superior officers during the war. He aimed his criticisms at the Cold War, with a hat tip to the Korean War and McCarthyism—which putting his antigovernment and antiwar philosophies in the context of World War II makes so clear.

The Catcher in the Rye by J. D. Salinger

Published: 1951
Category: novel
Banned for: parents' hypocrisy. But you know they totally loved reading it when they were kids, probably hid it from *their* parents. Maybe it's genetic that once adults hit a certain age they are contractually obligated to forget they were once rebellious teens, too. Sorry, kids.

> *"I'm standing on the edge of some crazy cliff. What I have to do, I have to catch everybody if they start to go over the cliff—I mean if they're running and they don't look where they're going I have to come out from somewhere and catch them. That's all I'd do all day. I'd just be the catcher in the rye and all."*

Why not wheat? Hmm, probably can't do gluten. OK, what about corn? That has a nice ring to it: Catcher in the Corn. We could do a Halloween reboot . . .

Holden Caulfield keeps getting booted out of schools for not doing, well, anything, and he's quickly adding Percy Prep to the list. He says goodbye to the only teacher he likes, who promptly launches into lecture mode. Teacher says: You're not applying yourself. Holden hears: *Wah wah waaaah.*

Holden bolts for his dorm. Roommate Stradlater is getting ready for a date with Jane, the only girl Holden finds attractive *and* can stand. Cauliflower boy's wound super tight, so this is a rare combo, believe me. He's also pissed because Stradlater has plenty of experience with the ladies. (See where this is going?)

Even better, Studlover makes Holden write his English paper for him. So Holden writes about his own dead little bro, who wrote poems on his baseball mitt so he could read them while stuck in the out-field. *Aww, cute.* Except, duh, Strad doesn't like it. Plus, he refuses to say what happened on the date, which really cheeses Cauliflower off. Holden takes a swing but misses, so Stradivarius clocks him instead.

Remember when New York was a total dangerous disgusting mess? OK, fine, YouTube it. Holden hops a train into the city. There he meets the mom of a fellow student, but she shuts him down when the little cougar cub tries to put the moves on her. When he decides not to go home, he gets chummy with a cabbie (gross) and invites him out for drinks. Um, no. Then he checks into a skeezy motel, yet is somehow *totally surprised* that the other guests are perverts. One guy's a cross-dresser, and in another room a couple spit on each other as foreplay, which turns Holden on (double gross). But if Holden *really* likes a girl, he'll treat her with respect. Uh huh, yeah, sure.

He wanders the Rotten Apple, doing his best to get into trouble. First, he calls a former stripper whom a friend knows. She rejects him. (Rejected by a stripper? *Yeowch.*) Next he checks out some clubs, but all he sees are ignorant women and phony men. So many phonies, it's like a needle stuck in the groove. (YouTube "record players" while you're at it.) Depressed, he goes back to the hotel, where the elevator operator gets him a hooker. (That'll cheer you up kid. At least until the herpes flares up.) Cauliflower boy freaks out and offers her $5 to leave. She wants $10, but Holden hasn't quite mastered the art of hostile negotia-tion yet. She comes back with elevator guy, who beats him up and takes the other $5. Now Holden really has a sad. He's bored, horny, and out ten bucks.

By this time, poor widdle Holden's practically in tears, so he calls Sally. She's hot, and they've dated, but he doesn't actually like her. They go ice skating at Rock Center, where he tries to convince her to run away with him to a cabin in the woods where he'll get a job as a gas station attendant. Total dream come true, right? Sally shoots him down (surprise), so Holden calls Jane. No answer. Then he goes out for drinks with a friend from school and drunkenly pesters said friend with creepy sex questions. Weirded out, his friend tells him to get a shrink. So Holden drunk dials Sally. Because that's never a bad idea.

He breaks into his parents' apartment to see his sister, Phoebe. She's excited to see him but starts on her own lecture about him flunking out of school *again* and getting over their brother's death. Have you lost count of the lectures yet? Because more are coming. Did no one think that backing off a little might help? No? OK, back to the guilt trip. . . . Holden tells his sis that his only dream is to catch kids running through a field of rye before they plunge off a cliff. *Um, WTF?*

Finally, he visits a former teacher, who (wait for it) lectures Holden about doing something with his life. Holden is exhausted, so he crashes on the couch. He wakes a few hours later with Teach's hand on his forehead. Pervert! Holden freaks and runs away. Because it couldn't possibly be a kind man trying to take care of a feverish kid. (Something about wandering the city for three days in the middle of winter, getting bombed and smoking, without a coat or sleeping or eating makes him sick. Strange, I know.) Nope, gotta be a pedophile.

When he meets up again with Phoebe, he tells her he's running away but then kiboshes that plan when she wants to go with. She's mad, so he takes her to the zoo and—*Oh look at the cute little monkeys!* While Phoebe rides the merry-go-round, Holden finally has a happy thought. About effing time.

Holden gets really sick (shocker) and ends up at a rest home for people with tuberculosis. Not nearly as cool as an asylum, true, but Holden still gets to enjoy yet another friggin' lecture, this time from the shrink. He concludes by saying he's going to apply himself in school and that he misses everyone he wrote about. By which he probably means just the hooker.

J. D. Salinger became a cantankerous old coot after *Catcher* brought him glory and truckloads of cash. He slowly cut himself off from the world and didn't allow anything he wrote after 1965 to be published, and he even quit doing interviews after 1980. Basically, he retired to a cabin in the woods and got a job as a gas station attendant.

A Clockwork Orange
by Anthony Burgess

Published: 1962
Category: novel (dystopian)
Banned for: ✓blasphemy ✓drugs ✓foul language ✓immorality ✓misogyny ✓pedophilia ✓rape ✓sadism ✓socialism ✓violence. In the seventies, a bookseller in Utah was actually arrested for selling *Clockwork* in his store. This novel is a book banner's wet dream.

"It's funny how the colours of the real world only seem really real when you viddy them on the screen."

Same goes for books of the real world. Now cue up the Hunger Games *Blu-ray and bring me a glass of milk-plus.*

Let me preface this little synops by saying that Alex makes me want to rip his gonads out through his esophagus. You'll see why in just a moment.

Alex is a parent's worst nightmare, especially if those parents have a daughter who likes bad boys. Perhaps he once had a soul, but the garbage he eats, drinks, and otherwise ingests long since dissolved it—and he likes it that way. Not. Hot. If that's what gets you going, I know a nice man who can fit you with a lovely white coat. Keep you all snuggly warm.

Alex's hobbies include: downing shots of milk-plus at the Korova Milk Bar, stomping hobos, listening to Beethoven, and thievery, violence, and mayhem. Fun! Might want to keep your valuables locked up and a can of mace within easy reach, but other than that you're golden. You might also want to lose the dignity.

In the disturbingly near future, Alex takes his gang of boys, whom he lovingly calls his *droogs,* on nightly violent orgy rampages, beating, raping, and killing random people. They even invent their own language: Nadsat, a bizarre marriage of English and Russian. Probably a shotgun wedding, considering who created it.

So one day they're getting themselves psyched up for a night of ultra-violent fun. They throw back some milk-plus (milk plus drugs, natch) and pile into a stolen vehicle for a joyride. Along the way, they beat down a guy walking home from the library; rob a store, leaving the husband and wife owners in a bloody heap on the floor; and break into a little cottage where they beat the husband senseless and rape his wife. You know, just another night on the town.

The next day he decides to skip school. WTF? He doesn't obey any other law, but he still goes to school on occasion? What kind of—

Deep breath. Out goes the anger . . . until you see what Alex does next. He's bored, so he goes, "Here's some candy," to a pair of ten-year-old girls. I'll let your sick and twisted imagination conjure what happens next. Then times that by ten and you might be getting close. Later that night, his buds decide he shouldn't be boss no more, so they set him up to take the fall when they rob some old lady. Sitch gets outta hand, and Alex kills her.

He's arrested, convicted of murder, and sent to the pokey. He'll have so much fun in there. Inmates *lurve* child molesters. He gets into even more trouble in prison—is anyone surprised by this?—so they enroll him in a super-secret program to test aversion therapy on him. Basically, they send him to some over-the-top secret government facility where they perform mind-altering behavior modification to rid him of his violent tendencies. Excellent. Pass the popcorn.

It's called the Ludovico Technique, wherein they inject him with drugs that make him sick. But they do so while he's watching über-violent movies, so his brain associates violence with being sick. Only problem is that the soundtrack to one of the violent films included Beethoven. So now he not only can't stand any kind of violence without getting violently ill, he can't listen to his cherished Ludwig van anymore. Boo freaking hoo.

When his many victims discover that he can't fight back, they beat him to a bloody pulp. Eye for an eye, amirite? Then he runs into the guy living in a cottage, whom he'd beaten up. Sadly, the wife died after Alex and his droogs raped and beat her.

The husband doesn't recognize him at first because the boys were wearing ski masks to hide their faces. So he's actually sad when he hears of Alex's nonviolence "plight" and wants to use his story as an example of why the current government is bad. But then grieving hubby recognizes the ridiculous slang that Alex created, and he has some of his buddies haul the kid off. They lock Alex in a room with classical music blasting 24/7 to the point where Alex leaps out a window to commit suicide.

He wakes up—you've got to be kidding me—in the hospital with all the anti-violence programming broken. The government will give him a job if he says that they actually fixed him. They certainly did, and so he goes back to his violent lifestyle.

Or not, if you go by the original version published in the UK. The American editors thought it would be more realistic to end on a violent note. If, however, you read the original, the final chapter has Alex getting bored with the violent life and deciding to get married and have kids. Aw, isn't that sweet. Evil sociopath wants a family. It ends with him pondering whether his son will be violent like him. Um, ya *think*?

Apparently, **Anthony Burgess** got the initial idea for *Clockwork* after some American soldiers who'd deserted their posts during the London Blackout of World War II raped his wife. Wow, you could've fooled me. Let's just hope she never read the book.

The Count of Monte Cristo by Alexandre Dumas, père

Published: 1846
Category: novel (serialized)
Banned for: being written by Papa Dumas. The Church in Rome put all of his work on the *Index Librorum Prohibitorum*. Making the cardinal a super-nasty bad guy in *Three Musketeers* (page 223) might have had something to do with it.

"How did I escape? With difficulty. How did I plan this moment? With pleasure."

Excellent. You have learned well, my young Padawan.

Edmond Dantès is supa-fine. He was just promoted to ship's captain, plus he has a babelicious fiancée, Mercédès, waiting for him in Marseilles. So when he's arrested because three pricks get jealous, let's just say those men won't be getting away with it once Dantès is released from the clink . . . *never.* The conspirators want him dumped in a jail cell so deep he'll be forgotten. The place for that is Chateau d'If, which isn't so much a prison as it is a living hell. Say hello to the rest of your life because no one has ever been able to escape. *Bwahaha!*

His three "friends" all hate him for one lame reason or another. First, we have Fernand Mondego, who's jonesing hard on the fiancée. When Dantès is locked away, Fernand is there to comfort her. Isn't that convenient. Next we have Danglars, who's pissed that pretty-boy Dantès got a captainship before him. I know, let's ruin a young man's life because someone has entitlement issues and can't deal with rejection. Don't forget about Caderousse, one of Dantès's neighbors who just hates that the kid has such a good life. No one is allowed to be happy if he's not, dammit!

Villefort, the prosecutor, figures out pretty quick that the three men are just out for blood. Right when he's about to release poor Dantès, he learns what treasonous thing the kid was supposed to have done: He'd promised his old captain that he'd deliver a letter to a loyal Bonapartist from the Little Man himself, who is currently imprisoned on his own tiny island in the Mediterranean. Well, that's not *horrible* since the letter never got there, and he didn't know squat about what it said. But wait—the Bonapartist recipient is none other than Villefort's father! Dun dun *dunnn.*

So Dantès gets screwed to protect prosector man's career—and on his wedding day, no less. Ouch.

A couple years go by, and Dantès has nearly lost his marbles after sitting in his itty-bitty cell devoid of all human contact. They don't give him anything he could use to end the torment, either. Years of bore-dom. Makes you claustrophobic just thinking about it. *Shudder.* Or hungry for a fried ham-and-cheese sandwich. *Mmmm . . .* food. They're a little hard up for that in solitary.

Then one day he hears someone digging nearby, so he figures, hey, I'm sitting here doing nothing *for eternity,* so why not play in the dirt? He starts tunneling and meets up underground with the ancient Abbé Faria, who's been stuck in his cell much too longer. They start dig-ging together, and the abbé, who earned his cell for having unsavory political views (which tend vary depending on who is in power, so pick your poison), teaches Dantès all kinds of cool stuff, like science, his-tory, and languages. Life in the slammer ain't quite so bad when you've got an intellectual tutoring you for free—"free" being a relative term here. Anyway, they dig for years, and just when they're about to break through—the abbé dies. Which bites the dust, even though the old guy found a kind of freedom. OK, not really.

Dantès isn't stupid—especially after all that learning—so he hides the abbé's body and sews himself up into the burial sack when the guards come to heave-ho the stiff into the ocean. Now that Dantès is loose, he sets his sights on Revenge Central. He's had fourteen years to devise punishments for his betrayers. Pull up a chair because this is where things start to get good.

One thing our boy learned in all those years with the abbé: the location of an Italian family's humongo treasure trove buried on the island of Monte Cristo. Hey, isn't that—Why, yes. Yes, it is.

So the new count of Monte Cristo plots for a few more years, setting everything in place to make his revenge absolutely *parfait.* He slides his way into Parisian society, where he sets up some mighty fine traps. The first snaps up Fernand, who now styles himself the Count de Morcerf and who had, unsurprisingly, "earned" his fortune by betray-ing his Greek boss. Once the old guy was out of the way, Fernand sold the man's wife and daughter into slavery before vamoosing with the moolah. Stay classy, Mondego.

Monte Cristo gets word out about the treachery and even has the formerly enslaved daughter (whom he purchased and then set free) testify against the creep. Mondego's life is ruined, but MC isn't done yet. Fernand ended up marrying Dantès' fiancée (like that was a surprise), so MC makes sure he loses his wife and son as well. No, he doesn't kill them; you're so bloodthirsty. He makes sure they know what kind of criminal Fernand really is. So they ditch him and take new names since their current ones are worthless if they want a decent life. Poor Fernand is all alone, so he eats a bullet. Coward.

Next comes Danglars, who is taken down by the thing he loves the mostest: money. MC rigs a few things, and the guy loses everything. That was easy. Caderousse feels kinda guilty about what he did, so MC goes easier on him. He gives him a sweet little diamond. Wow. That was actually nice. Except when Caderousse leaves with it, his friends murder him for it. *Snap.*

Last he takes down Villefort, who had an affair with Madame Danglars years before. Turns out, they had a kid that Villefort tried to kill at birth, but someone saved the boy. Lil' Ville grows up to become engaged to . . . Danglars's daughter? Yup, the young lovers are actually half siblings. Might want to ask Moll for some advice on the whole sibling-marriage thing (page 152). At least they didn't find out *after* they got married. Ick.

But Dantès isn't done yet. Before springing all his traps, MC taught Villefort's wife all about the fun science of poisons. She's actually the prosecutor's second wife, so she figured that she needed to eliminate the competition—that is, the daughter from his first marriage—so her son will get everything. She ends up poisoning a bunch of relations just to make sure. When grieving hubby figures out what she's done, she poisons herself *and* her son. Overkill much?

Monte Cristo does eventually find some happiness (rather than joy in revenge, which surprisingly isn't the same). The Greek girl he saved from slavery is kinda cute. Huh. I guess you *can* buy love.

Alexandre Dumas was a tad sensitive about his family. Mommy was French, but daddy was born in the Caribbean, the biracial kid of a French nobleman and a slave. Best not to mention it, however, or he'll tear you a new one—in the most eloquent way, of course. "It is true. My father was a mulatto, my grandmother was a negress, and my great-grandparents were monkeys. In short, sir, my pedigree begins where yours ends." Ouch. Also, mispronouncing his name will only prove to others that *you* are the dumbass. (Hint: It's pronounced *doo-MAH*.)

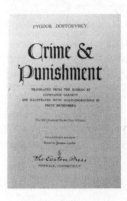

Crime and Punishment by Fyodor Dostoyevsky

Published: 1866
Category: novel (serialized)
Banned for: serving as a poor model for young people. Please tell me, book banners, what makes a *good* model for young people? How about an innocent book like *Winnie the Pooh*? Nope, someone banned that one, too. This is why we can't have nice things.

"Pain and suffering are always inevitable for a large intelligence and a deep heart. The really great men must, I think, have great sadness on earth."

Yes, Rasky, geniuses like you have such a hard life. Why don't I get my tiny sad violin to accompany your despair? #martyr

Raskolnikov is a dirt-poor dropout. Are we supposed to be surprised by this? He thinks he's a genius, as does every other average person in the world. But he has this brilliant theory. Oh, great. Here we go. BRILLIANT THEORY: People who will go on to do great things for the world are allowed to commit any crime they want, so long as they'll eventually do something to benefit humanity.

Uh. That's quite a theory. But then it gets better (worse?). *Any crime* includes murder. So he tests it out by killing an unscrupulous moneylender. I mean, really, if anyone should die to prove his theory, it should be someone bad, right? Of course. He's cleansing the world of bad people, and loan-sharking is so much worse than, say, murder.

When he breaks into an old moneylender's apartment one night, he goes all Lizzie Borden on her. When her half-sister walks in on the fun, he starts chopping her with an axe, too. He'd planned to rob them because he could do so much good with the money. I mean, Napoleon killed a couple people with all his wars, but he's doing so much to help the world, right? So it's all good, yo.

But murdering two people freaks him out a little bit. Ya think? He ends up stealing only a few things, which he later hides under a rock. He makes it home and then frantically tries to clean the blood off his clothes. Wait, you're only thinking of this *now?* Someone needs to watch more *CSI*. Almost immediately he gets sick with a really bad fever and is out of it for several days. Aww, so sad. Why, he could even die. Which would be a shame because . . . ?

When he gets better, the guy his sister is planning to marry stops by for a visit. But that dude can't marry Rasky's nice, sweet sister. He's a self-righteous jerk! It's obviously Rasky's job to judge the fiancé because he's such a paragon of human virtue himself.

By now, he's really curious to know what everyone's saying about the murders. He's been trapped in his apartment for days and is too poor to buy a wireless router. So he gets the newspapers from the days he was in his post-murder hangover to see all the lurid accounts of those poor women's deaths. Yeah. While he's out and about, he runs into the policeman who's investigating the crime.

Don't freak out. Don't freak out. "Hey, inspector. How's that, uh, murder thing going? The investigation." *Act normal. Stop twitching.*

Rasky word-vomits all over the place, almost confessing to the crime, but pulls himself together enough to get out of there. For some reason, the inspector suspects Rasky might have had something to do with the murders. Excellent deduction, Sherlock.

Now another jerkwad is after Rasky's sister. Oh, look. It's her widowered former boss. What is it with men always trying to get freaky with their kids' governesses? Would you like to answer that question, Rochester (page 108)? Around the same time, Rasky befriends Sonya the hooker, who—wait for it—has a heart of gold and is only selling her body to support her family. But what's really sad is that two of her friends were just murdered.

How's that guilty conscience coming along, Dexter? Not so good?

He finally confesses to Sonya, and who should be listening in but creepy ex-boss, who has his own skeletons in the closet. (He had nothing to do with his wife's tragic demise. Of course not. God rest her soul.) The creep tries to blackmail Rasky's little sister into sleeping with him. She says no way—*finally* someone with common sense—so the douche canoe commits suicide later that night. What, Rasky wouldn't take care of it for him?

Sonya finally convinces Rasky to confess to the police, which he does, and gets an eight-year sentence in a Siberian work camp. So you're telling me that he hacks apart two defenseless old women with an axe and gets a grand total of *eight* years? You have got to be freaking kidding me. So not OK.

Even better? Sonya tags along so she can help him become a better man. What is wrong with people? Sonya, sweetie, he's a *murderer*, and probably not much better than the johns you serviced. Yet you move to a frozen wasteland to help him through his imprisonment? You might want to get your head examined, dear, because that's not sanity talking.

Fyodor Dostoyevsky had some of his own happy fun times in prison. Granted, it was for political reasons that stemmed from reading banned books. Ahem. The government feared that he and his friends would start a revolution, so he was sentenced to death, but then Tsar Nicolas I changed his mind about the executions. Nicky waited until the very last minute to call it off, though—Dosty and the other prisoners were literally standing in the firing line. Then it was off to Siberia for four years. Which is totally the way to convince someone not to take down your corrupt, totalitarian government.

The Crucible by Arthur Miller

Published: 1953
Category: play (drama)
Banned for: the Commies are coming! Yeah, not so much. But who needs evidence when there are ~~witches~~ Commies to hunt? Which pretty much sums up (a) the impetus for writing the play, and (b) the reaction from censors and people whose panties kept on twisting. Because anyone who satirizes a modern-day witch hunt is obviously a very bad man . . . and a Commie.

> *"Because it is my name! Because I cannot have another in my life! Because I lie and sign myself to lies! Because I am not worth the dust on the feet of them that hang! How may I live without my name? I have given you my soul; leave me my name!"*

> *Whoa, calm down there, Johnny boy. Fine, keep your name, but Beelzebub is totally taking your soul . . . which, in case you didn't know, tastes like chicken.*

Get your torches ready, kids, because we're going on a ~~Commie~~ witch hunt!

Let's start with a group of teenage girls getting freaky in the woods, dancing around nekkid and casting love spells with the slave Tituba—you know, like thou doest. In ~~1950s Hollywood~~ Puritan Massachusetts, that's a big no-no. Too bad the town pastor happened upon the bacchanalia. Such a party pooper, that one.

Some of what happened that night scarred the younger girls so much—drinking chicken blood? Seriously?—that they went comatose and wouldn't wake up. Yea verily, 'tis not so good. When they still won't wake days later, preacher man sends for Reverend Hale, the closest expert on witchcraft and demonic activities because this is *obviously* the work of witches and not just a bunch of bratty tween girls being overly dramatic and trying to get out of trouble.

When Hale shows up, the situation heats up like the devil tinkering around with the thermostat in hell. The girls awake, and their friends all join the reindeer games by flailing and screaming about being forced to do wicked things by witchy Tituba. Home girl knows she's screwed, so she says what her masters want to hear. She confesseth to witchcraft and then accuseth others. Yeah, this is gonna get ugly.

The principal accuser of witchiness, Abigail Williams, has a big ol' crush on John Proctor, a married man with kids not much younger than her. She'd been the farmer's "helper" until Mrs. Proctor (first name: Goody; middle name: ~~Twoshoes~~ Elizabeth) kicked her out for having an affair with her husband. Unfortunately for goody Goody, Abby wants her dead so she can become the next Mrs. Proctologist. Guess who's about to be accused of witchcraft? Mmmhmm.

To cover their lies, the girls form a gang, led by Abby, that terrorizes Salem. She relishes her power over life and death a li'l bit too much, though, accusing anyone who's ever annoyed her. Bye bye, Nurse! See you later, Goodwife Corey! Then the moment she's been waiting for: getting rid of Goody Elizabeth Proctor.

Hale carefully questions the Proctors. The big test to prove their innocence? Reciting the Ten Commandments. Which, I mean, *come on*. John does a good job, until he forgets the one about—you guessed it!—adultery. Oops. John's mission becomes saving his wife from hanging. She's so honest that she'd never lie. Unfortunately, someone forgot to mention that to Elizabeth. When John admits his infidelity to discredit Abby, the court asks Lizzie if she knew of the affair. She tells a little white lie—nope, didn't know—that condemns John as the liar. Well, crap.

But wait! Elizabeth can't be executed. She's pregnant. *<gasp>* So she's safe for now because the court is sensible enough to protect the unborn child. Just barely. But John's in hot water—and prison. Perhaps that "God is dead!" speech wasn't such a good idea after all.

To end the whole sordid thing after months of drama, they convince Proctor to sign a confession, and dude totally caves. How could such a principled guy lie to prevent his death? Man, it's almost like he'd rather live and be with his family than greet the gallows because of some twisted young brat. Imagine that. (It probably helps that in real life he was sixty years old and not a brawny spring chicken like Daniel Day-Lewis.)

So no witch burning here, kids, just a bunch of hangings instead— except the old codger forcibly crushed to death under a pile of rocks. Twenty-seven people accused of witchcraft died; of that, twenty-one were hanged and five died in jail. Let's hear it for the legal system!

Arthur Miller must have been clairvoyant. He wrote *The Crucible* after the House Un-American Activities Committee interrogated a friend about participating in the Communist Party, only to be called before it several years later himself. Miller never folded or named names. John Proctor would've been proud. Single tear. The House's conviction of Miller was overturned a few years later.

Death of a Salesman
by Arthur Miller

Published: 1949
Category: play (drama)
Banned for: criticizing consumerism, which is what happens when you bite the hand that feeds you.

"I realized that selling was the greatest career a man could want. 'Cause what could be more satisfying than to be able to go, at the age of eighty-four, into twenty or thirty different cities, and pick up a phone, and be remembered and loved and helped by so many different people?"

Jet lag, lumpy mattresses, bed bugs, travel fatigue, doors in the face . . . that's the life all right.

Spoiler alert: A salesman dies.

Willy Loman—*low man* on the totem pole of life (so many lolz, so little time)—is not a happy man, despite naming his youngest son Happy and burdening the poor kid with unrealistic expectations. No, Willy is a traveling salesman with an ever-expanding capacity for bringing the crazy.

When Willy returns from a failed sales trip, he's a tad grumpy. His wife, a bit concerned about his wrinkled pair of crazypants, convinces him to ask his boss if he can work in his hometown to avoid all that travel. Willy spends the evening badmouthing his kids. The oldest, Biff, has done nothing with his life. He was a big football star back in high school. He had dreams. He coulda been a contender. But no, kid had to go and flunk out of high school and hasn't done anything since. Not to worry, though, because Biff and Happy trash-talk their dad right back. Fun for the whole family!

Biff: Pops has been whackadoo lately.

Happy: Yeah, he keeps talking to invisible people. Totally creeps.

Willy: What are you two knuckleheads doing? Sitting on your butts, like usual?

Biff: No. Maybe. Yes.

Happy: Tomorrow Biff's, like, totally going to pitch his old boss with the most amazing business proposal *evar*. It'll be epic!

Willy: Believe it when I see it. *(mumbling)* I tell you, Ben, kids these days . . . *(wanders off)*

Biff: Uh, who's Dad talking to?

Happy: Ben. As in dead Uncle Ben? So wrong.

Next day, Willy and Biff have their respective meetings—and fail spectacularly. Instead of getting a better arrangement, Willy gets canned. Even worse, Biff's old boss has no clue who he is. "I told Bill that if they move my desk one more time, then I'm quitting, I'm going to quit. I told Don, too, because they've moved my desk four times already this year, and I used to be over by the window . . ." With such colossal failures to celebrate, they go out to dinner, just the guys. The meal consists of sour grapes, bitter whining, and biting tongues. Delish. Still at it, Willy flashes back to an especially memorable business trip while Biff was in high school. Good ol' Biff surprised dad by showing up unannounced to find Pops working extra hard with a young woman in the hotel room.

Not what it looks like, son. I take my clients' needs very seriously.

Which explains Biff's disinterest in (a) his father, (b) being a sales-man, and (c) pretty much everything. With papa channeling the nut-house, the boys skedaddle, leaving Willy confuddled at the restaurant. Mom's not thrilled about that, so when Willy finally toddles home it all erupts in a big family fight. Biff gives dad the 4-1-1: Neither of them is anything special. They're all just normal people.

Quoi? They can't possibly be *average.* Salesmen are the bestest people in the whole wide world!—and not just because they can keep separate families in each of the great fifty states of the United States of Freedomer-ica! They cry, they hug, they bond. Biff just wants to be accepted for who he is. But Willy has developed a case of selective hearing, so he thinks Biff is promising to be a terrific businessman—just like dad. Papa's so proud that he drives his car into a light pole. Whoops.

Yeah, Willy figured the insurance money from the accident would enable Biff to start a business. Biff, however, doesn't want to be a business-man *like he said* right before the unfortunate "accident." Thanks, dad.

Arthur Miller wrote the first act of *Death of a Salesman* in one day. Perhaps some rather powerful feelings toward his Uncle Manny—a traveling salesman, if you can believe it—might have fueled his writ-ing fever. Nothing like working through personal issues on a national stage, amirite?

The Divine Comedy
by Dante Alighieri

Published: 1314
Category: epic poem
Banned for: being anti-banking, anti-kinky, anti-Semitic, homophobic, Islamophobic, and misogynistic by modern political correcticians. How dare that Dante have such medieval notions about society!

"Abandon hope, all ye who enter here."

That's the welcome sign? Would it have killed them to make it sound a bit nicer, like "Welcome to hell. Please enjoy your eternal damnation"?

Please pass forward your field trip permission slips. We're all going to hell. Make sure you wear something cool; it's gonna get hot down there. No flash photography, please. The bright light disturbs the natives, who think they're getting upgraded to heaven.

Dante's our narrator, and—hey look, there's Virgil (page 6), come to be our tour guide. Whazzup, buddy? Didn't think we'd be seeing you around here, considering you're a polytheist Roman poet who died before the birth of Christ. Sweet deal. Let's get going then. On your right, you'll see the Uncommitted. They spent so much time fence-sitting in life that they're still not sure whether they want to end up in heaven or hell. Seriously, guys, you're dead. Time to decide.

Next we come to the Acheron River, where the ferryman Charon will take us across into hell proper. To recap so far: We've got a Roman guide leading an Italian Christian across a Greek river into the Underworld. Right. Clear as brimstone. This boat's only for those going to hell, though. The sinners who repent hop a different ferry to purgatory, where they suffer for a limited time only. The goody-two-shoes go straight to heaven, but we don't hang with those people. Too self-righteous, if you know what I mean.

Circle 1: Limbo. Sadly, this is not an eternal Caribbean dance party. Virgil chills here with his philosopher friends because even though they were super-awesome people when alive, they were never baptized. Sucks to be you! But not completely because it's kinda nice down here, with meadows and castles and stuff.

Circle 2: Lust. In hell, people are usually punished by the sins they committed in life. Sex punished with sex? Yes, please. Except that's not how it works. *Dammit.* No sexytimes for these folks. They're perpetually blown about by strong winds because they let lust blow them around in life (not like *that*). Everyone wave to Lancelot and Guinevere as they blow past!

Circle 3: Gluttons get the wrong end of the stick here. They lie around forever in a big, stinky pile of muck because they were pigs in life. *Boring.* Next!

Circle 4: Greed. Both the misers and prodigals are punished by punishing one another, one for hoarding their stuff, the other for wasting it. Talk about poetic justice. The misers play an eternal jousting match with the prodigals as they push big ol' stones in a circle, each pushing in a different direction until they meet and crash. Then they have to turn around and go the other way until *bam!* Perpetual bumper cars, without the rubber bumper. Ouch. Hey, isn't that a pope? Wait, some of those guys look like clergymen. Men of the cloth in hell? No comment.

Circle 5: What do wrathful people do for eternity? Mud wrestling, of course! They wallow in it while hitting and biting each other. Fun the first century or so, but it gets old after awhile—and messy. OK, now we're heading into the lower circles of hell, so it's gonna get a bit toasty.

Circle 6: When people say heretics will burn in hell, they're not kidding. Fiery tombs all over the place. Yikes.

Circle 7: Here the Minotaur guards the violent peeps, punished in three different ways, depending on their violence in life: against others, against themselves, and against God. In the outer ring, sinners take a nice relaxing dip in a boiling river of blood and water. How badly they violenced others is how deep they sink in the river. Alexander the Great? Up to his eyebrows. The second ring is for suicides, who are turned into thorny bushes and trees. Not *so* bad—until Harpies come rip them apart. The innermost circle is for blasphemers, usurers, and sodomites. They live in a beautiful desert of burning sand and flaming stuff falling from the sky. Make a wish . . . now duck!

Circle 8: Fraud. This level is divided into ten different pits where each kind of shyster gets a special punishment. Flatterers get stuck in a big pile of crap because that's what came out of their mouths in life. Sorcerers and fortunetellers get their heads stuck on backward so they can never see in front of them—the future—again. Hey, watch out for that—*ouch!* That's gonna leave a mark. Snakes whose bites do all kinds of funky things chase thieves, while a sword-wielding demon hacks sowers of discord into pieces. Good times!

Circle 9: Traitors get lucky number nine. Each of these sinners is stuck in ice, with the worst group completely encased in awkward positions. Looks like someone took Freeze Tag a bit too far.

Now we hit the center of this hell-flavored lollipop: Satan! Yup, the Big Baddie himself is stuck waist-deep in ice. Dude has three heads, one white, one black, one yellow. He also has three sets of wings and arms, though I'm really not sure how they all fit onto a single Satan. It's like Mr. Potato Head gone horribly wrong. He has perpetual snacks in the form of the worst backstabbers of all time. You've got Cassius and Brutus in two of the mouths for stabbing Julius Caesar, and Judas Iscariot in the really nasty middle mouth. Mmm, traitor-cicles. Judas is extra special, so he gets a nice *deep* back massage from the Devil's claws.

OK, it's been fun, but time to ditch this amusement park. Where's the exit? We have to climb down Satan's fur? Um, ew, but OK. After that, it's just a matter of passing through the center of the Earth and popping up on the other side. Hey, Dante, could you send Professor Lidenbrock (page 111) Google Maps directions on how to reach the center? They keep getting lost. Thanks, you're a peach.

Dante Alighieri wasn't afraid of skewering his enemies by sticking them in hell. By all accounts, he rather enjoyed it. (And who wouldn't?) But it sucked when his political party—the White Guelphs: anti–Holy Roman Empire, pro-pope, against papal influence over Florence—was booted out and he was sentenced to permanent exile under penalty of death should he return. No biggie. Florence eventually rescinded the order—in 2008.

Doctor Zhivago
by Boris Pasternak

Published: 1957
Category: novel
Banned for: not toeing the Party line. The Soviet brass hated beautiful love tragedies caused by political upheaval. The ban on the book in the Eastern Bloc finally lifted in 1988 when the puppet governments fell from power.

"The roof over the whole of Russia has been torn off, and we and all the people find ourselves under the open sky."

Which means snow over all the furniture. Great. I can't even imagine what the heating bill is going to be like this year. Here, put on another sweater.

Married to one woman, in love with another, ends up with a third. Tragic love story, here we come!

The twentieth century wasn't all that nice to Russia: revolution, war, and the rest of the world's hatred because their athletes kept winning all the gold medals at the Olympics. Ahem. For Yuri Zhivago, that time also sucked; his dad went on a partying and spending binge and lost the family's everything. Then he took off. Skeezy lawyer Viktor Komarovsky also helped whittle the money away by putting a good chunk of it into his own account. Professional hazard with lawyers, I suppose. Yuri's mom dies when he's still young, so his Uncle Kolya finishes raising him. YZ moves to Moscow for school. Betcha can't guess what he studied in college. There he marries Tonya, and they have a son, Sasha.

Once he becomes a doctor, the Imperial Army drafts him as it battles most of Europe in World War I, which sucks. Don't worry, YZ, the wars *plural* and suffering will only last forever. He gets wounded and is put in the care of a nurse named Lara. Stars align, and heavenly choirs of angels sing as bright light shines on her *(cue Lara's theme)*.

Turns out, Yuri's seen Lara twice before. The first time, as a medical student, he went with the doc who helped Lara's sick mom. Does attempting suicide by drinking poison count as being sick? OK, yes, she was sick. Mom got a little upset when she realized that her lover, Komarovsky, was also seeing her daughter, Lara. Gross. So this Coma dude messed up both YZ and Lara's lives? Nice guy.

Yeah, not so much, which becomes apparent when YZ sees her for the second time. He attended a Christmas party to dress the bullet wound of a high-profile prosecutor, whom Lara had shot. Whoops. She was aiming for Coma dude. Komarovsky is rather forgiving, though, and keeps her from being prosecuted by pulling some strings.

Still a bit miffed at Coma for ruining her life, Lara runs off and marries Pasha. She loves him *sooo* much and wants to be with him all. the. time. He feels a tad smothered, so he finds a way to "disappear" while at war. Not one to be discouraged, Lara becomes a nurse to find him. ("Honey, I brought soup!—and shoes. I'm sure your feet are cold. Would you like me to rub them for you? Pasha! Where are you?") But then she meets YZ, and she's all "Pasha who?"

Yuri eventually returns to his wife and kid. Bye bye love, hello responsibility. With the country at war with (a) itself and (b) the rest of the world, life's a leetle tough. Eventually, they get tired of being cold and hungry, so they make their way to the fam's old estate, now a communist collective.

One day YZ decides to check out some books at the library, so he goes to the nearest city and—you guessed it—runs into Lara. They do their thing, which lasts a few months, before Yuri feels guilty and breaks it off. He's on his way home to tell the wifey when . . . a local guerilla group conscripts him. Bad time to be a doctor. Jeez. Docs in the grand ol' US of A just have to pay off student loans for the rest of their lives. Actually, that might be worse. Indentured servitude FTW!

Anyway, he escapes and heads back to find . . . hmm. Whom should he look for first? Wife and son? . . . Lover? . . . Let's go with option two. YZ finds Lara and then learns that his family was exiled to Paris, which isn't exile so much as lifelong vacation. Here, have a pastry. But at least they're safe. Hopefully. He and Lara spend the next few months together until they have to go into hiding because Lara's "missing" hubby actually became a general in the Red Army, and he's now on the outs with those in power.

Then who should find them but Komarovsky. Yay? Boo? Not clear at this point. He convinces Lara to take her daughter and leave Russia. She only agrees when YZ says he'll follow her. Which is a total lie. So now that both his wife and his lover are safely out of Russia, what does he do? He goes to Moscow and lives with another woman. Obviously. They have two kids together.

He gets a new gig at the hospital in Moscow, but on his first day of work he has a heart attack and dies. Well that's . . . tragironic. Lara attends his funeral and asks YZ's lawyer brother how she can track down a child she gave to strangers. Apparently she had another baby Zhivago, but Coma didn't want kids around. You people are messed up. So what happens to Lara? Who knows. Most people guess she died in jail during Stalin's Great Purge. Lovely.

Boris Pasternak knew he was climbing into a vat of boiling water when he smuggled the manuscript for *Zhivago* out of the USSR for publication in 1957. (Russian publishers refused to touch it. I'll give you ten guesses why.) It's said that he told the Italian publisher who finally took it on, "You are hereby invited to watch me face the firing squad!" Wait, literally? Either way, bravo, Boris. You've got balls, bro.

A Doll's House by Henrik Ibsen

Published: 1879

Category: play (drama)

Banned for: respecting women. Really. The über-conservative old white men who ran Norway couldn't believe that Ibsen would even *suggest* that women were just as good and smart as men. I'll show you smart . . .

"I have been performing tricks for you, Torvald. That's how I've survived. You wanted it like that. You and Papa have done me a great wrong. It's because of you I've made nothing of my life."

If you'd taken that act to the street, Nora, you probably could've paid off that debt much faster.

It's Christmas, everyone! Well, Christmas Eve, but close enough. Everyone's excited for the holiday—except Nora Helmer, who just found out she's being blackmailed. Oh joy ~~to the world~~.

She might have committed forgery and perjury by signing her father's name to get a loan—without telling either her father or husband. Torvald, her hubs, was super sick and needed to recuperate in Italy, so she figured out a way to pay for it. And he thought they were paying for it how? Doesn't matter. Nora is still an evil, wicked woman! How dare she take care of her husband? Why, it's almost like she's not completely reliant upon him for everything in life—including her happiness. Letting women think and make decisions for themselves? Society's foundation will surely crumble.

Torvald treats her like a doll, too silly to understand how the world works. "That's why old white men run everything, sweetie. So the world doesn't collapse when it's *that time of the month*. Now be a good girl, and fix me dinner. And bring my slippers. Oh and . . . "

Even though he doesn't know it, Nora's worked really hard, scrimped for years, and nearly has paid off the debt. You go, girl. Well, she doesn't *technically* work because women don't do that in Victorian Norway, but she saved up her weekly allowance—yes, an allowance—and paid the loan off bit by bit. That Nora's got moxy.

Unfortunately, the menfolk don't like that, so she had to do everything in secret and keep quiet when hubby rails on her for spending so much money on his Christmas present. So wasteful!

Now back to the blackmail. Torvald just got a promotion at work to bank director. W00t! The first thing he's gonna do once he's in charge? Can that skuzzy Nils Krogstad, who once forged someone's signature on a document. Only problem: Krogstad is Nora's secret loan shark. Yeah.

Krog tells Nora that if she doesn't convince Torvald not to fire him, he's going to show Understanding Hubby the contract on which she forged daddy's signature. Crap. Nora knows her husband, which means a no-go on influencing his decision. She is, after all, just a silly woman. So emotional. It's cute, really.

Next day, Nora's a tad agitated—as in bouncing off the walls to keep from freaking out. She tells her recently widowed friend, Mrs. Linde, everything. The woman offers to talk to Krog and retrieve the letter before Torvald can see it. Problem solved.

Except Mrs. Linde used to be in love with Krog but married a richer man because—do you even need to ask? Now that she's available, however . . .

The next night while everyone's at a costume ball, Mrs. Linde has a little *tête-a-tête* with her former lover. She convinces him to let things go so they can be together. He's all for that, so he calls off the whole blackmail thing. Torvald and Nora get home a bit late, but the night is still young—at least for Tor.

Torvald: Hey, baby. *Rawr.*

Nora: Um, maybe you should open the mail.

Torvald: That can wait un—

Nora: OPEN IT!

When Understanding Hubby finds out about the forgery, naturally he blames her for everything.

Torvald: You've ruined my life! I hate you!

Then another letter arrives from Krog, returning the forged contract to Nora.

Torvald: Oh, sweetie, look at that. Everything's OK now. Come here and give daddy a hug.

Nora: Bite me.

Torvald: *(confused)*

Nora: You're an ass. I'm outta here.

That **Henrik Ibsen** believed in equality between the sexes didn't sit so well with many Norwegians, so he and the fam vamoosed to Italy—and didn't return to Norway for twenty-seven years. Sunny beaches vs. bitterly cold winters? Smart move, I'd say.

Don Quixote of La Mancha by Miguel de Cervantes

Published: 1605 and 1615
Category: novel (in two parts)
Banned for: royally pissing off the pope. Roasting pretty much every major institution landed the book on the *Index Librorum Prohibitorum,* the Catholic Church's official list of banned books. Ooh, shiny.

"For the love of God, sir knight errant, if you ever meet me again, please, even if you see me being cut into little pieces, don't rush to my aid or try to help me, but just let me be miserable, because no matter what they're doing to me it couldn't be worse than what will happen if your grace helps, so may God curse you and every knight errant who's ever been born in the world."

So a simple thank you for saving your life is too much to ask? Typical.

Oh, glorious Spain, land of fiestas and siestas, a place where the code of chivalry . . . is dying. Yeah, not so many knights in shining armor anymore, except in those fantastic books about chivalry that Alonso Quixano has been reading. He reads them so much that he eventually *becomes* a knight like the ones in his books. What sort of magic is this?

Senility. Yeah, *abuelo*'s gone so cray-cray that he's suiting up in personality number two: Don Quixote de la Mancha, a chivalrous knight who bests evil and rescues fair maidens from harm's way. *Ay ay ay.* But our courageous knight is pushing fifty and, let's be honest, probably hasn't worked out ever. His armor's a bit rusty, and his steed, Rocinante, is looking ready for a field trip to Elmer's these days. His ladylove, Dulcinea del Toboso (a.k.a. neighboring farm girl Aldonza

Lorenzo), has no clue who Don is or that he's made her into some unrealistic fantasy that fuels his delusions. She might want to look into restraining orders.

Unfortunately, Don has a nasty habit of picking fights with big strong men traveling in groups. The first time he gets beat down, a neighbor finds him on the road and carts him back home. Don's niece isn't thrilled to see him all bruised and broken, so she has all his books burned and his library sealed. Instead of, say, helping him work through his delusions, she tells him a wizard stole the library. Makes perfect sense.

It doesn't help, though, because losing his books strengthens Don's obsession with stopping wicked plots and protecting the innocent. You know what that means, right? He needs a minion. So he convinces an illiterate farmer to be his squire by offering him a governorship over an island. With Sancho Panza to aid him, Don Quixote sets out for adventure.

They're riding along, *tra la la*, when all of a sudden Don spots a GIANT. Not just one giant, forty of them. Attack! Rocinante ~~ambles~~ races toward the closest one, and Don tilts his lance and stabs—a windmill. Seriously, there *were* giants, but an evil wizard changed them to windmills at the last second. Damn you, Voldemort! <*shakes fist*>

Next they come upon a terrible scene: A pair of shadowy, hooded enchanters are holding a beautiful princess captive. Don Quicky launches his assault—and attacks two friars traveling with a lady and her attendants. The "battle" ends when the lady tells her companions to "surrender" to Quixote so they can move on. Seriously, guys, just humor him.

While Don and Sancho rest by a pond, a group of travelers stops to water their horses. Rocinante gets a little frisky with the lady ponies, so the travelers beat the decrepit horse off with clubs, which Don (obviously) takes as an attack, so he runs to defend his horse . . . and gets himself and Sancho beat down in the process.

In the second book they spend most of their time getting mocked and manipulated by a rather mean duke and duchess and their sycophantic hangers-on. Good times. At one point, Sancho even gets his governorship. Hey, congrats, buddy! You must be so—oh. Another prank.

Don Quixote does get some action in when he faces the knight of the White Moon in battle, who makes him promise that, if beaten, Don will call it a day and go home. That's an odd request for a kni—oh, he's not really a knight: He's an old friend who wants to get Don home where he belongs. In the end, Don Quicky returns home and eventually recovers his sanity. Which is boring. Crazy Don's much more fun than mopey Alonso. Can't we slip him some angel dust or something?

Plenty of hoighty-toighty scholars say that **Miguel de Cervantes** wrote the greatest novel of all time. Pretty cool, but check this: Those same scholars call Spanish the language of Cervantes. To have one of the most spoken languages in the world nicknamed after you = the pinnacle of awesomeness.

Dracula by Bram Stoker

Published: 1897
Category: novel
Banned for: containing layers of repressed sexuality. ~~Penetrate~~ Stake evil sexualized vampiresses all you want, just don't get all Freudian on us. Some people like vampires just because they're, um, snazzy dressers. And they sparkle. No repressed fantasies here.

"The blood is the life!"

My life, yes. Your life? Not so much, dear count.

When young British lawyer Jonathan Harker travels to Transylvania to meet his new client, Count Dracula, he really isn't expecting . . . pretty much anything he encounters. Especially not becoming a prisoner inside Castle Dracula or being attacked by three villainous but super-sexy female vampires. (Count them—one, two, three. *Ah, ah, ah!*) Just remember, John, your darling virginous fiancée, Mina, is waiting for you back home—and any woman aware of her sexuality is *eeeevil.*

Despite the damper it puts on his, um, business relations, Harker escapes. He only gets as far as Budapest, though, before brain fever disables him. Yep, brain fever. Totally a thing. Meanwhile, Mina is gossiping with sweet little gal pal Lucy, who has not just one or two, but *three* offers of marriage—*ah, ah, ah!*—all from the same group of friends. She picks Arthur, basically at random. But then a Russian ship runs aground nearby, the crew all missing or dead. The cargo? Fifty boxes of dirt from Castle Dracula. *(Cue sinister music.)*

Soon after, Lucy starts getting sick and sleepwalking, and two small marks appear on her neck. That's what you get for necking with a corpse, darling. She goes to jilted wooer Dr. Seward, who has no clue what in hell—or possibly escaped from it—is going on with her. He calls in his mentor, Professor van ~~Halen~~ Helsing, who immediately recognizes the signs. So convenient, having an expert on the occult handy, innit? Van Halen orders garlic strewn about Lucy's bedroom. She feels a bit chipperer the next morning, so Mina heads off to help poor Harker in Budapest. Things go relatively well until:

Lucy: Mum, I told you not to clean my room!

Mum: Yes, dear, but that garlic is stinking up the house.

Lucy: It'll stink worse when I'm undead.

Mum: Stop overreacting, dear. Cuppa tea?

Unsurprisingly, Lucy's health plummets. They give her blood transfusions, but nothing works. Then a wolf attacks, scaring Lucy's mom to death, literally, and killing Lucy. But wait—Lucy's not really dead! Yay?

Van Helsing has quite the time convincing the doctor, the former fiancé, and their American friend Quincey (better known as proposals one, two, and three) of this until he shows them Lucy's tomb, where they find corpse lady snacking on some kid. Which totally convinces them to stake the former object of their ~~Lucy~~ lusty desires.

Remember: Any woman aware of her sexuality is *eeeevil.* Innocent Lucy good, sexy Lucy bad. Get her! While she's taking a little bat-nap, they stake her, behead her, and fill her mouth with garlic. That's one way to get revenge on a former lover. Makes appearing on an episode of *Cheaters* kind of appealing, doesn't it?

John and Mina return from Budapest, married, and join the stalwart band of vampire slayers. While they plan their next move, they stay at the asylum where Dr. Seward works. That doesn't go too well when one of the crazies lets Dracula in to snack on Mina. I mean, if you can't trust a complete and total lunatic, who can you trust?

The team finally tracks down the boxes of dirt in which the count's been hiding during the day, and they purify them. One, *one* box ruined! Two, *two* boxes ruined! . . . Fifty! All *fifty* boxes ruined! *Ah, ah, ah!*

Evicted from his dirty digs, Drac heads back to his crib with the Scooby Squad in hot pursuit. They split up (of course), Mina with Van Halen and the rest of the boys together. Turns out, though, that when Dracula was sucking Mina's blood, he also had her drink from him *(ew)*. It gave him power to control her, but it also turned her into a two-way radio. She can sense the count's surroundings, so they can track him. Take that, Vlademort!

Mina and the prof make it to the castle in good time, so they do a bit of tidying up and get rid of Dracula's three hoochies in the process. The guys, still hot on Drac's tail, catch him right before he reaches his castle, which now he can't enter. Sucker! Night has just fallen, but the guys are ready and slash Drac's throat and stab him through the heart with a knife. Don't you boys know anything? I don't care if Stoker *did* create most of modern vampire lore. It has to be a wooden stake . . . because that's how it is in the movies. Unfortunately, they didn't do a super-great job of protecting themselves, so Quincey dies. If only they'd had Buffy with them.

Bram Stoker was actually a crap writer and totally lucked out with this one. Most of his books completely tanked. It's almost like some otherworldly being controlled his mind and compelled him to write a fascinating tale about an *obviously* mythical monster. Yep, that must be it.

Faust by Johann von Goethe

Published: 1808
Category: drama (closet, meaning to be read rather than performed)
Banned for: all that talk of freedom and the will to choose—a dangerous thing, dontcha know. Which is why the German government halted an 1808 production of the play in Berlin. It might give people *ideas*, and then where would we be?

"Alas, I have studied philosophy,
the law as well as medicine,
and to my sorrow, theology;
studied them well with ardent zeal,
yet here I am, a wretched fool,
no wiser than I was before."

Ain't that the way. All this learning mumbo-jumbo
gets us nowhere quick, I tell ya.

Turns out that Mephistopheles, a.k.a. the Devil, is still peeved about losing that bet with God over Job. Who knew? So he challenges God to another competition: that Meph can tempt God's favorite human, scholar and alchemist Heinrich Faust, into all kinds of sins and debauchery. God totally won their last bet, so He says, "Deal."

How did Faust get to be so special? Well, he studied a lot, to gain ALL THE KNOWLEDGE. He finally has all earthly knowledge, but since he's not yet a spirit he can't have heavenly knowledge. Out of despair, Heinie brews a suicide poison. So sad for you. To have the best education ever, spend your life doing whatever your heart desires, and never worry about poverty or the ever-impending threat of murder or mutilation? Boo freakin' hoo. Cry me a Rhine, why don't you.

But hearing Easter celebrations makes him change his mind. Must have been one hell of an egg roll. Frustrated, he goes for a walk, and

a cute widdle poodle follows him home. Aren't you cutest! Then—
poof—dog turns into the Devil. Which goes to show that you can't
trust those yappy fluff balls.

What do you get when you make a deal with El Diablo? A crappy
ROI, that's what. Just ask the guys at Lehman Brothers.

Meph: So you want all the knowledge. What's it worth to ya?
How's about your soul?

Faust: I don't really use it that much, so OK. But you have to give
me a moment of pure transcendence, and you'll never accomplish that.
Hahahah!

Meph: Don't be so sure, you cocky little nerd. I have the tricks you
wouldn't believe. Just ask Oprah. Here, you've got to sign this pact in blood.

Faust: Gross, but OK.

Afterward, Meph takes Faust out for a night of clubbing and booz-
ing around town.

Meph (whistles): Look at that sweet, innocent virgin. She could use
some manly attention.

Faust: Hey, baby. Nice shoes, wanna sin?

Gretchen: Never! . . . How?

Faust: Let me seduce you.

Gretchen: Teehee!

She lets Faust give her mom an Ambien to knock the old bat out
while she and Faust get their sin on, but it accidentally kills dear mama.
They get jiggy with it anyway. By the time Faust comes for his next visit,
Gretchen's brother Valentine is there. They fight, and Faust stabs Val,
killing him, and takes off, leaving Gretchen alone to deal with the mess.

Meph drags Faust off to party with some witches, and they debauch
a bunch more.

Faust: I wonder how Gretchen's doing. Maybe I should go check on her.

Meph: I'm pretty sure she's in prison for murdering your baby.

Faust: What? I have a kid?

Meph: Had. Past tense.

Gretchen (in prison): I killed the baby! (is crazy)

Faust: That sucks. My bad for leaving you.

Gretchen: (Power of love returns her sanity.) Faust! It's you!

Faust: We should probably vamoose because we're both wanted for murder.

Gretchen: I can't leave! I have to die so I won't feel guilty anymore.

Meph shows up and gives Faust a get-out-of-jail-free card, but then an angel appears.

Meph: Dude, lost cause.

Angel: Nuh uh. She's going to heaven! *(Blows raspberries.)*

Faust: Thank you, Lord!

Meph: Stop that! You're supposed to thank *me* for everything.

Faust: But you ruined my life with all this sinning and debauchery!

Meph: You're welcome.

We're gonna skip most of part two because it's *really* long and boring. Lotta nonsense about Faust experiencing all the earthly pleasures and seducing Helen of Troy—you totally saw that one coming, right? At the end of his life, Faust, bitter and disillusioned, curses the Devil and believes in God again. Then he dies. *Wait, what the hell?* Faust doesn't get dragged down to hell? Even after he corrupts an innocent, murders someone, and commits every last sin in the Devil's handbook, he still manages to waltz through the pearly gates? That's messed up.

Deathbed repentance: 1. Being good: 0. (Goethe wasn't Catholic, so do the math.)

It took *decades* for **Johann von Goethe** to finish *Faust,* but it takes even longer to slog through the damned thing. You're welcome.

For Whom the Bell Tolls
by Ernest Hemingway

Published: 1940
Category: novel
Banned for: its pro-Republican stance in fascist Spain.

"We do it coldly but they do not, nor ever have. It is their extra sacrament. . . . They are the people

of the Auto de Fé; the act of faith. Killing is something one must do, but ours are different from theirs."

Bless me, Father, for I have—AAAAHHHHHH!! <dies>

You might call Robert Jordan a mercenary because, well, that's what he is. What else would you call a bored young American who suits up with the Commie Russians backing Republican guerillas in the Spanish Civil War? No, not Occupy Spain. Besides Americans are always happy to stick their noses in other peoples' wars. Turns out a lot of those Spaniards didn't like that Francisco Franco staged a coup and turned their sunny country into a giant bloodbath. Ever tried to get bloodstains out of a bolero jacket? Not easy. (Don't ask.)

Really, though, Jordan just likes making things go 'splodey—and who can blame him? Destruction is fun, especially when it involves *un ¡kaboom! muy grande*, like taking out the only bridge into town. The problem? You might not come back alive. Which is fine for Jordan—until he meets dashing beauty María at the guerilla camp. She's one hot mama despite her anger at being raped by fascist scum right after they executed her parents off a cliff. Girl's got issues.

Surrounded by war and certain death, it's pretty much instalove for the duo, with Cupid firing his arrows among soldiers shooting bullets. Either that or impending doom makes people horny. Possibly both. But now that, *swoon*, they've found each other, the world fills with hope once more. Birds sing in harmonious delight . . . along with the *¡ratatattat!* of gunfire. Yeah, not so much. It basically sucks big hairy donkey balls: Bobby and María know that they'll probably both die soon. *Así es la vida (loca).*

Hooking up with the guerillas not only brings Robbie *amor*; it also lands him a nemesis. Pablo doesn't like this Café Americano trying to take control of his band of not-so-merry soldiers. In the meantime, Rob and María get it on. *Muchissimo.* At one point, the earth even moves. Yes, my friends, we have Ernesto Hemingway to thank for that vomit-worthy romantic cliché: "Did [you] feel the earth move?" Thanks a lot.

Pablo only cares about *numero uno*, though, so he decides to steal some of Rob's dynamite so he can't blow up the bridge. Oh no he didn't! <*snap*> What's a trained explosives guy to do? Find another way to blow stuff up, obviously. So Robbie rigs the whole shebang, then blasts yon bridge sky high.

Rob gets maimed when his horse is shot out from under him by a tank. Talk about overkill. Instead of letting one of the guerillas put him out of his misery before the fascists torture him then toss him off a cliff, he sends his buds off to protect María while he takes out another soldier or two before—

The end.

Wait, that's it? No happily ever after? Dark, man. Dark.

Ernest Hemingway covered the Spanish Civil War as a journalist in the late 1930s and witnessed all kinds of atrocities. Not that he'd ever write a book based on his personal experiences. Hey, at least they don't have to fight bulls in the jungle.

Frankenstein by Mary Shelley

Published: 1816
Category: novel (epistolary)
Banned for: being too obscene and indecent for South Africa.

> *"I, the miserable and the abandoned, am an abortion, to be spurned at, and kicked, and trampled on."*

Animal sez: Nobody love me, everybody hate me, I'm gonna go eat worms. Raaarghrgrhg!

Before we start, let's clarify one thing: it's *Dr. Frankenstein* and *his monster*. Frankenstein isn't the monster, unless you consider mad scientists monsters . . . which is kind of the point that Mary Shelley was trying to make. Now, let's begin . . . in the Arctic. Really? Huh. Didn't see that one coming.

Captain Walton is exploring the North Pole so he can become famous. He and his crew see a hugemongous figure running in the distance. Shortly thereafter, they find a human Popsicle by the name of Victor Frankenstein, who tells Walton his story:

As a lad in Switzerland, Frankie loved science. Because the Swiss are as bad at that as they are at picking sides, he goes to Germany to study, particularly chemistry. Like any good college goth boy will do, he finds a way to bring dead stuff back to life. Mary's a bit fuzzy on the details of how Victor stitches together his monster. It's a combination of "*The thigh bone's connected to the hip bone. The hip bone's con—*" and, um, grave robbing. Yeah, Frankie sneaks around and comes back with body *parts*. Gross.

By the time he's finished sewing and super-gluing the . . . whatever . . . together, he looks down and sees that he's created a ~~masterpi~~ thing. But this Mr. Potato Corpse can't feel anything—at least not yet. It needs a bit of a jolt before that happens. Clear! *Dzzzttt! Dzzzttt!*

"It's alive! *Alive!*"

Frankie's pretty excited . . . until he takes a closer look at what he brought to life: an eight-foot-tall hodgepodge of stolen body parts with dull eyes and withered skin that barely holds everything together. He thought this would be a good idea why?

Monster: *(sits up)* Hey, dad.

Frankie: *Aaahhhh! (runs away)*

When Frank finally returns to his lab, the monster has gone. Hmmm. A terrifying undead creature that doesn't know anything about the world on the loose? That's not good. Frank realizes his boo-boo and sets out to find the monster before anyone gets hurt, but first he goes home for a visit. Priorities, people. *Uh oh* turns into *too late* when he learns that the nanny murdered his little brother. Gasp!

Except Frank saw the monster near the scene of the murder. He doesn't want anyone knowing about the monster, though, so he lets an innocent woman hang. Which is a shame, because it's so hard to find good help.

Even though the creature's a bit—OK, *very*—ugly, it's pretty smart and knows its creator royally screwed up by bringing it to life. No one wants it, which gives it a sad.

Frankie goes all stalkery on a nice little family but then is totes surprised when they freak after seeing the big lug. Really? Bud, look in a mirror. But let's take a moment to pound some MEANING down your throat: Frank's a monster on the *outside,* but the people are the monsters on the *inside.* Whoa, deep.

Monster: Dude, my life sucks. Make a woman for me.

Frankie: What? No! That would be horrible!

Monster: Do. It.

Frankie: *(gulps)* But what if you had children? Horror, madness, and woe! You could overrun the world.

Monster: Hey, that's not a bad idea . . .

Frank agrees to make her if only to get the monster off his back. So demanding. Frankie takes off for Scotland to create the female, but when he realizes the chaos it could create, he destroys ~~her it~~ whatever. Which seriously peeves the creature. The story devolves into a game of revenge, with the creature murdering Frankie's best friend and framing him, then murdering Frank's wife on their wedding night. OK, not cool. Revenge becomes a game of death tag as they chase each other all the way up to the Arctic.

So now we're back with Captain Walton, whose ship is stuck in the ice. Making them sitting ducks. *(Cue ominous music.)* Doesn't take long before the creature corners Frank, and it's lights out. Sayonara, Frankie! Walton comes upon the creature cradling Frankenstein's body. Turns out, killing his creator didn't help, so he decides to kill himself on a funeral pyre—subtle—so no one will know he ever existed. Except Walton, who tells his sister, who tells everyone she knows, and . . .

In 1816, **Mary Shelley** (then Mary Godwin) and a group of friends, including her married lover/future husband Percy Shelley, and Lord Byron (yeah, that one), were stuck indoors at a villa in Switzerland because of bad weather. They read spooky stories to one another and then had a contest to write their own gothic horror story. Mary wrote *Frankenstein* (with Shelley's help, some say); Shelley wrote a fragment of a poem; Byron wrote a creepy fragment of a novel; and Byron's doctor, John Polidori, wrote what became "The Vampyre," the first vampire story in English. Now you know who to blame for *Twilight.*

Gone with the Wind
by Margaret Mitchell

Published: 1936
Category: novel (historical, romance)
Banned for: mild language, accurately depicting reality, and inciting awful southern drawls.

"My dear, I don't give a damn."

Rhett, peanut, you're saying it wrong. The movie version is always right.

At plantation Tara near Atlanta, Scarlett ~~Johansson~~ O'Hara hasn't a worry in the world. She's not what you'd call pretty, but she's oh so charming that she becomes the belle of every guy's ball. So to speak. Kindly overlook that she makes "high maintenance" look like a breeze.

It's the perfect day to have a barbecue. But what's that noise? Oh, that. Just cannon fire announcing the start of the War of Northern Aggression. Damn Yankees. Way to ruin a picnic, guys. When the local manboys hear about the fighting, they all join the Confederate Army pronto. Because there's no better way to prove your manliness than to die a horrifically painful death on a blood-soaked battlefield with thousands of your closest friends and relatives.

For Scarlett, the greatest tragedy is Ashley Wilkes, resident dreamboat. The problem? He knows Scar a bit *too* well, so he realizes life will be miseryballs if they got married. So he gets engaged to his cousin, Melanie, because we're in the South and that's how we roll, y'all. Spurned, ScarO throws a fit that Rhett Butler witnesses. He thinks her temper's cute; she thinks he's an ass. Thus begins the grandest "I hate you because I love you" romance since Heathcliff stalked Cathy's ghost (page 268).

In retaliation, ScarO marries Melanie's brother, Charles. You show him, honey! All the men folk go off to war, and Charles dies of measles, leaving Scarlett a pregnant widow at sixteen. New from MTV: *16 and Pregnant and Confederate*. Scar is devastated, but not like everyone thinks. What others think: *Poor dear, crying heartbroken over her lost love*. What she thinks: *Ashley's married. I hate Melanie. Goddammit, my life sucks!*

Life's a drag for a widow. She has to wear black all the time and can't talk to men. It helps that she inherited Charles's fortune, but still it's so *boring*. Plus, the war is, like, totally annoying. ScarO has to volunteer at the convalescent hospital. Dudes be all stinky and bleeding and dying all over the place. How's a southern belle supposed to have some fun?

Adding insult to tending horrid injuries, she has to help set up a fundraising ball for the hospital—and she can't even dance because she's a widow. *Burn*. Plus, men bid to win a dance with a lady for charity, so how's she supposed to one-up all the other gals now? Don't worry, honey. Rhett will take care of that. He bids $150 in *gold* to dance with Scar. Haters be hatin', but ScarO be dancin'.

Y'know, these two would make the perfect match—if they could keep from strangling each other every two minutes. He's a rich blockade-runner only interested in profiting from the war, not fighting in it. She's a rebellious young widow. The war continues, blah blah blah. Food becomes scarce, people keep dying, and it's generally horrible—but Scar's having fun because people don't have time to worry about "propriety," so she can hang with Rhett whenever she wants.

Melanie is preggers and ready to pop when General Sherman marches up to Atlanta's door. They can't evacuate the pregnant lady, so Scar has to help deliver the kid. Gross. With bouncing baby boy in tow, Scarlett gets herself and Mels out of Dodge—with Rhett's help, of course. They escape the burning ruins of Atlanta and head on back to Tara, which is also a mess.

When a looting Yankee soldier swings by for a chat, Scar shoots him in the face, and then loots *him*. Melanie's totally got her back, standing there wobbling with a sword in hand. Girl power, indeed. To keep everyone fed, Scar has to work in the cotton fields. Why, it's almost like *she's* a slave. But she does what needs doing because sisters are doin' it for themselves. Finally Scar reluctantly admits that Melanie isn't *that* bad. But she still totally hates her for marrying Ashley. The skank.

The war ends, but now carpetbaggers are threatening Tara. Desperate, Scar begs Ashley for help, but he says nope. So they make out, because that's how southern gentlemen roll. Scarlett's more interested in money than pride, so she convinces her sister's fiancé to marry her instead to pay the ginormo taxes on Tara. Land over family, it is. Then she pushes new hubby out of the way to take over business matters. Wha? A woman better at business than a man? Inconceivable.

The sitch gets worse when the KKK forms to "protect" white folk from the dangerous blacks. When a black dude assaults Scar, her hubby and Ashley go get their Klan friends to give the man a talking to—and new hubby ends up dead. Scarlett, sugar, think you could go a bit lighter on the husbands? Always an opportunist, Rhett finds Scarlett at home, drunk. So he proposes. She *sort of* has her wits about her because she says no, but then they make out and she says yes. Way to stick to your guns, honey pie.

They go on a long and expensive honeymoon in New Orleans, and when they get back she builds a humongoid mansion in Atlanta. Shunned by society, she still chases after Ashley but realizes it's more the love of friendship than the passion she felt for him when younger. Jealous, Rhett sort of rapes Scarlett—but not legitimate rape because they're married, even though she kind of did say no.

She loves Rhett, but the morning after their, um, special night, he takes off for several months. Usually when Scar gets preggers, she's really put out by it. (However will she get back her bikini bod in time for summer?) So it's weird that she's glad that their illegitimate-rape night resulted in pregnancy. When Rhett returns, though, he taunts her about it being Ashley's baby. She tries to slap him but falls down the stairs instead. Bad move. She loses the baby and nearly dies.

Later they have a daughter named Bonnie, whom Rhett spoils like crazy. When she's four, he buys her a pony. Except Bonnie falls off the pony and dies. Let's be nice because he's so heartbroken, but seriously, *who does that?*

Rhett seeks solace in bottle and brothel. Melanie dies after having a miscarriage, and Scar *finally* realizes how much she relied on her and what a patsy Ashley has been all along. When she runs to tell Rhett and declare her love for him, he says her love done wore him out and he makes his famous parting shot. Fine, just get it over with. I'll start it for you: "Frankly, my dear, . . . "

Margaret Mitchell was ten years old before she realized that the South lost the Civil War, so good thing she (kind of) gets history right in her only published book (other than that slaves loving their masters bit . . . minor glitch). "For all I know," Mitchell said of the lovelorn couple after the book ends, "Rhett may have found someone else who was less—difficult." Ya think?

The Good Earth by Pearl Buck

Published: 1931
Category: novel
Banned for: not being Communist. Banning books is one of the Chinese government's favorite hobbies even today, but they took it a step further on this one and banned Buck from the country.

"Out of the land we came and into it we must go—and if you will hold your land you can live—no one can rob you of land. . . . If you sell the land, it is the end."

Three words: location, location, location.

~~Everybody~~ Wang Lung ~~tonight~~ is a poor farmer in the Chinese countryside at the turn of the twentieth century. His dad takes him to the wealthy Hwang house so they can buy a slave to be his wife. One way to avoid being single, I guess. So Wang has a wife! O-Lan unfortunately has fat . . . feet. Didn't know that was a thing, did you? Yup. Being a slave, poor O couldn't mutilate her tootsies as was all the rage in China at the time. No newfangled Golden Lotus bound feet for Wang, which is *so embarrassing*. Whatever will he do? They get along, so it's all good . . . until he can buy a concubine.

They both work really hard on his land and start to succeed in life. The neighbors, though, are living a tad too extravagantly—have you seen the price of hookers and heroin these days?—so they sell some of their prime real estate to Wang. In the meantime, O gives birth to two boys, which is awesome because boys are good luck and it means she doesn't have to kill any newborn daughters. When a freeloading uncle hears about their success, he forces Wang to lend him money. Chinese custom dictates that respect for elders, especially family, trumps all, so he has to fork (chopstick?) it over even though the uncle spends it all on booze and gambling.

So things are going sort of great until famine hits. Then it's all, "Why did we give the scuzzy relatives the money we need to, you know, feed our kids?" O-Lan had a girl earlier, so when a second girl comes along, she suffocates her because there's not enough food for everyone. To survive, the family flies south for the winter. Wife and kids beg while daddy drives a rickshaw to earn money. They have land in the countryside, but dirt's not all that nutritious. (Don't ask.) They barely get by, so for a while they consider selling their remaining daughter into slavery. So you're telling me that in the grand order of things, women are better than garbage but worse than dirty mutts. Good to know.

What do you do when you have no money but there's political unrest? Looting! They join an unruly gang of rioters smash-and-grabbing stuff from some rich guy's house. Er, he'll never miss all of his possessions anyway. They return to their land and have über-successful harvests for several years. Possibly because they're dirty thieves. They get rich again, and Wang starts thinking too much with his, uh, wang. He can pay others to work for him, so he has time to kill and nags his selfless, devoted wife because she has big feet. Ugh.

Wang and his wang fixate on the hooker Lotus because he likes her bound feet, and he cannot lie. The whorehouse madam can't deny that when the girl walks in with her itty-bitty feet and a round big toe to eat, Wang gets sprung—and that's enough of that.

O pops out a few more kids but then she gets sick, and Wang realizes what a colossal ass he's been. Dedicated wife is dead, and all he has left are greedy relatives and rebellious kids. Before he dies, Wang makes his sons promise that they'll stick to the land that's been good to them all along. Uh, yeah, sure, Dad (*fingers crossed*). They sell off the land before papa has a chance to settle into his grave, let alone spin in it.

Pearl Buck grew up in China, the daughter of a self-martyred Presbyterian missionary who didn't believe that women had souls. Even better? Her favorite toys as a kid were the mutilated hands and feet of newborn girls left out to die, which she took home and buried. I'm not even going to touch that one . . .

The Grapes of Wrath
by John Steinbeck

Published: 1939
Category: novel
Banned for: "spreading propaganda" unfavorable to Turkey. Wouldn't it have been easier just to, I don't know, confiscate and destroy the books instead? Oh, they did that, too.

"This here is my country. I b'long here. An' I don't give a goddamn if they's oranges an' grapes crowding' a fella outa bed even. I ain't argon."

I don't know about you, Grampa, but I find that things get a little messy when you sleep with fruit.

Tom Joad just got outta the joint after serving four years for killin' a man. He heads back to his family's Oklahoma farm where he finds . . . nothing. "Anybody home?" Nope. The Dust Bowl done ate their farms, so they've all hightailed it to California, where the weather is nice and they can work on farms picking fruit from the bountiful trees as angels strum their harps while resting under palm trees drinking cocktails with those cute little umbrellas.

Unfortunately, with the whole family packed into their heap o' metal truck, it becomes a game of Oregon Trail where everyone slowly dies of dysentery—except the Joad family members just drop dead or run off on their own. First up is cantankerous ol' Grampa Joad, who kicks the bucket just days after they start their road trip. Then, once they get all the way to the coast, Granma cashes it in.

Now, there are fruit picking jobs in California. Problem is, everyone else fleeing the Midwest is out there, too. The locals don't like these "Okie" invaders, but unfortunately for the Lala Landers, these migrant workers are legal, so they can't kick them back across the border. Let's take stock, shall we? We've got starving migrants without, well, anything, working long hours at jobs that pay less than squat so they can't even feed their kids. The landowners don't want to pay them more because, hey, cheap labor. People should just be glad they're not shipping all the fruit picking jobs off to China. Oh, wait . . .

Tom tries to do best by his family, but it's tough when they're starving and none of them can find work. So sad. Plus, Tom's friend Jim Casy, an ex-preacher, gets into trouble when he knocks out the sheriff while arguing about the workers forming a union. Jim gets arrested, and police break up Hooverville, the tent camp where all the migrants "live." Those trouble-making preachers, always trying to do good.

The Joads end up at a government-run camp, which is nicer, but they're still not happy. What, you expect the government to take care of you while you sit around starving all day because even though you search tirelessly for work there isn't any? Ugh, such a drain on society.

They should just let you starve. You're already doing that? Oh, well, carry on then.

Tom starts to get some work, but then he overhears a super-secret convo between some police officers who are planning to stage a riot so they can shut the camp down. Not so good. Tom tells a few others, and they're able to calm the situation so the police don't go all Rodney King on the migrant workers.

But in the end, it doesn't matter. The Joads move on and find work at a peach farm . . . only to realize that they were hired as strike-breakers. Ah crap. Even worse? Casy is leading the strike. Things definitely aren't so peachy now. As he and Tom chat after the working day is done, coppers sneak up and hit Casy over the head, killing him. Tom understandably doesn't take that very well and starts beating the cop responsible. The policeman's buddies jump into the fray, and Tom's nose gets all broke, but he gets away. He grabs the family and they scram, eventually finding work picking cotton and a new home in the form of a boxcar. There doesn't happen to be a rowdy bunch of kids living in the car next door by chance.

Everything's going fine, with Tom hiding out nearby in a cave to avoid a trip back to the slammer—until his kid sister threatens to sic her murderer brother on a bully. Whoops. Tom takes off again, but this time he decides to do something worth getting beaten for: He takes up Casy's work to organize the migrant workers. Strike! Strike! Strike!

Tom has another sister who gives birth to a stillborn. But hey, it's all good. When flooding forces them out of their ~~fabulous new home~~ boxcar, they take shelter in a barn where a boy and his dying father are staying. The dad can't keep down solid food, but as luck would have it, a source of fresh milk just arrived. Tom's sister kicks everyone else out of the barn and nurses the dying man. Tough call, but the sympathy factor beats out the creepiness factor. Probably.

John Steinbeck was no pushover when it came to researching his books. He actually lived with a farming family in Oklahoma and made the trek west with them to California. Talk about walking in your characters' footsteps. Ouch.

Great Expectations by Charles Dickens

Published: 1860
Category: novel (serialized)

"It was so heavily overhung with cobwebs that its form was quite undistinguishable; and, as I looked along the yellow expanse out of which I remember its seeming to grow, like a black fungus, I saw speckle-legged spiders with blotchy bodies running home to it, and running out from it."

Well, now we know what happened to all of Charlotte's daughters.
<shudder>

Little orphaned Philip Pirrip lives with his sis and bro-in-law near the marshes of Kent. What's there to do in Kent? Well, there's . . . uh, Pip hangs out with his dead parents at the cemetery. Which isn't creepy at all.

An escaped convict comes along and friends Pip on Cemetery-Book so they can play Hide and Seek around the tombstones. Pip's not very good at this game, though, so it ends rather quickly when Convict Magwitch threatens to skewer the little, um, pipsqueak unless he brings back food and a chisel to break the guy's shackles. Pirrip scurries off to help, but the con also sucks at Hide and Seek, so it's back to prison for Pip's new—and only—friend.

Later, Uncle Pumblechook (yes, seriously) takes Pip to see Miss Havisham, a crazy old bat dumped on her wedding day a million years ago, which made her totally bonkers. As in, running the funny farm. She wears the same dress every day—the one she wore to her not-quite-wedding. (Sometimes you need to say *no* to the dress, ladies.) Also, apparently bitterness and manhate can age a woman prematurely—to say nothing of living in a decrepit mansion surrounded by moldy food while wearing a decaying dress. Even though crazy cake lady's really only fifty-ish, she looks like a cross between Madame Tussaud and the Crypt Keeper. Amazingly, she's still single.

Chilling with perma-bride must be fun, because Pip hangs with her all the time. Though it might have something to do with Havisham's adopted daughter, Estella. The girl's a beauty, which makes it all the more delightful that Miss Havisham crazifies her and makes her into a man-eater, teasing and taunting poor boys to make them think she actually likes them—then ripping out their still-beating hearts to feast upon them. (*Kali Ma Shakti*—oh wait, wrong movie.)

Pip falls hopelessly in lurve with unattainable Estella, who practices her cruel womanly wiles on him. When a mysterious benefactor later pays for Pip to get an expensive wardrobe and edumacation, he assumes that Miss Havisham is finally taking pity on him and making him into a gentleman worthy of her daughter. (Hint: yeah right.) So he ditches his family and friends to become a prissy gentleman so he can win the cold heart of London's reigning beyotch, racking up all kinds of debt while he's at it.

Turns out that Pip's mysterious benefactor is the escaped prisoner he helped years before. You don't say. But the surprises don't end there! One of the con's evil cronies is none other than the guy who jilted Havisham after stealing all her money. Even more shocking, the convict is Estella's papa! Oh, the twists and turns—so twisty, so turny.

The whole thing quickly unravels, however, when Estella marries Pip's nemesis. Heartbroken, Pip visits Miss Havisham, who must *really* be crazypants now because she actually apologizes for using Estella to get revenge against the male race—and pretty much succeeding only in screwing with Pip. Miscalculated a bit, did we?

He leaves just before perma-bride's dress catches on fire. Totally an accident. Uh huh, sure. He rushes back in and saves her, though she still dies a few weeks later. Pip ditches England to work as a merchant abroad. When he returns several years later, he runs into—wait for it—Estella! What are the chances? This is Dickens, so about 100 bloody percent. Turns out her hubby was a jerk (*gasp*, really?) but he's dead now. So Estella's single.

Or not. After the nemesis, she married a farmer. So she and Pip say hi . . . and that's about it. He winds up a bachelor for the rest of his pathetic life.

Psyche!

Fooled you, didn't I? You thought it would end all sad. It did, actually, but one of **Charles Dickens**'s friends, Edward Bulwer-Lytton—best remembered for the worst opening line *of all time* ("It was a dark and stormy night . . ."), so consider the source—made him redo the ending. Now Pip and Estella run into each other and hit it off because she's magically nice now. Who needs real-world disappointment when you can have imaginary hope?

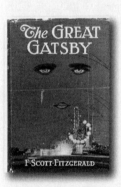

The Great Gatsby
by F. Scott Fitzgerald

Published: 1925
Category: novel
Banned for: naughty language and referring to extramarital affairs. Because no one ever does stuff like that.

"Gatsby believed in the green light, the 'orgastic' future that year by year recedes before us. It eluded us then, but that's no matter—tomorrow we will run faster, stretch out our arms farther. . . . And one fine morning— 'So we beat on, boats against the current, borne back ceaselessly into the past.'"

One fine morning we all wake up and croak? Well, if that isn't a depressing story. Remind me to never write a Great American Novel. It's all death, death, death, throw in some crippling and maiming, and then more death with a side order of woe.

Let's party like it's 1929! Well, 1922 actually . . . with plenty of jazz to keep things lively. Not a care in the world if you ignore Prohibition and swill giggle water like everyone else. Ain't life grand?

Nick Carraway hails from the Midwest but has come to New York to learn the bond business (loan certificates, not Ian Fleming). He rents a nice place on Long Island with all the other nouveau riche. His next door neighbor—Jay Gatsby, who throws extravagant parties every Saturday night—is as mysterious as the Gothic mansion in which he lives. Note to self: Borrow cup of sugar from the neighbors. What? I like baking on the weekend.

One night Nick goes to visit his cousin Daisy Buchanan, who's married to egotistic Tom. While dining at their mansion, his ~~meddling~~ always helpful cousin sets him up with Jordan Baker, a professional golfer and complete pessimist. Nick starts hanging out with Tom, who introduces him to his mistress, Myrtle, and her husband. Nice to meet you all? Tom drags both of them to a party in the city at the apartment he rents for Myrtle. The festivities end when jealous Myrtle starts shouting Daisy's name. Tom backhands her, breaking her nose. If that isn't love . . .

When Nick finally receives an invite to one of Gatsby's shindigs, he's baffled to learn that his fellow guests don't know a thing about their host either. But that only makes Gatsby more interesting. His enigma makes girls swoon and tongues wag. Oh, Gatsby, you're so mysterious, and you throw the absolute bestest parties *evar!* Except Gatsby doesn't party with his guests or even drink. What kind of crap host does that? Who *is* this man? Let's play the gossip game and find out. Gatsby is:

A. An Oxford man
B. A German spy during World War I
C. An American officer during the war
D. A bootlegger
E. Straight from the swamps of Louisiana
F. A killer

If you answered C and D (and possibly F because of C), you win!

Gatsby takes Nick out to lunch and introduces him to some of his notable—and notorious—business associates. Gatsby astonishes Nick by telling him that he and Daisy were in love five years before. Gatsby went off to war, and Daisy married Tom. Oh, love, how fickle your pickle.

So every Saturday night Gatsby hosts an elaborate party in the hope that Daisy will attend. At each disappointing party, he gazes at her house across the bay, where he can see a green light at the end of the dock. (I already told you, Hal Jordan. Gatsby doesn't *like* like you. So go, and take your green lantern with you.)

Nick sets everything up, and Gatsby reunites with his *twu wuv*. She's happy to see him as well, and they kick things off again. Daisy (and Tom) finally show up to one of Gatsby's parties—but she doesn't like it. Sad Gatsby is sad. She's supposed to be impressed!

Later, the whole gang meets up for some fun in the city. Tom stops for gas at the station owned by Myrtle's husband, who confides in Tom that he thinks his wife is having an affair. Uh, yeah, good luck with that one.

They head to the Plaza, where they rent a suite, and the party *really* gets going. Tom confronts Gatsby about his affair with Daisy. *Ruh roh.* Then Gatsby tells Daisy to leave that jerk for him. But Daisy won't and reveals that, once upon a time, she actually loved Tom. Gatsby is stunned, but Tom isn't finished and accuses Gatsby of being a bootlegger. *How did he know?*

Overwrought, Daisy makes Gatsby take her home in his yellow Rolls-Royce. Surely that will improve the situation, *non?* Unfortunately, Gatsby lets Daisy drive, and she doesn't notice when an equally distraught Myrtle runs into the street after fighting with her husband. *Nohmygosh!* But it's too late: Daisy kills her husband's lover without even realizing it. Ain't that how it always happens?

Tom stops by the gas station a few days later and learns of Myrtle's death. *Somehow* the husband finds out that Gatsby owns the car that killed his wife. Since Gatsby is playing the fall guy to protect Daisy, she's in the clear. But Gatsby on the other hand . . . yeah, not so much.

Myrtle's husband finds Gatsby lazing away in his pool and shoots him, then turns the gun on himself. *But Gatsby was the hero!* Even more tragic, almost no one shows up for Gatsby's funeral, though a Mr. Gatz attends. Turns out Jay Gatsby was the son of a destitute farmer in North Dakota. His dad was mighty proud that his boy made somethin' of himself. (Let's just hope he never finds out about the whole criminal thing.)

Fed up with the falseness of the wealthy, Nick moves back to the Midwest. The end.

You'll never believe this, but many of the events in this book come from **F. Scott Fitzgerald**'s youth. *No, not possible!* He, of course, played the part of the great Gatsby, minus the bleeding out in a swimming pool. Someone clearly had issues.

Gulliver's Travels by Jonathan Swift

Published: 1726
Category: novel (satirical)
Banned for: discussing public urination. Seriously. Politicians *hated* Swift. Hey, at least this time he didn't tell people to eat babies.

"I cannot but conclude the Bulk of your Natives, to be the most pernicious Race of little odious Vermin that Nature ever suffered to crawl upon the Surface of the Earth."

Cruel, Britannia. Cruel.

After a shipwreck, surgeon Lemuel Gulliver finds himself in Lilliput where a whole bunch of teeny tiny people live. They tie him down with their itty-bitty ropes and shoot him with their itsy-bitsy arrows. Awesome. I missed my acupuncture appointment, guys, so thanks!

When they realize that Gulliver isn't a threat, they take him to see the Wizard emperor, who finds him endlessly entertaining—and big. Don't forget about the BIG. Gulliver eats more than a thousand Lilliputians combined, though, which seriously puts them out. But they're happy he's there when he serves as their super ~~secret~~ weapon against their enemies, the Blefuscu. The two nations are warring over which side of the egg they should crack, big or little. I prefer mine shaken, not stirred.

He wins the war for Lilliput—things did get a bit tense when one ship rammed him in the shin—but they're not so hot for him when he extinguishes a fire with the most readily available source of liquid. That's right, kids. He pees on the palace. Honestly, that's what you get for sending a man to do the job: piss-poor work. Anyway, time for Gulliver to skedaddle, which he does by building a boat and sailing for England. He stays home with the wife and kids for a couple months, but then he's off again. "Hi, honey! . . . Bye, honey!"

Next he lands in Brobdingnag, where he's the Munchkin. The woman who finds him puts him in a cage as a pet. Wook at the cute widdle Guwivver. He's eventually sold to the queen, where he entertains all the giants. It all gets a bit weird, though, when the overlarge ladies let him play on their naked bodies. Sometimes bigger isn't better, gentlemen. (Think really nasty pores and grooming habits.) He escapes when a giant eagle carries off his cage and drops it into the ocean, thereby losing its lunch.

So it's back to the sea, where he's attacked by pirates. Then off to Laputa, a floating island inhabited by scholars. Those philosophers and academics get their jollies by performing science experiments on the inhabitants of the land below. Yay, for progress? Yeah, maybe not. A few more stops bring our weary traveler to the land of the Struldbrugs, who are immortal. Living forever is awesome . . . until everyone goes senile. Never mind, I take it back.

After returning home, he's off for one last trip, this time as captain. The crew mutinies and locks him in his cabin for *mucho tiempo*, which does a number on his mental faculties. Doc goes cuckoo. They make it to the land of the Houyhnhnms, a race of sentient, talking horses that rule over the paleo-licious Yahoos. So apparently Mr. Ed was vanguarding a vast equine takeover? (One out of three Internet search engines agrees.)

It takes him a bit to learn their language, but once he does they have grand discussions, and he comes to love their noble race. He wants to stay with them forever . . . so too bad they see dude nekkid soon after and realize he looks a bit too much like the Yahoos for comfort. So they vote him off to an island, where a passing ship from Portugal picks him up and takes him home.

It's a remarkably tragic comment on humanity that Swift had to add preface material to explain that *Gulliver's Travels* is fiction—as in NOT REAL. There were still blank spots on the map in 1726, so he could make up all kinds of fun stuff . . . but so did others, including sailors who claimed that they traveled with Gulliver on his adventures. <facepalm>

Also, you might find this hard to believe, but Irish satirist and all-around wit **Jonathan Swift** was actually a *priest* (which technically makes him a father mocker). Wait, you mean some of the clergy actually have a sense of humor? Shocking, I know. They even made him dean of St. Patrick's Cathedral in Dublin. Almost makes you want to go to church, doesn't it?

The Tragicall Historie of
HAMLET
Prince of Denmarke.

Hamlet by William Shakespeare

Published: 1600, give or take a few years
Category: play (tragedy)
Banned for: references to the occult.
Because talking to ghosts is so much worse than murder and suicide.

"To be, or not to be, that is the question."

You can count me in the "not be" camp if I have to read any more ~~*travesties*~~ *tragedies. #depressing*

Hamlet has mommy issues . . . and daddy issues . . . and uncle issues. Let's not even get into his love life. Unfortunately, his preferred method for dealing with it all involves sticking pointy objects in other people's gullets. As any shrink will tell you, that's not exactly a healthy outlet for his frustrations.

I can't really fault him, though. I mean, dude has it pretty rough for a prince. First, out of nowhere, his dad up and croaks. Making matters worse, with the king gone, Uncle Claudius yoinks the throne and marries Ham's mom, Queen Gertrude. That's not creepy, marrying your dead brother's wife. Nor is it what Queen Elizabeth I's father, Henry VIII, did when he married Catherine of Aragon, the widow of his late older brother, Arthur. Nope, nothing to see here, folks! Hamlet should already have a therapist on speed messenger, but we're just getting started.

When Daddy's ghost comes back to haunt poor Ham, he's somewhat receptive to the ghost's message:

Ghost: My brother murdered me by pouring poison in my ear while I was taking a particularly good cat nap.

Ham: Gross, Dad. I don't need to hear about your earwax problems.

Ghost: You must kill Claudius to avenge me! He stole my crown, my woman, and my life! Besides, what's a little murder in the family?

Ham: I dunno, dad. That's pretty intense.

Ghost: Revenge!

Ham: OK, fine. I can haz revenge for you.

Ghost: Good. Also, be nice to your mother.

Ham figures that the easiest way to throw Clod off his scent is to act off his rocker, because acting nutty is always a good way to go unnoticed. Ham keeps putting off the vengeance thing, not sure if he can commit the big M—even if it is his mean, creepy uncle.

Then he concocts the perfect plan: Put on a play about a murder just like daddy's and see how dear uncle reacts. Yeah, not the best idea after all.

King Clod isn't terribly fond of Ham-for-brains by this point, so he sends two of his nephew's best friends to *sort things out (wink wink)*. When Hammy figures out his uncle's devious plan, he makes sure his friends get the rope instead. So now Rosencrantz and Guildenstern are dead.

The Hamster ups his crazypants quotient, but then his girlfriend, Ophelia, outdoes him by actually flipping her lid. Probably didn't help that Hammy accidentally killed her papa, Polonius. To be fair, it's really hard to tell whom you're stabbing when someone is eavesdropping behind the curtains. Can't blame Hammy for such an honest mistake; he was only trying to murder the king.

Ophelia doesn't take the news so well and goes for a permanent swim. Her brother, Laertes, declares vengeance against the man who murdered his father, and—wait a second. This sounds oddly familiar . . . anyway, now we come to the climax where *everybody* dies. Laertes poisons his sword. Claudius poisons some wine. Laertes stabs Hamlet with his sword. Hamlet pokes Laertes back. Mama Gertrude drinks the wine meant for Hammy. Not to be outdone, Ham sticks Claudius with the sword *and* makes him drink the wine.

Prince Fortinbras of Norway walks in on the mess of corpses splayed everywhere and becomes king by default because everyone else is dead. Hopefully he can have the throne dry-cleaned before he takes it. Bloodstains are a bitch to get out of fine fabrics. Just ask Lady Macbeth (page 135).

The original story—sans all the fretting, moping, and whining—took place in Denmark around the thirteenth century or so (after the dinosaurs but before the flushing toilet). **William Shakespeare** wrote *Hamlet* about a decade after his own son, Hamnet, died. Coincidence? Possibly, but let's not think about what it says about that father-son relationship. Anyway, Hamnet was only a 'tween, so no vengeance required, thankfully.

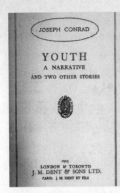

Heart of Darkness
by Joseph Conrad

Published: 1899
Category: novella
Banned for: the word "nigger" . . .
because rewriting history is the best way to change it.

"But his soul was mad. Being alone in the wilderness, it had looked within itself and, by heavens I tell you, it had gone mad."

Yeah, yeah, he's going to love the smell of napalm in the morning. We get it.

Hey, kids, it's *Lord of the Flies* (page 132) for grownups!

Sailor Charlie Marlow wants to travel to Africa. I hear the dense jungle of the Congo is lovely this time of year, *n'est-ce pas?* The best way to visit Africa while (a) earning money and (b) possibly not dying is to work for one of the European mining companies, such as The Company (not menacing at all when you say it like that), which hunts elephants for their ivory. Makes you want to take piano lessons, doesn't it. No?

So Marlow becomes captain of a steamboat, though it'll take him awhile to get to his floating pile of logs and steam. First he has to get to Africa, hike inland for two weeks to reach the Central Office, then fix his broken steamship before he can set out. Makes you tired just thinking about it. On the sea journey to The Company's first station in Africa, a French ship fires its cannons into the deep jungle. As in they're literally attacking the landscape.

After docking, Marlow gets his first sight of African life: a long chained gang of "criminals"—that is, enslaved natives. He also first hears about Mr. Kurtz. Kurtz technically went to Congo as an employee of The Company to "harvest" ivory, but he really wanted to test his theory about civilizing the savages. They're not really people, you know, because they don't have souls. Obviously. Kurtz helps the ignorant savages see why they're heathen, godless creatures that need the ever-wise white man to show them the right way to live. Because they don't have their own cultures and customs that Europeans are destroying in their quest to civilize the world. Nope, not at all.

Marlow reaches the central office after a good fifteen-day hike through dense jungle. There he finds . . . his sunken steamboat. Oh, and they make him repair it himself. It'll take three months to fix up the floating death trap, but they need to check on the peeps upriver soon. It's been so long since they last said wassup that they don't know who's alive or dead. Comforting.

While working on the boat, Marlow overhears a convo about how a year ago Kurtz asked to be left alone, but he keeps sending tons of shipments of ivory back to the main station. So obviously nothing weird is going on. With the boat fixed, they head out, bringing along with them ~~slaves~~ workers to take care of running the ship. Apparently his African shipmates are cannibals. Don't worry, they won't eat your spleen while you sleep. But you should probably learn how to sleep with one eye open.

As they chug along, they pass villages with tribesmen on shore who jump and shout as they go by. Marlow humbly realizes that he shares humanity with these prehistoric creatures. Why, he can even feel some deep-down savage part of himself respond to their shouting. How cute. Some while later, thick fog holds them up. Sitting idle because they can't see anything, they hear a chilling scream—but nothing else happens. Anticlimactic much?

When they start up again after the fog clears, they're attacked as they pass through a narrow part of the river. More steam, please! The guy standing in the pilothouse with Marlow takes an arrow to the chest and dies. But Kurtz is probably dead already, so it doesn't even matter.

They reach the inner station two months after departing, so apparently they were rowing the whole way there. As they come to a clearing, they see an old decaying building surrounded by a nice picket fence with human skulls serving as . . . um, ew.

Their boat was attacked because the tribes feared that they'd take Kurtz from them. They also find out how he got so good at harvesting ivory: He raided neighboring villages with the help of the local tribe, which thinks of him as a god. So Kurtz, can we talk for a minute here about this whole "civilizing the natives" idea? It doesn't appear to be working very well. You've basically become a feral beast worse than the "savages" you tried to convert. Any thoughts on that? No, we don't need to discuss this outside like men. Please put the knife away.

Marlow finally gets to meet Kurtz, who turns out to be really sick, and not just mentally. Couldn't have anything to do with a guilty conscience, could it? Still, Kurtz doesn't want to leave because he has to finish his work. The company manager who came along on the excursion says not a chance. You're going home, mister. Manager's a tad upset that Kurtz's methods were so violent that they've probably ruined The Company's reputation in the area. Because that's the only violent and inhuman act the Europeans have perpetrated on any of the native inhabitants of the land. Right.

That night, Marlow wakes up, and Kurtz is gone. But Marlow sees a trail where crazy dude crawled away on all fours. Marlow heads him off but quickly realizes that if Kurtz yells loudly enough the tribe will come and kill them all. So he threatens to beat Kurtz up if he doesn't go back to the station. Nice. Beat a dying man. Yes, he is a lunatic, but still.

Before the boat heads back the next day, tribe members bid a sad farewell to Kurtz. A few days later, as ~~Marlon Brando~~ Kurtz is dying he shouts, "The horror! The horror!" Then he dies.

Marlow returns to Europe, though he hates being around normal people who haven't gone through hell and back in Africa. He visits Kurtz's fiancée and gives her his papers and stuff from Africa. She assumes that Marlow admired and loved Kurtz because everyone who ever knew him obviously did. <*cough*> When she asks about Kurtz's last words, Marlow lies like a gentleman: "He, uh, called your name before he died. What's your name again?"

Marlow finishes telling his story to some passengers on a boat that he captains back in England. As the sun sets, he looks up the Thames toward London through the twilight. Hey, it looks like we're really sailing into the heart of darkness now . . .

Joseph Conrad was born of Polish parents in Ukraine, but they took off for Western Europe when the Russian government sent his dad packing to Siberia because they thought he was plotting against them. Yikes. He never saw dear old dad again. Sad. Conrad didn't learn English until he was twenty-one, which is pretty impressive considering that he was writing novels in English not long after. He traveled to Congo as a sailor but later had to return because of health. Totally unrelated.

The Hound of the Baskervilles
by Sir Arthur Conan Doyle

Published: 1901
Category: novel (serialized)

"All my unspoken instincts, my vague suspicions, suddenly took shape and centred upon the naturalist. In that impassive, colourless man, with his straw hat and his butterfly-net, I seemed to see something terrible—a creature of infinite patience and craft, with a smiling face and a murderous heart."

You know, I never did trust that Vladimir Nabokov (page 129).

The executor of Sir Charles Baskerville's will pops by the office of one ~~infamous~~ detective Sherlock Holmes, where he tells a spooky story of a demon dog that hunts down the Baskerville men, and—it just struck again! *OooOOOooh.*

With the old baronet dead by way of demon dog, the new baronet sails from Canada to claim his inheritance. Holmes and Watson meet the new guy, Sir Henry, who is already getting creepy messages about the bad doggie via notes left by a, um, shoe thief. Makes total sense. Holmes is way too busy to take the case—Thursday is when he washes his hair—so he sends Watson instead.

When the good doctor gets to the Baskerville estate, the police are chaotically tracking down an escaped convict on the nearby moors. More worried that a mythical poochie will kill their master and not, say, *an escaped convict*, Watson gets back to the problem at hand. Genius.

He interviews the household servants, Mr. and Mrs. ~~Drew~~ Barrymore. There's something sneaky going on with them, but Watson just takes notes. It's not like he could solve the mystery himself or anything. Nope. Later Watson goes for a walk, where he runs into one of the neighbors, Jack Stapleton, out chasing butterflies across the wild moors. Totally normal.

Jack's sister, Beryl, shows up, has a nice chat with Watson, then tells him to leave town. Thanks, lady. Nice to meet you, too. A few days later, the Stapletons meet Sir Henry for the first time, and it's love at first sight for Beryl and the baronet. Her brother doesn't seem too keen on their little romance, though—if "not too keen" means shooting fiery darts from his eyeballs.

While Watson is trying to sleep, he hears someone in the hall outside his room. *Creepy creep creep.* He goes to investigate and finds Mr. Barrymore standing at a window in another room, holding up a candle and looking out onto the moors. Um, OK. Turns out the escaped convict is Mrs. Barrymore's brother. She and the Mr. have been leaving food out for her bro and then alert him that it's time for din din by shining a candle out a window. The things people had to do before cell phones.

Sir Henry tries to catch the brother, but he escapes. Instead, the baronet makes a deal with the Barrymores that if the brother leaves the country, he'll be pimped out with money and clothes so he can get on his merry little way. In the meantime, someone else has been lurking on the moors. Watson goes to investigate and finds an ancient hut with signs of recent habitation. Wily Watson waits for the mysterious person to appear and pounces—on Sherlock! What up, Holmes?

They catch each other up on the various clues, and it looks like the brother and sister team are actually Mr. and *Mrs.* Stapleton. That's right; they're married, which explains why Jack didn't like Sir Henry putting the moves on his sister-wife. While they're chatting, the detectively duo hear a scream. They run out to find Sir Henry dead. . . . Wait, no. It's the corpse of the convict, who's wearing Sir Henry's clothes. He broke his neck by running off a cliff as he was being chased by the Hound. Bad doggie!

Holmes explains the whole crazy story: Stapley is next in line to inherit the Baskerville goods. Apparently no one in the family knew about him. They thought his father died years before, but he was chilling in Costa Rica (natch). Stapley has problems with money, as in he spends it all, plus some, and now he needs more. So he gets a little murdery to speed up the inheritance process. Ain't nothing but a hound dog attacking the victims, just a regular old pooch gussied up in a bit of phosphorous to make him look ghostalicious. Stapley stole a boot from each victim so the doggie could get their scent. Shoe thief! Which also explains why the doggie took out the wrong mark. Dude was wearing Baskerville's duds. That bites.

Sir Arthur Conan Doyle was a tricksy sprite and not just because someone who created such a logical detective totally believed in fairies (seriously). No, two years after he got sick to death of writing Sherlock Holmes stories, he killed off his cash cow. Fans completely wigged, so he wrote another Sherlock tale. What in dog's name was he thinking? *Hound* supposedly takes place before the events of the previous book (in which Sherlock bites the bullet), but Doyle caved and brought Holmes back to life in later stories. You thought Sherlock died? *Hahahah!* Nope, just faked his death.

The House of Mirth
by Edith Wharton

Published: 1905
Category: novel

"But we're so different, you know: she likes being good, and I like being happy."

Oh you sly, dirty minx.

Lily Bart is a simple woman with simple wants: namely a rich, socially connected husband. That's not too much to ask, is it? Really, a girl in Gilded Age New York has to have priorities, and love just isn't one of them—unless it comes with a sizeable income, of course. Lily might do a bit better with her goals if she weren't, say, addicted to gambling. Probably not a great hobby for a single twenty-nine-year-old woman with expensive taste.

She sets her sights on the rich Percy Gryce, and she almost has him—if only she hadn't ticked off a certain Mrs. Dorset by hanging out with the married woman's lover, Lawrence Seldon. Oopsies. So Old Dorsie tells Percy all the horrible gossip she's heard about Lily. That gambling habit doesn't look so hot now, honey. Sad part? Lily is actually in love with Seldon, and he loves her back, but he isn't rich enough for her. Why must love and gold-digging be so complicated? *Le sigh.*

Still trying to get by until she can marry the big bucks, Lily attempts a more reputable form of gambling: the stock market. She gets her friend's husband, Mr. Traynor, to invest some dough for her. He sends her money that her investments are throwing off; she goes shopping and lunches with friends. Gambling, shopping, gambling, shopping—isn't life grand? Unfortunately Traynor's a total schmuck who has the hots for Lily, so he's actually giving her the interest that he's earning from his own Wall Street shenanigans, and he considers it a "loan"—unless she'll spend more time with him. The nerve! She stands up for herself and says nothing doing. How much does she owe him? Oh, just . . . $10,000. The frak?

To escape all that drama, she takes off on a last-minute Mediterranean cruise with Mr. and Mrs. Dorset, plus a young Mr. Ned Silverton. But it turns out she only got an invite so she could distract the Mr. while the Mrs. got it on with Silverboy. Awkward. It gets even worse when Lily gets all buddy buddy with some European nobility, because jealous Mrs. Dorset is really jealous now. She boots Lily off the boat and starts some delicious rumors about how Lily was having an affair with Mr. Dorset. Quelle peach.

Lily returns to New York to find that (a) she's been shunned from "proper" society, and (b) her aunt died and left her only $10,000—plus she has to wait a year before she can have any of it. She expected to inherit all of auntie's fortune, but that went to someone without a, um, gambling problem.

Life's not looking so hot for Lily. Especially when she has to get a job as a secretary and then move into a boarding house. Working for a living? The horror! Poor Lily hasn't a friend in the world, except for Lawrence Seldon. He's planning on proposing to her. Except Lily finally gets her inheritance check, makes another check out to Mr. Traynor to pay off her debt, then gargles a bunch of sleeping pills and dies.

But he was going to propose! He would have made everything better, and she would have learned her lesson and . . . eh, too late. She's dead, and Seldon realizes that she'd been in trouble the whole time but never asked for his help. He wasn't rich, but he certainly wasn't poor. Poor Seldon.

Good thing **Edith Wharton** never had to worry about money. With family money and all the moolah she made from *The House of Mirth*, she was pretty much set. Shockingly, though, the elite in New York didn't enjoy her critical assessment of the upper crust. Many of them expressed their displeasure by writing lofty yet condescending letters to the *New York Times* following the paper's glowing book review.

The Hunchback of Notre-Dame by Victor Hugo

Published: 1831
Category: novel (historical)
Banned for: an archdeacon practicing black magic. Not the best way to stay on the good side of the Church in Rome. Otherwise, you land on its banned books list.

"Nothing makes a man so adventurous as an empty pocket."

It's true. When I don't have change or gum on me, I get into all kinds of trouble.

Quasimodo isn't what you'd call an attractive man. The hunched back and malformed face aren't really helping in the looks department. The friends department, either, now that you mention it. He's also deaf after ringing the bells of Notre Dame Cathedral for, like, ever. But hey, there's a festival coming up, and he's just been elected pope! . . . of fools. Yay? Not so much. For the Festival of Fools, revelers parade around with the ugliest man in Paris and, well, let's just say that Quasi fits in better among the gargoyles chilling on the cathedral.

So they've got him hoisted on a fake throne, prancing around Paris, *la la la*, when Archdeacon Frollo tromps up and makes Quasi go back to Notre Dame. Jeez. He was just starting to make frie—OK, never mind.

OK, OK, he's *going*. But why do you need him so much at right that very moment? To kidnap a gorgeous gypsy dancer named La Esmeralda, of course. Got it. The archdeacon of Notre Dame is a nasty man who has taken to practicing black magic and alchemy. Some, er, *interesting* extracurricular activities there, Frollo. But as Quasimodo's only semblance of a father, he can make the beast do pretty much anything he wants. All right, fine. He'll follow orders, but when Quasi goes to grab her, a hot strapping soldier saves the day.

Esmeralda: Oh, Captain Phoebus, you're my hero! *(flutter, flutter)*

Frollo, of course, has already booked it, so Quasi gets all the blame, which means enduring torture out in the middle of Place de Grève so everyone can gawk at that freaky hunchback getting it. It's not so much the pain that's killing him as dying of thirst in the middle of a plaza while people look and laugh. The only person nice enough to bring him water? Esmeralda, whom he tried to kidnap. Aw, isn't that . . . creepy. Quasi falls head over heels as he's stretched out for punishment. But he's also in wuv. You do realize, Quaz, that this can't end well. Esmeralda is in love herself—with that dashing Captain Phoebus—who is only in lust with her. They arrange a secret rendezvous so Esme can be with her love and the soldier can get some. Frollo, obviously in love with the girl and also a ginormous creep, follows them, gets mad jealous, and stabs Phoebus. A lot.

This time, Esme gets the blame—for Phoebus's murder. Plus, everyone kinda hates her already because she's a gypsy and they think she's a witch, so they'll use whatever's handy to take her down. Executing an innocent woman for being a witch? What is this, the Middle Ages? Oh. It is? Sorry. Go on.

When they're getting ready to string her up at the gallows, Quaz swings down from the bell tower using one of the bell ropes. Daring rescue by the least dashing man possible. Probably a good thing, though, because Phoebus is alive but doesn't want people to know (a) that he survived and (b) that it was him who was doing a little somethin'-somethin' with the gypsy girl because (c) he's already engaged. Ass!

Esmeralda's safe in the church now because, as Quasi was swinging his way back to the cathedral, he called, "Sanctuary!" Which means no touchbacks. Frollo lets her stay, though he's still just trying to get up her skirt. She and Quaz hang out a bunch, and after a while she isn't as grossed out by him as she was before, so she actually looks at him now. Aw, Quaz has friend!

Eventually the peeps in charge decide to take away her right of sanctuary. Can they do that? They're in charge, so they can do whatever they want. When a bunch of criminals and other street dwellers bum-rush the cathedral to take Esme safely away, Quasi thinks they want to hang her. So he bumps some heads around and kills a few of them. Whoops. Then when the soldiers come for Esme, he thinks they're the good guys come to save her. Bigger whoops.

All Quasi can do now is watch her hang. Sadness. Lots of it. While he and Frollo are watching the execution, the archdeacon starts laughing. Quaz is so upset that he pushes Frollo off the cathedral and—*splat.* Triple whoops. Kid, you're not doing a good job of helping people out lately.

Quasimodo loses everyone he ever loved in one day. A couple years later, when a gravedigger comes across Esmeralda's grave, he finds the skeleton of a hunchback curled up around Esme's. And that's the story . . . *(sobs)* . . . of Quasi– . . . *(hiccup)* . . . –modo, the *(blows nose)* hunchback of Notre Dame. *(bawls)*

When **Victor Hugo** wrote *Notre-Dame de Paris* (the French title and name of the cathedral), the cathedral itself was a mess. No one took care of it, and it takes a lot of money and effort to restore a building that large. Like ginormous. But the book was so amazingly popular that tourists flocked to the city just to see it, which kind of embarrassed the Parisian government. "Oh, I didn't know you were coming . . . or I'd have cleaned the place first. Please don't touch anything." Tourists saved the cathedral—yay!—and two centuries later they still overrun both the church and Paris, making a nuisance of themselves.

The Importance of Being Earnest by Oscar Wilde

Published: 1895
Category: play (comedy)
Banned for: the author being gay. *Earnest* was the toast of the town until Wilde went on trial for preferring guys over gals. The producers shut the play down immediately. *Dandysaywha?*

"I never travel without my diary. One should always have something sensational to read in the train."

Dear Diary, today was rather uneventful—until pirates showed up with their fire-snorting monkeys.

John Worthing is known as Ernest by his friends in London and Jack by his friends and relations in the country. Nice to meet you . . . all. At least your parents didn't name you Aldous or Rudyard (pages 23, 119). Oh, right. You don't have parental units. Sorry, dude. My bad.

Yeah, so John was an orphan, which means girls totally ignored him. Not a playboy who does nothing to earn the moolah? Pass. I mean, he totally could have been the spawn of circus folk, and nothing good ever comes from marrying into the freak show. Without a cool name, there's no way the chicks will swoon over him, so he makes up a super alter ego named . . . Ernest. Really? He *picked* that? Wow.

He's in lurve with his BFF Algernon's hottie cousin Gwendolen, but her over-starched mumsie, Lady Bracknell, says not hardly. Gwen says yes anyway. Good thing JohnJackErnestJingleheimerSchmidt chose a stellar new name because Gwendy's obsessed with a capital ~~stalker~~ O with the name Ernest. It's totes her fave.

What's-his-name tells Algernon to pretend to have a wicked bro named Ernest so he can get his groove on in London without getting in trouble back home. Good plan. Except for the high probability that someone will figure it out, and then he's screwed. Jingleheimer also has a secret (babelicious) ward named Cecily off in the countryside. Algernon invites himself over to his friend's digs without telling him. "Uh, would you believe wrong train?" To scramble the scene even more, Algernon tells them he's Jack's naughty brother, Ernest.

Confused yet? Good.

Cecily has a thing for bad boys, so she's crushing hard on Algernon. Then Jack arrives to find his "brother" putting the moves on his charge. Busted! The real fun hasn't even started yet, if you can believe it. Enter future mother-in-law from hell with Gwen in tow. Hijinks ensue, and the ladies get all bent outta shape when they discover they both love Ernest. Time's up, boys. The crap has met the fan. So they have to tell the girls the truth: They're both big fat liars. Yeah, baby!

Wait, what? Oh. Hey, that means the girls *aren't* in love with the same guy. *Phew*. Who cares that their beaux created party alter egos? But wait! Fun's not over yet. They also discover that Cecily's governess "accidentally" lost Algernon's brother in a train station when she was babysitting him like forever ago. Which really does make Jack Algernon's older brother. Even better? His name really is Ernest, and everyone learns the importance of being honest. Hahahah—huh.

Oscar Wilde is considered the greatest comic playwright since Shakespeare, and dude only wrote nine plays. Not bad. He saucily mocked the prudey Victorians, and the sexually repressed masses ate it up . . . until they discovered that Wilde was "*fabulous*." Did he regret not keeping his exquisite wardrobe tucked safely in the closet? Nope. (His wife did, though.)

Ivanhoe by Sir Walter Scott

Published: 1820
Category: novel (historical)

"For he that does good, having the unlimited power to do evil, deserves praise not only for the good which he performs, but for the evil which he forbears."

OK, so what if someone does neither evil nor good? That's a wash, right? The path of least resistance is completely underrated.

Cedric is not happy with his son, Wilfred of Ivanhoe, for a couple of reasons. #1: Wilf fell in love with Rowena. Aw, how sweet. Except Cedric is also her guardian and wants her to marry some other guy. Hey! He's your son. Why don't you want him to be happy? Probably because of #2: Wilfred, a Saxon, is bestest buds with King Richard, a Norman. *Le eep.*

King Richard . . . Richard . . . Why does that sound so familiar? What's he like, again? Has the heart of a lion? Ohhh . . . *right.* But what's so bad about the Normans? Well, they're actually French, and they might have conquered England a hundred years before. Got it. Let's conveniently ignore that the Saxons invaded England while the Romans were in charge five hundred years prior, and the Romans conquered the Celts five hundred years before that. Ahem.

Anyway, Wilfy's family disowns him, so he heads off on the Crusades with Ricky. Excellent way to make your son loyal—to the other side. *D'eau!* When Wilf returns, Richard has been taken prisoner in Austria, which is nowhere nearby, and Prince John might have helped with that. He wants the throne for himself. Man, all this family loyalty is making my eyes water. Unfortunately, Wilf doesn't have a family home anymore, so he jousts in a tournament—and wins. His handle? The Disinherited Knight. Yeah. That'll fool 'em. #namefail.

Well, he did have a little help in the tournament from the mysterious Black Knight. As winner, Ivanhoe gets to crown the queen of Beauty and Light, so he picks . . . wait for it . . . Rowena! Shocker.

Happy day! Except for the minor problem that Ivan the hoe is severely wounded. Puts a damper on the celebration. He's tended to by Rebecca, whose father is . . . a Jew! And a moneylender. *Gasp!* Say it ain't so, 'Hoe. Sadly, it *is* true. Even though Rebecca and her pops are good people, we couldn't possibly overlook the travesty of their being Jewish. So Ivanhoe, did you happen to meet anyone Rebecca might know while you were off crusading in the Holy Land? Oh, so the Crusaders were too busy massacring the Jews to invite them to tea? Curious.

While tending to her charming, gorgeous, manly, strong, did I say handsome? patient, Rebecca falls in love with him. But it'll never work: He's a Christian, and she's a Jew. Let's ignore that Jesus and his apostles were all Jewish, which technically means the first Christians were Jewish and Christian *at the same time*. Whoa. Either way, none of that "Love thy neighbor" stuff here.

Meanwhile, *eeevil* Prince John hears that dear brother Ricky might have escaped from prison in Austria. It's not like Johnny boy would do anything worthwhile, like run the country fairly and effectively. With bro on the loose, John convenes his minions and cohorts to figure out how to steal the throne permanently. All right, boys, commence plotting!

Back at the tourney, a nice little group of Saxons and Jews head home, feeling rather triumphant at Ivan's big win. Even though he's still laid out from his injuries. And the Saxons are schmoozing with Jews. Otherwise everything's good—until they're attacked and the whole party is captured. Dagnabbit, Ivan! You're useless. You're some epic chivalrous knight, so you're supposed to do knightly stuff. Those injuries look like superficial flesh wounds to me. Ugh, fine.

Turns out, one of the prince's minions is in love with Rowena, so he steals her. Another of the knightly cohorts tries to seduce Rebecca and ends up falling in love with her. Guys, it's usually not a good sign when you have to tie a girl up to marry her. Just a thought. Don't worry, though; the chivalrous knight has chivalrous knights of his own on the way to rescue them. Papa Cedric comes—though probably only for Rowena. Harsh. The mysterious Black Knight also shows up to do some damage. He even brings some friends along. Hey there, Robin ~~Hood~~ Locksley. How goes it in the Forest of Sherwood? Nice of you to join us for the storming of the castle. We're totes gonna have a blast.

With such a dream team of knights out to kick some cans, they quickly spring Ivan and friends from the joint. Well, all but one friend. Seems the knight who took a shine to Rebecca took her away with him to the temple of the Knights Templar, who aren't presidents of the Jewish fanclub. So they accuse her of witchcraft because a beautiful woman obviously used magic to make someone fall in love with her. Always the woman's fault when kidnapped by some lusty jerk, got it. Feeling a bit better, Ivanhoe rides in to rescue Rebecca, but the knights have already sentenced her to burn. Anyone have marshmallows? Since this is the era of chivalry, the knights allow Ivan to fight as her champion in a trial by combat. Explain to me again how fighting to the death is an indicator of guilt or innocence. I'm not quite grasping the concept, especially when one person is going to die no matter what. Oh, maybe that's the point. Hmm. Dark.

Well, the Templars play all tricksy by choosing the kidnapping knight to fight on their side. So he either defeats her champion and she dies, or he dies in combat. Let's just say that the kidnapper is just a tad conflicted. Well, more than a tad. He's so conflicted that it kills him. Literally. Dude falls dead off his horse.

Bravo, Scott, for writing the *lamest* excuse for a *deus ex machina* in the history of deuces, deoi, whatever. You deserve a round of applause just for having the sheer guts to put something like that in a book and expect us to take it seriously. Oof.

Anyway, turns out Mr. Black Knight is none other than . . . King Richard! You don't say. Never saw that twist coming. Wow. Everyone ends up fairly happy-ever-after. Ivan and Rowena get married, and Rebecca and her dad move to Granada. Which is . . . good?

Sir Walter Scott would have made an awful knight. A bout of polio as a kid left him unable to walk for many years. But he was made a baronet after he found the long-lost Scottish Crown Jewels. For realz. They were hidden somewhere in Scotland to keep Oliver Cromwell from melting them down . . . about two centuries earlier. Seems the jewels were hidden a bit *too* well—until Scottie finally found 'em in 1818. Good job, Walt.

Jane Eyre by Charlotte Brontë

Published: 1847
Category: novel

"I am no bird; and no net ensnares me; I am a free human being with an independent will."

Yes, dear, of course you are. You're very independent. Make sure to tell yourself that when Rochester introduces you to his crazy pyromaniac wife.

In the Victorian era in England, the term "gothic" meant creepy old castles and horrible, unimaginable things happening to innocent girls—not sparkly teenage vampires allergic to anything with color, wearing too much eyeliner, and playing human pincushion.

Jane Eyre is not a sparkly vampire. She is just an orphan that nobody wants. (Tomato, tomahto.) All of her relatives hate her. In fact, they hate her so much that they ship young Jane off to a boarding school where everyone hates her, too. Except her best friend, who promptly dies. *Sniff.* What sucks more is that Jane doesn't even have good looks to save her from bullies. What is poor plain Jane to do? Fight back with snark, of course. It works spectacularly, and suddenly everyone loves Jane. Happy totally fictional sunshine day!

Years pass, and Jane decides to get a job. She posts an ad seeking work, then, *ta-da*, one immediately appears. We should be so lucky. <sarcasm> But Jane is off to Thornfield Hall where she will teach the ward of broody Mr. Rochester. Enter Céline, spoiled French spawn of Rochester's dead lover. But of course Céline is not Rochester's daughter, wink, wink, nudge, nudge.

Unfortunately, someone forgot to tell Jane that office romances get messy—especially if you all live in a creepy manor with mysterious locked doors. No need to worry that something might be creeping around at night, watching you sleep. It's part of the charm; a special amenity, if you will.

Like every respectable gentleman, Rochester strings Jane along and makes her think he's going to marry someone else. He even flaunts the woman in front of Jane to make her crazy jealous in love. Then, because he's totally in his right mind, he pretends to be a gypsy to see if Jane really loves him, probably more to torment her than anything, though secretly he loves her. Such a catch, that Rochester.

He and Jane declare their love and get married. Almost. They're at the altar saying their vows when a strange man dashes in, yells, "I object!" then drags the wedding party back to Thornfield. Turns out Rochester already has a wife . . . a batshit crazy one with a penchant for pyromania. Whoops. Not a problem, though, since he keeps Crazy Wife #1 locked in the attic. It's not like she'll escape and light his bed on fire again. Right?

Jane isn't super keen to be Crazy Wife #2, so she takes off and moves in with a pastor and his sister. Since Jane is so plain and untalented, every man wants her, pastor included. The pastor proposes, saying that she'd be the perfect missionary wife in Africa. It'd be a great partnership; who needs love? Um, no thanks. She says no deal, let's just be friends. Meanwhile, she inherits a buttload of money that she doesn't want. Let me repeat that: Jane is the sane one.

Soon after, she hears Rochester's disembodied voice calling to her, which obviously means that he wants her back and not that she's gone bonkers and is hearing voices. Jane hightails it back to Thornfield . . . which is now a burnt ruin. Apparently Crazy Wife #1 took her little mania a bit too far, lighting blazes with glee, then flinging herself from the highest tower. Rochester tried to save her—talk about wasted opportunity—and is blinded for the effort.

Then Jane and Rochester get married for reals, have kids, and live happily ever after. Hey, even strong, independent women deserve a happy ending. Well, strong characters anyway. **Charlotte Brontë** came from a literary family, with sisters Emily, who wrote *Wuthering Heights* (page 268), and Anne, who wrote *Agnes Grey*. (Sadly, Anne isn't cool enough to get an entry in *Faker's*. Let's hope the other two don't rub it in her face. Sisters can be so mean.) After attending boarding school as a child and becoming a governess, Charlotte married a pastor she didn't love, then died of pneumonia while pregnant a year later. Single tear.

Journey to the Center of the Earth by Jules Verne

Published: 1874
Category: novel (science fiction, serialized)
Banned for: No need to go to outside sources for your censorship needs; just get your own personal censor, like Verne's publisher Pierre-Jules Hetzel, who changed potentially problematic things like Captain Nemo's heritage in *Twenty Thousand Leagues Under the Sea* so as to not offend Russia, where his books were very popular. But don't worry. Publishers nowadays would never do anything like that.

> *"Descend, bold traveler, into the crater of Snæfellsjökull, which the shadow of Scartaris touches before the Kalends of July, and you will attain the centre of the earth; which I have done."*

Any chance you could give us a clue about what we'll find at the center of the Earth? No? Useless.

Professor Lidenbrock, a scientist in Hamburg, is über-excited when he finds an original copy of an Icelandic saga written in archaic runes by some nutjob named Arne Saknussemm. A page-turner, I'm sure. While he's translating the text to Latin—because that's helpful—he happens upon a cryptic note on one of the manuscript's pages. Will kids *ever* learn not to deface books? With such an intriguing clue to, um, *something,* the professor becomes obsessed. But the Hamburger can't figure out the funky code even after translating it, so he locks himself, his nephew Axel, and the maid in the house—without food—until they decipher it. Dude. *Chill.*

Except, it's a clue to something amazing: the center of the Earth. Betcha didn't see that coming with such a vague book title. They finally figure it out when Axel is sitting in the hot, stuffy study, bored out of his marbles. He uses his uncle's translation to fan himself—because that's the best thing to do with work you've labored over for days—and realizes that it's written *backward*. Oh, you tricksy Icelanders.

After much too long, with wussy Axel F playing a broken record of *Are we there yet?* the whole way to Iceland, they arrive in Reykjavík and hire a duck hunter named ~~Bjork~~ Bjelke to guide them to the Sna . . . the Sne . . . the volcano. Most people don't realize that duck hunters are experts at navigating underground caverns where birds don't actually fly. Really. It's stapled to their diplomas. Anyway, they hike down the crater, which takes them down down to the underground, and eventually into a ginormous cavern filled with petrified trees and giant mushrooms. Everything your geology teacher taught you is wrong. Molten core of metal and rock? *Pffft!*

Electrically charged gas *(*cough*nitrous*cough*)* lights the underground world below the freakishly high ceiling. Coming to a colossal super-deep underground ocean, they build a raft and set sail for the center of Planet Earth—dun dun *dunnn.* Turns out exploring by water was a smart move because soon they spot a fight between two gargantuan dinos. An electric storm nearly destroys their raft, but they make it safely to land where they find even stranger stuff, like humungo insects and a herd of mastodon. Aw, look at the shaggy elephants. Which means your biology teacher lied, too. The biggest surprise comes when they spot a really big caveman—like, twelve-feet-tall big—but our adventurers skedaddle without introducing themselves. Rude.

They finally come upon a passageway that Saknussemmmmm marked: THIS WAY TO THE CENTER —>. Unfortunately, cave-ins block the path. So what do our intrepid explorers do? What you'd expect from a bunch of men: They blow it up.

They're smart enough to hop back on the raft so they don't get blown to bits, but, like most improvised tasks that involve men and explosives, they create an even bigger problem. Oh, and it wasn't actually a path to the center, but a massive pit. Not even duct tape can fix that. With another ginormo hole now attached to the bottomless pit, the water from the underground sea takes the boys for a ride. They go whooshing down the hole, tossing and tumbling for hours until they reach a volcanic tube. Things get a bit toasty, though, so it's a relief when they shoot out of an active volcano. (Paying attention, Six Flags? Best. Water slide. Ever.) They land on Stromboli, which is delicious, and also an island off the coast of Italy.

They return to Germany as heroes, the Hamburger heralded as one of the greatest scientists ever, and everyone buys it when they say, "So we crawled inside a volcano, and it took us to a really cool place with giant mushrooms, and we saw dinosaurs and cavemen that were ~~twelve~~ twenty feet tall, and then we shot out another volcano. I swear."

Pics or it didn't happen.

With his many futuristic novels, **Jules Verne** earned the title of Father of Science Fiction, a distinguished honor in nerddom. The Frenchman wrote about space travel, aviation, and underwater exploration long before they became reality. So *are* there dinosaurs at the center of the Earth? Iceland, anyone?

Jude the Obscure by Thomas Hardy

Published: 1895
Category: novel (serialized)
Banned for: pretty much everything. People hated *Jude the Obscene,* which some actually called it. Hardy mocks (a) religion, (b) higher education, (c) marriage, (d) non-incestuous relationships, and (e) society in general. Some people can't take a little criticism.

"I can't bear that they, and everybody, should think people wicked because they may have chosen to live their own way! It is really these opinions that make the best intentioned people reckless, and actually become immoral!"

*Go you, Jude. You keep justifying your heart out. Let's see how
well that works out for you, shall we?*

Welcome, folks, to the most depressing book you might ever (fake) read.
Really. Hardy is a master at killing happiness. ALL THE HAPPINESS.

Jude Fawley is a smart boy; really smart, like teaching himself
Greek and Latin. He dreams of attending ~~Oxford~~ Christminster and
becoming a scholar. In the meantime, he works as a stonemason to
save up for college. Then he meets the conniving Arabella, who seduces
naive but horny Jude, fakes a pregnancy to force him to marry her, and
abandons him two years later. Hawt.

Note: Copyright law prevents me from directly quoting "Hey
Jude" by The Beatles without forking over a buttload of money to Sir
Paul and ~~Dragon Lady~~ Yoko, so let's all hum along while we take a sad
life and make it better.

Jude heads to Christminster once again to pursue his dream. There
he meets and falls in love with his cousin Sue Bridehead. (Nothing like
keeping it in the family, kids, as you're about to see.) It's there that he
introduces Sue to his former schoolteacher, Mr. Phillotson, whom she
later marries, even though she's in love with Jude, disgusted by ~~Dr.~~ Mr.
Phil, and hates even the thought of sex. Yeah, she's a total catch. Surprisingly, things don't go so great. When Phil gets frisky one night, Sue
leaps out a window rather than let him touch her. She doesn't die, but
this still doesn't seem like healthy marital behavior, you know?

All Jude's dreams come true—except the whole college thing—
when Sue runs away with him. They live like friends with*out* benefits
for a while, but Jude finally convinces her to get their family freak on.
They're both still married to other people, so they skip that bother,
which scandalizes the neighbors and makes for difficult living when
they're constantly evicted and Jude fired because of their immoral ways.
Naughty, naughty.

Over the next three years, they have a couple of screaming brats,
then—*surprise!*—Jude finds out he already had one. Oh, Arabella, you
slutty minx. Marry Jude when you're not pregnant but scram when you
are. Unfortunately, their son is weird—like *Children of the Corn* weird.

They call Mini Jude "Little Father Time" because he's so serious and morbid. When little guy with the scythe thinks that he and the other children are a burden on their parents and will soon be abandoned, he hangs the other kids and then himself. If only he'd had an emo T-shirt to express himself.

When Jude and Sue get back from grocery shopping—kids, we're home!—they find three little bodies swinging in the closet. Sue understandably loses it, thinking this a punishment from God for living in sin with her cousin. Because God obviously likes it when bad things happen. Um, no. Soon after, she miscarries, thereby losing *all* of her children. Sad Sue is sad, so she goes back to church—and creepy Phillotson—to repent of her terrible ways. This destroys Jude's heart as thoroughly as if it were eaten by a cat.

Arabella comes trotting back and, once she liquors him up real good, convinces Jude to remarry her. But Jude can't live without Sue, so he sets off in bitter bitter cold—a bit like her heart?—to plead with her to come back. Doesn't work, but it does give him pneumonia. With Jude on his deathbed, Arabella pretends to take care of him but, *yaaawn*, gets bored and goes off to partay instead. He dies alone and a failure for not getting a piece of paper that says he's S-M-R-T. Sue becomes despondent living with Dr. Phil. Arabella doesn't care and trots off to ensnare a new man.

Moral of the story? If you let her into your heart, it gets better—or, you know, not.

Readers weren't terribly happy with **Thomas Hardy** after the publication of *Jude*. Can't imagine why when all he did was attack the institutions that Brits cherish most: marriage, scholarship, and social class. Opposition to *Jude* got so bad—an Anglican bishop actually burned his copy of the book—that Hardy vowed never to write fiction again. Which is why you probably had to read his happy-go-lucky poetry in school, too. Also, speaking of cats . . . Hardy's body lies in Poet's Corner in Westminster Abbey, his heart (supposedly) buried at his first wife's grave back home. The story goes that someone left the heart sitting out for a bit on the kitchen table, like people naturally do, and a hungry kitty happened by and, well . . . *gulp*.

The Jungle by Upton Sinclair

Published: 1906
Category: novel (serialized)
Banned for: socialism. The Nazis burned it—no surprise there, as it was a socialist call to action—but get this: The Russians banned *The Jungle* because it didn't espouse the *right* kind of socialism. Picky, picky.

"They use everything about the hog except the squeal."

Pigs wallow in filth and eat slop. Their breath, including the squeal, has got to be fatal. Probably doesn't taste all that great, either.

It's Jurgis and Ona's wedding day. Yay! All their ~~friends~~ fellow Lithuanian immigrants gather in a bar in Chicago's Packingtown, one of the city's ~~loveliest neighborhoods~~ biggest slums. Sigh. Ain't love grand?

Barkeep: Congrats on the wedding. Tab is a hundred bucks. Now pay up.

Jurgis *(panics)*: Hey, guys, it's not an open bar. Really. Guys? Where'd they all go?

Barkeep: Will that be cash or outta your hide?

Welcome to America! Jurgis believes big in the American Dream, so he'll just work extra hard and pay off that tab quick as can be. Hahahah! *(wipes tear)* Oh, you immigrants are so cute when you're naive n00bs. He does find a job pretty fast, as do several members of the extended family. Excellent. Let's buy a house!

Jurgie: Huh. There's a word in this agreement I'm not familiar with: S-W-I-N-D-L-E. And the house comes with lemons?

Landlord: Oh that. It's just the special type of flooring. Yeah, that's it. And you gots to use lemon polish on it.

Jurgie: OK. *(sighs)*

Not such a great deal after all, huh Jurgs. So all the members of the fam, including Ona and one of the kids, have to find work. They quickly learn the rules of working in the nasty factories in the district, mostly through trial and error. Lots of error.

Rule #1: Don't die. Dear old dad finds a job, which promptly kills him because it's too labor intense. Well, that's one fewer mouth to feed. #brightside?

Pretty soon life sucks for all of them. Jurgs joins a union. Awesome. That'll get him decent wages and safer conditions, right? Not so much. What he gets is a better education about the political corruption, bribery, and criminal behavior that make up the essential business aspects of factories in Packingtown. Sweet!

Rule #2: Don't complain. Someone forgot to mention this one to Ona's cousin, who loses her job when she complains that she was cheated out of pay. "You don't like that? Fine, now you get none of it!"

Rule #3: Don't get injured. Jurgs sprains his ankle and is out for three months. Wait, seriously? Three *months*? Dude, alternate ice and a heating pad, and you'll be fine in a few days. Then Ona gets pregnant. Cute, right? Just until the little parasite in her guts makes working a backbreaking job more difficult. Still, she works until the kid pops out, and then she's back on the job seven days later. Getting preggers did save her from being forced to join the prostitution ring her ~~pimp~~ factory boss runs, so, um, bonus?

All better, Jurgis finally heads back to his old job . . . that he doesn't have anymore. Better luck next time, bub. He looks for work and finds a job in the butt-nastiest place of all: the fertilizer factory. The less you know, the better for your gag reflex. What could possibly be so bad about working in these factories, though? I mean, this is America, land of germaphobes and hand sanitizer. Well, his first job was working at a meat-packing plant, where the animals were basically tortured before slaughter. Lovely. But it gets better. Factory workers had to butcher diseased animals, pass off vomit-worthy meat as fine, and often let rats dance on animal carcasses before processing. This book was the reason the FDA and other agencies were created. Really. It's so bad, Jurgs turns to the best friend of the downtrodden: booze. Now who wants the mystery meat loaf?

Rule #4: Never retaliate. One night Ona doesn't come home from work. That's not good. Jurgie goes to the factory—where he sees that her boss has raped her. Oh, did I forget to mention that she's pregnant again? Leaves a pleasant taste in your mouth, doesn't it? Jurgie is (understandably) upset, so he beats the snot out of the scumbag.

Of course, the stupid immigrant is at fault, so after an unfair trial, he goes to jail. When he gets out a month later, he arrives home—to no home. Yup, the fam's been evicted, so they're living in a hellhole of a boarding house, where Ona goes into labor much too early. If life doesn't suck enough, both Ona and the baby die.

Devastated, Jurgie turns to his best friend (the bottle). They chat for a good long while, but finally a family member talks some sense into him: "Um, hello, you've still got a son. Take care of him."

So Jurgs gets back on the wagon and looks for work. He gets a good job at a steel mill—hallelujah!—and then his son drowns in the mud-filled streets. He is (naturally) anguished, so he abandons his remaining family members and wanders off to become a tramp. As in hobo, not prostitute. But don't worry, that comes later. He eventually returns to Chicago and starts working again. But then he breaks Rule #3 again and has to camp out for a bit at the hospital. They've got him all patched up—but without any money, food, or job. So now he becomes a bum.

There are *some* nice rich people, though, like the guy who gives the beggar Jurgis a $100 bill. Sweet! When he goes to break it at a local bar, the bartender helps him out by giving him 95¢ as change. I think the math might be off just a bit. Someone want to recalculate that really quick? For some strange reason, Jurgs isn't happy about that and attacks the bartender. So he earns another stay in jail. He makes a buddy while doing his time, and when they get out they decide to work together . . . as burglars. Jurgs is certainly coming up in the world, eh? Eventually, he joins the mob and becomes a scab: scab as in strikebreaker, not congealed blood and crusty skin. But as a factory worker, he has more than his share of those, too. Then he sees evil rapist boss and beats the tar out of him. Again. And goes back to jail. Again. And goes back to being a beggar. Again.

He hasn't seen the fam in a while, but he runs into someone who knows them. Turns out, Ona's cousin found a new career (prostitution) and a new hobby (morphine). Life pretty much bites the big one until he stumbles into a socialist rally, and hope returns. Socialism is the answer to every problem in the world ever, and could never be corrupted into something terrible and more oppressive than the conditions he's living in.

Upton Sinclair got a bit grumpy when the public's outcry over dirty, diseased meat upstaged his tragic socialist propaganda story portraying the plight of the common factory worker. Eh. What can you do? People tend to think with their stomachs.

The Jungle Book by Rudyard Kipling

Published: 1894
Category: novel (children's, serialized)
Banned for: profanity and—dare I say it?—*slang*. The horror! I would *never* countenance the use of such degrading language as slang in books. *<coughs>*

"There is no harm in a man's cub."

Unless you're into that kind of thing, in which case: Grrrr!

Bad news for the wolf pack: *Eeevil* tiger Shere Khan is hunting in their part of the jungle. Why's that so bad? Because this tiger has a taste for the people. When the villagers retaliate, who will they come after? Da wolves.

Up to his usual shenanigans, Khan (da tiger, not da Mongolian general) is hunting a baby. When the wolves hear something prowling around their cave, they spring out . . . to find a leetle nekkid human. Anyone know India's number for Child Protective Services? Mama Wolf sees nekkid man cub and wants to keep her new pet. She names him Mowgli, which means frog. Kind of weird because the kid isn't green, but who cares? Mama has a new froggie!

They powwow with the rest of their pack. They're about to toss the kid out or invite him to dinner when Baloo da bear and Bagheera da panther, who was raised by humans, offer to teach Mowgli the bare necessities of life. When Mowgli reaches the mature old age of seven—what do you mean, "human years"?—Baloo yells at him for not paying attention. Imagine that, a boy zoning out during school. That would never hap—*hey!* I'm telling a story here. Mind on task, please.

Then a bunch of cheeky monkeys swoop in and kidnap Mowgli, taking him for a ride, swinging through the treetops, until they reach an abandoned human city. Baloo and Bagheera eventually catch up, but they take the scenic route so they can pick up a friend on the way. That's great. Go hang out while a bunch of reckless monkeys play catch with your man cub. Except, their friend is Kaa da python. What don't monkeys like? Snakes—especially really long ones fond of giving bear hugs. *Woof!* While Kaa hypnotizes the overly excited primates, the others vamoose with gusto.

Frogboy grows up, grows hair in various places, and learns of Shere Khan's *eeevil* plan: to have Mowgli ~~over~~ for dinner. When Khan springs his trap, the naked boy-wonder uses the one defense reserved just for man: fire. *Ooh, burn.* He chases off the scaredy cat. Yay! Hey, why aren't you guys cheering? Guys?

Might want to put out that fire, kid. Even though Mowgli defeated the *eeevil* kitteh, the wolf pack boots him out. Not a big fan of the fire thing. Time to be a man, kiddo.

Back with the humans, Mowgli's miserable. They make him wear clothes, learn manners, and speak their language. The villagers see how restless he is, so they put him in charge of the buffalo herd. Because sitting around all day following buffalos is so exciting that it will instantly cure him of boredom. Or they just don't want to hear his constant litany of "I'm *booooored*."

Not long after, one of Mowgli's wolf bros warns him that Shere Kitteh Kahn is coming for dinner, with Mowgli on the menu. He positions half the buffalo herd to block the opening of a canyon where Khan is taking a cat nap, then he stampedes the other half down on the tiger. Look out, ~~Scar~~ Shere Khan!

When a hunter after Khan's pelt sees Mowgli with it, he throws a hissy fit and tells everyone in the village that Jungle Boy is a shapeshifting sorcerer. The villagers are idiots, so they believe him and kick poor Frogboy out. He goes off alone into the jungle. His wolf bros still chill with him, though, so there's that. Where's Tarzan when you need him?

Rudyard Kipling had *swastikas* printed on his book covers? He couldn't have been a Nazi . . . because he wasn't. The swastika is a traditional Indian symbol for the sun, bestowing good luck and well-being. Then the Nazis kifed it, so Kipling had it removed from his books so he wouldn't be linked to those *eeevil* men—but people do anyway. He died in 1936, just before World War II started.

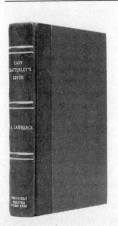

Lady Chatterley's Lover
by D. H. Lawrence

Published: 1928
Category: novel
Banned for: sex. The British publisher of the sexy uncut version of the book went on trial for obscenity in 1960.

"A woman has to live her life, or live to repent not having lived it."

Sing it, sister. But can we clarify what you mean by life?
Promiscuous sex: good. Obeying rules: bad?

There are actually three versions of the book in print: mild, steamy, and smokin'. Obviously we're going for the *obscene* version of events. Buckle up!

Constance Reid marries the baronet Clifford Chatterley, a war hero tragically paralyzed during the Great War. What wife wouldn't be *constant* to a man who required so much help and attention? Well, she is at first, but he becomes emotionally distant and spends most of his time writing. Connie has no one to love *(wink wink)*.

Her painterly bohemian dad, Sir Malcolm, raised her in rather interesting circumstances, so by the time she gets married she's had some experience in the ways of love. Everything was going great with Cliffy on their month-long honeymoon, but once they got back, Cliff went off to fight in World War I, where he was paralyzed—from the waist down, of course. Connie gets to play naughty nurse for a bit, but the role starts to grate on her, so she hires Mrs. Bolton to do it. Which is good news for Connie because Sir Cliffy subtly morphs into one of those haughty intellectuals with a side order of disdain for the working class. Charmed, I'm sure.

Meanwhile, Connie's getting an itch that Cliff just can't scratch anymore. Wait, wait. Hold on there, son. You're saying that women want the sexytimes as much as or even *more* than men? Outrageous! Tell me more.

Cliff's ~~notes~~ short stories land him all kinds of attention from the literati, so that's fun for a bit, discussing Big Important Philosophical Things 'n' stuff, but Connie's getting bored again. Nor is she getting any, so there's that. One of the writerly people who visits Cliff hooks up with Connie briefly, but it wasn't all that great for her. "It's not me, it's you."

But then she meets the gamekeeper just back from war, the sexy hunk of man Oliver Mellors, all of whose limbs are still working. Connie finds him *fascinating*, but he ignores her. She tries harder, so he ignores her *and* is rude to her. In this case, playing hard to get totally works. She has to have him.

Connie: Hey there, hot stuff. *(sex sex sex sex)*

Oliver: Go away. I'm your employee. Plus, you're rich and have lots of smarts, and I don't got none of that book learnin'.

Connie: *(stares at his rippling abs)* I don't care.

Eventually she wears him down when they "accidentally" run into each other at a shack out in the woods. The sex is good, so they have plenty more "coincidental" encounters, rocking it in the love shack. It's a little old place where they can get together. Oh yeah. These brawny working class guys are *real* men. Not like her wimpy smartypants hubby. Love isn't about intellectual and emotional garbage. It's about bumping uglies and releasing endorphins while screaming out your partner's name. Is it getting warm in here?

Connie takes off for a vacation to Italy, but when she returns all hell has broken loose. Oliver's wife—whom he tried to escape by going to war: "Honey, I'd rather die than spend another moment with you, so I'm joining the army. Bye!"—is making his life miserable. She spreads all kinds of rumors and gets him fired from his job on the estate. When Connie confirms some of those rumors to Cliff, he refuses to get a divorce—even though (drum roll) she's pregnant. I don't think we need to ask for a paternity test on this one.

Meantime, Cliffy's grown rather attached to Nurse Bolton, who has become like a lover/mother in a really twisted way. "Hey, pretty lady. I think it's time for you to change my nappie." He refuses to give Connie a divorce, so she takes off to stay with her sister. Oliver gets a job at a farm and waits for his divorce to come through, and . . . that's it. Really, that's how it ends. For the romantics among us, there's hope, and the pessimists won't care either way because the world is a horrible place, and we're all going to die.

D. H. Lawrence was totally into sex and the occult. Dude eloped with the wife of one of his professors, swung both ways—hello, sexy farmer William—and wrote pamphlets in defense of smex and porn. Conventional morals? *Pffft.* So nineteenth century. Now turn your head and cough.

The Last of the Mohicans
by James Fenimore Cooper

Published: 1826
Category: novel (historical)

> *"The pale-faces are masters of the earth, and the time of the red-men has not yet come again. My day has been too long."*

Yeah, I've had a long day too. You can't imagine how horrible the commute is. Then I spilled ketchup on my shirt. Now what were you saying?

Historical accuracy? Pshaw, this is historical *fiction*. Who worries about factual details when sexy frontiersmen are running around half-naked? Certainly not Cooper (or Michael Mann, who didn't keep romances properly aligned or all the survivors alive in his epic 1992 movie version. Shhhh. Don't cry, it'll be OK.)

Hawkeye, a white scout, hangs with his Mohawk friends all the time. He's a sexy beast, but would he be as sexy with a different name? Natty Bumppo, for instance. Yeah, stick with Hawkeye, bud. No lady's going to want to bump uglies with a Bumppo.

Cora and Alice are off to visit their dad, Colonel Munro, with Major Heyward, some of his soldiers, and ever-faithful guide Magua . . . until they realize that Magua has been taking them the wrong way—into an ambush. Turns out Magua hates their papa and wants to steal the girls to make one of them his bride. Then comes our Natty hero with his trusty rifle, Kildeer—impressive names, Coop, however do you come up with them?—to save the day. His Mohican friends Uncas and Chingachgook help out, too. (Mohicans were also known as Mohawks, and, no, they didn't walk around with ridiculous, foot-long, perma-spikes on their heads.)

The ladies are taken safely to the fort . . . which is under attack from the French. Frying pan, fire . . . eh, probably all the same at this point.

While they're sitting around dodging cannonballs, romance gets a-burnin'. Major Heyward sidles up to Alice while Cora takes a liking to sexy Mohawk Uncas. No big deal, right? WRONG! Couple 1 = Congrats! Couple 2 = How could you possibly like someone outside your own race? The horror!

Despite the drama, there's still a war going on outside, and it's not looking so hot for Colonel ~~Mustard~~ Munro.

French: Surrender!

Mustard: Never!

French: Surrender, or we kill you. And your kids!

Mustard: OK, we give up.

While the Brits are abandoning fort in the usual orderly style, the French-allied Hurons decide to do a little hunting—of the departing English soldiers and their families. Magua captures Cora and Alice and drags them off to the Huron camp. Hawkeye and friends play dress up to sneak into the village and rescue the women. They get Alice, but when they go after Cora, tribal rules say that everyone but Cora can go because Magua has claimed her as his wife. But she never said "I do."

They give Magua and Cora a three-hour head start. Not kidding— it's part of tribal etiquette. They sit around for three hours, and then *ding!* time's up. When they catch up to the bad guy and the damsel in distress on a steep mountain trail, a fight ensues, and both Cora and Uncas die. Natty gets there too late to do anything other than shoot Magua. Leaving ~~four little, three little, two little Indians~~, one little Indian. Boy.

Perhaps **James Fenimore Cooper**'s greatest detractor was none other than viper-tongued critic Mark Twain (page 3), who wrote a long essay destroying the *Deerslayer* novels that ends with this zinger: "A work of art? It has no invention; it has no order, system, sequence, or result; it has no lifelikeness, no thrill, no stir, no seeming of reality; its characters are confusedly drawn, and by their acts and words they prove that they are not the sort of people the author claims that they are; its humor is pathetic; its pathos is funny; its conversations are—oh! indescribable; its love-scenes odious; its English a crime against the language. Counting these out, what is left is Art."

Oh, *burn*. Also, Coop didn't particularly care about getting his facts straight. He spliced two tribes—Mohegan and Mahican, both of which still exist—into a bigger mythical one. Popular culture trumps historical accuracy. Again.

Little Women
by **Louisa May Alcott**

Published: 1868
Category: novel (children's)
Banned for: Some of the feminist persuasion—even during Alcott's era—argue that *Little Women* belittles women's fiction because it offers a nice homey portrayal of women who gather round the hearth with family and enjoy being there. They're joking, right? The ladies *must have it all*—career, spouse, children, two-car garage, Harvard education, summer home in the Hamptons—to find fulfillment as a woman. There are women who actually choose to be homemakers, even when they aren't chained to the stove, barefoot and pregnant? Inconceivable.

"Oh, my girls, however long you may live, I never can wish you a greater happiness than this!"

Marmee, could we cut back on the sappiness?
People are starting to gag.

Daddy March is off fighting for the North in the War Between the States, while at home Marmee is raising their four daughters, which is probably the more dangerous of the two. Ever try to break up a cat fight? Don't. Meg is eldest and prettiest, though without ambition; tomboy Jo loves books; Beth, the sweet, musical one, is going to die halfway through, so don't get attached; and bratty artistic Amy is (obviously) the youngest.

The family used to have money, but now they done gone broke. It doesn't stop do-gooder Marmee from dragging her daughters along on her noble errands. "Seriously, mom? We're visiting the 'poor' again? I'm pretty sure the neighbors can tell it's soup from a can." Enter Laurie, the crush-worthy boy next door. Literally. Dude lives one house away. Let's review, shall we? Jo is the tomboy girl, and Laurie is the crushable boy. Got it? Good. He and Jo are BFF, but he's just like an unofficial bro to the whole fam. They even put up a post box between their houses so they can send secret messages to each other. *<retch>*

Amy is a smitten kitten, so one day she is sneaky sneaky and follows Laurie and Jo as they go to a local pond to ice skate. Amy ends up skating on thin ice—*badum ching!*—and nearly drowns when she crashes through to the icy water below. Laurie saves her, which only adds to his crush-worthiness. "My hero! I totally didn't plan for that. Not at all. But now you're going to have to carry me in your arms all the way home. What strong biceps you have."

Marmee gets a letter saying that Daddy March fell sick during the war, so she heads off to D.C. to nurse him. While she's gone, chaos ensues. Beth, the responsible one, helps out a sick family. Bad move, girlie. She gets scarlet fever. They send Amy to some relatives to make sure she doesn't catch it too. Say goodbye to your childhood crush, dear.

Marmee comes home from taking care of dad, only to be thrust into playing nursemaid again. Gee, thanks. Beth survives—barely—but never fully recovers. *(Cue foreboding music.)* In the meantime, Laurie's tutor, Mr. Brooks, falls in love with Meg, and they get engaged and almost immediately become a boring married couple.

Fast forward two years. Jo is supposed to jaunt off to Paris as a companion for a rich aunt, but Amy gets to go instead. But that's not fair! *(weeps uncontrollably)* Jo wants to be . . . wait for it . . . a writer. Which couldn't possibly have anything to do with Alcott's profession. Nope, not at all. Jo moves to New York, where she meets the distinguished Professor Bhaer, a dirt-poor German who left a university position back in Berlin for the siren song of America. You realize sirens sing sailors to their deaths, right? He helps Jo with her writing, but she moves home soon after, with the unspoken command that he come for her later. Let's hope this one isn't as dense as most men.

Laurie finishes college and comes home to propose to Jo, but she turns him down because she's a complete idiot. Upset, he takes off for Europe. Get your tissues ready, ladies, because Beth dies soon after he leaves. But she was so nice and everyone loved her. Too bad, so sad. Moving on!

While Amy and Laurie are gallivanting around Europe, they run into each other. Now that Amy is fitting into her ~~bra~~ britches a bit better, Laurie takes a closer look and likes what he sees. Ooh, baby. They get married before coming home. Surprise! Jo doesn't care too much because her little tomboy heart is set on old man Bhaer, who fulfills all her romantic daddy-issue dreams when he comes for her. Maybe it's more than a coincidence that *Little Women* falls right before *Lolita* alphabetically. Granted, Jo isn't really underage, but still. Old man. Gross.

Everyone lives happily ever after except sweet Beth because she's dead.

Louisa May Alcott belongs to the club of women writers who wrote about great romances but never married. Unrealistic fantasies, perhaps? She might have had her own secret-ish romance, but she worried more about establishing her independence than finding a husband. Dear Ms. Alcott, you rock. Love, women everywhere.

Lolita by Vladimir Nabokov

Published: 1955
Category: novel
Banned for: pedophilia—shocking, but true—on nearly every continent. (Apparently penguins can't read.) Bravo, Vlad, for grossing out *the whole world*.

"Lolita should make all of us—parents, social workers, educators—apply ourselves with still greater vigilance and vision to the task of bringing up a better generation in a safer world."

Let me get this straight. We're supposed to read this pronouncement by the shrink sarcastically because there's no moral to the story? What the frak? Wanna see how romantic it is for creepy old men to seduce young girls? Hand me a nutcracker.

Hey, kids! Ready to spend some time in a thoroughly disgusting, creepy place where pedophilia's cool and everyone's doing it? No? Too bad—because this book is completely and utterly effed with a capital UP. For your sanity (and possibly your virgin eyes) here are two versions of this one:

My Poor Eyes (condensed for your sake)
Humbert Humbert, a pedophile, preys on Lolita, corrupting and then turning her into his spoiled little sex doll. He marries her mom to get close to her, but then Mom gets hit by a car. He has his way with the little one, they take a long road trip, but then another creepy pedo kidnaps her. After two years of searching, Humbert finds her preggers

and married to some other dude because her kidnapper abandoned her when she wouldn't get all up in his child porn orgy. Humbert murders the (possibly bigger) creep. Lolita dies in childbirth, then Humbert has a heart attack and dies in prison. *Gah.*

You Asked For It (condensed with enough detail to make you want to gouge your eyes out—see page 164)

Dr. John Ray Jr. begins our lurid tale with a fascinating case study of child-loving gone wrong. The lawyer of a guy who died in jail while awaiting trial sent him the manuscript because it's just so. well. written. Gag. While he admits that the events described are horrifying, the doc explains how beautiful and persuasive Humbert's writing is. And that's what I had for lunch. Sorry.

First, we have Humbert Humbert, resident pedophile and total sociopath. Then we have wicked little Lolita, who is of course at fault for tempting grown men with her seductively childish ways. Obviously. As a tween, HH lived in the Mediterranean, where, like Edgar Allan Poe, he fell in love with a twelve-year-old named Annabel Leigh. She died a few months after they met but before they could get it on. So she's to blame for dude's screwed up sexuality. Obviously. Nice try, HH.

He grows up to be an English teacher, an excellent choice because he has to spend all his time with kids—when he's not in the nut house or working odd jobs. At one point, he married a grown woman, but apparently he couldn't get over his obsession with "nymphets," a.k.a. sexually aware girls. Vom.

He moves to the States, where he rents a room in the house of the widow Charlotte Haze and her twelve-year-old, Dolores, a.k.a. Lolita, a.k.a. sweet little girl savagely ripped from the innocence of childhood by nasty old man. Mom doesn't realize what a creeper is living in their house, so *she* falls in love with him, and both mommy and daughter fight for HH's attention. Humbert Humbert, bringing families together since—ick.

HH is a sicko, so he chooses the young girl but then marries her mom so he can stay close to her. EWW. Mom sends Lolita to summer camp, but then she finds HH's journal, in which he details his pervy love for the girl and desire to kill the mom. Who journals shizz like that? Mom's upset—understatement of the year—and runs into the street where she gets hit by a car and dies. Convenient.

So Daddy Humbert picks Lolita up from camp to go on a year-long cross-country road trip. When they get to the hotel the first night, Humbug tells her that mommy's dead, and then she seduces him. *What the*—? You seriously expect us to believe that, you perv? Ugh. I don't care how "*beautiful*" his writing is. Bring me pliers and a screwdriver, and I'll make this a *novella*—if you get my drift.

During their road trip, HH becomes even more obsessed with Lolita. (How is this even possible? Gross.) She figures out how to manipulate him, throwing tantrums and holding out on sex to get what she wants. Ew. Eventually they settle down, and HH gets a job teaching at a college. When Lolita starts flirting with boys her own age—and this should surprise you why?—he takes her off on another road trip. Jealous much? But then she gets sick and has to go to the hospital, where another nasty pedophile kidnaps her.

After searching relentlessly for two years, HH finally gets a note from L asking for money. She married some other guy and is preggers at seventeen. HH begs for her to return to him, but she says no dice. When HH figures out who kidnapped her, he finds and shoots the creep. Too bad he didn't turn the gun on himself. So HH ends up in jail for murder—but not for child molestation, sexual abuse, rape, or being a complete and utter blight on the face of the planet? Moral of the story—and I don't care what Nobby says, there totally is one—castrate the perverts.

Vladimir Nabokov, you frighten me. Yes, it's *fiction*, and you actually lived a quiet life at home with your appropriately aged wife and son and butterflies, but still . . . the imagination that spawned this heinous feculence isn't something I ever want to understand. However brilliant you are. Buh-bye.

Lord of the Flies
by William Golding

Published: 1954
Category: novel
Banned for: violence—go play your
Modern Warfare video game instead.
The new features let you rack up more
points per kill!

"Ralph wept for the end of innocence, the darkness of man's heart, and the fall through the air of a true, wise friend called Piggy."

Well, look at that. Pigs can fly!

In the not-too-distant future, a group of middle school–age boys is evacuated from England because of nuclear war. Enemy fire downs their plane, which crashes on an uninhabited island in the middle of the ocean. Tropical island surrounded by sun, sand, and sea? Score! Hey, Ginger, Mary-Anne, bring these boys some drinks, and make sure they come in coconut shells with little umbrellas.

Not quite. All the adults on the plane died in the crash. No girls, either. There aren't even cannibals—yet (page 196). The island blows (not literally; we don't burn this island down until a bit later).

After the initial chaos, Ralph blows a conch shell to call the other survivors scattered through the jungle. Ralph is oldest and biggest, so they vote him ~~team captain~~ leader. Really it's because he's beautiful and speaks like a politician, which peeves Jack—all *big strong hunt good*—who thinks he should lead. Beauty over brawn, kid. Every time.

Ralph wants to build shelter and a signal fire in case a ship passes close enough to see it, but Jack wants to hunt. So Ralph puts Jack in charge of leading a group of choirboys to hunt pigs, which can only end well. Obviously. Ralph probably should have made it clear that he wanted them to hunt wild pigs and not the kid named Piggy. To make matters more interesting, before they start playing Survivor, one of the younger boys asks about the big scary beast he saw lurking in the jungle. Well that's great.

With Jack and his manly choirboys off on the hunt, the rest of them light stuff on fire with Piggy's glasses because that's what boys do. They're having so much fun playing with fire that they accidentally burn down a chunk of jungle—and the kid who is afraid of monsters. Talk about a weenie roast. Ralph isn't terribly happy about the pyro party, though, which destroyed a lot of food, shelter, and firewood. Islands don't grow on trees!

Meanwhile, most of the hunting party loses interest when they can't place their order at the deli counter, so they go play in the ocean. Except Jack, who keeps hunting even though he has no clue what he's doing. Ralph organizes the rest of the boys to make a shelter, but they get bored and go play in the water, too. Only Ralph and Simon stay behind to work. Meanwhile, in the water, a bigger kid starts heaving rocks at one of the younger boys. He's not actually hitting the kid—just testing the boundaries of their new society and getting off on the thought of hurting another human being. Because that's totally healthy.

Jack and the hunters figure out that painting their skin makes them better hunters. Soon they're doing war dances and acting like savages. The mighty hunters eventually bring back a pig . . . when what should Ralph see off in the distance? Smoke from a passing ship. Saved! But it chugs past because the signal fire burned out. Not saved. Whoops.

Ralph, who is doing everything but wiping their bums, wonders why no one is helping out with the fire and the shelters. But who needs to be rescued when you can do war dances and hunt wild pigs? Ralph finally tags along on a hunt and realizes how much fun it—

We interrupt this metaphor for the evolution of man and government to bring you an air battle overhead, during which a dead pilot falls to the island still attached to his parachute. A couple of boys out after dark find the dead guy hanging from the tree. Suffering from some kind of short-term memory loss, they decide it's The Beast. *Run away!*

Jack unsuccessfully tries to get Ralph voted out as chief, so he huffs off and invites anyone who wants to hunt to join him. Boys start sneaking off to be in Jack's tribe, where they kill another pig and stick its head on a pike. Simon stumbles upon the pig head and has a seizure, which might explain why the pig head starts talking to him.

"Let me introduce myself. I'm The Beast, but you can call me Lord of the Flies. I'm not The Beast—"

"But I thought—"

"Shut up, kid. I'm not done. I'm not The Beast because *you* are. The Beast is inside you. You're all turning feral. Cut it out."

Meanwhile, Jack's tribe is feasting on the pig they slaughtered. Ralph and Piggy show up for the party and find that the other boys have defected to Jack's team. They're all chowing down when Simon comes back to tell them what he found. Simon says, there's no beast. So they kill him instead. Hey, Simon didn't say!

The next night, Jack and his gang attack the other camp to steal Piggy's glasses so they can make fire. When Ralph goes to get Piggy's glasses back, he and Jack fight. Piggy foolishly tries to talk sense into everyone, so one of the wild boys pushes a boulder down the hill that knocks this little Piggy off a cliff. All the way down.

It all goes a bit *Hunger Games* from there: The remaining boys hunt Ralph instead of pigs. More fun when the target is as smart as you, I guess. They try to smoke him out, which basically sets the whole island on fire.

The wild boys catch up to Ralph on the beach. As he's running from them ~~Ralph wakes up and realizes that they've been dead all along~~. (Sorry, wrong plane crash.) Ralph runs into a British naval officer who came to check out the smoke ~~monster~~. As the boy tries to tell the adult what happened, all the other boys start bawling.

The officer is disgusted with them. How could proper English boys behave like animals? He tells them to get on his ship so he can take them back to civilization, where men kill each other at a distance by dropping bombs that level entire cities.

Moral of the story? Listen to the talking pig head, but don't tell anyone.

William Golding fought in World War II as part of the British Navy. He even stormed the beaches of Normandy on D-Day, which racked up about twenty thousand ~~kill points~~ casualties on both sides— proof positive, if you needed it, that men and boys can be feral beasts full of violent intentions.

Macbeth by William Shakespeare

Published: 1606
Category: play (tragedy)
Banned for: witchcraft. Those hags get such a bad rap. It's not like they *wanted* murder and mayhem. They just set it all in motion and stoked the fires. See? Harmless.

"Out, damned spot; out, I say."

If you're going to go around stabbing people to death, make sure you're dressed appropriately for it. Something easier to clean than silk or a fine brocade. Trust me.

Ah, Scotland, land of the blue *tuches*. Hey, don't look at me; I don't strip nekkid and paint myself for battle. Sadly, they don't really do that anymore . . . I think.

Most of the play takes place at the Macbeth castle in Inverness, with some stops at the witches' cave. The whole play can be summed up thus: Power, I wants it . . . so I shall takes it! But it's not really Macbeth who wants the power. Nope, it's his nagging wife.

Lady Mac: I married you because I thought you were a powerful lord, but here I am, stuck in this drafty castle, when I should be queen. You have no ambition. Honestly, if I didn't push you, nothing would ever happen. And why don't you ever take out the garbage? Gah!

Mac: Yes, dear.

Three witches show up, and things get weird.

Witches: Macbeth, you will be king, and your friend Banquo's descendants will be kings.

Mac: Uh, if you say so.

Banquo: Sweet!

Mac trots home, victorious from war. King Duncan visits Mac to congratulate him during a dinner party.

Lady Mac: Honey, you *know* how much I want to be queen. Besides, those creepy hags said you'd be king. Clearly you must murder Duncan while he's our houseguest.

Mac: Whatever you say, dear.

Duncan: Good job, Mac. I'm glad I have a general I can trust.

Mac: Uh huh. *(Stabs Duncan while he sleeps.)* Don't look at me. His chamberlains must have done it. Execute them! Oh, and since the king is dead . . .

Yoink! Mac steals the crown and makes himself king. Upon further thought, Mac realizes that Banquo's kids could dethrone him if both prophecies are real. So he has them killed on the way to a party at Mac's place. But Banquo's son gets away.

Mac: Dang you, Banquo! I'll deal with your kid later. Hey, what's that shiny thing?

Banquo's ghost: You murdered me!

Mac: Did not!

Lady Mac: Kindly stop freaking out in front of the guests, dear.

The witches show up again and make things worse.

Witches: Watch out for that Macduff character.

Mac sends his peeps to take out Macduff, who scrams for England.

Macduff: Run away! Honey, stay home with the kids. You'll totally be safe.

Mac: Not so fast! I'll take your castle and kill your family. What do you think of that?

Macduff: *Whyohwhy?* You asked for it, Macbeth. Revenge!

So Macduff comes back to visit Mac, this time with an army, and chops off Mac's head.

Kthxbai!

Which you totally saw coming, didn't you? Who needs witches to predict the future?

Sadly, it wasn't just Macbeth the king who was cursed. The play was too after **William Shakespeare** used *real* witches' spells in the play, which ticked them off. *Oooh. Spooky.* Anytime a person says the name of the play *within* the theater, it activates the curse, dooming the production with failure, death, and rioting. The only way to stop it? Performing one of a variety of rituals. My fave: Spin around three times really fast while spitting over your shoulder and shouting obscenities.

Madame Bovary
by Gustave Flaubert

Published: 1857

Category: novel (serialized)

Banned for: sex . . . in *France*, so you know this one's gonna be good. The author even went on trial for obscenity. He was acquitted, but there's no such thing as bad publicity, so *Madame Bovary* sold like hotcakes because people wanted to get their hot little hands on that naughty little book that caused all the fuss.

> *"She hoped for a son; he would be strong and dark; she would call him George; and this idea of having a male child was like an expected revenge for all her impotence in the past. A man, at least, is free; he can explore all passions and all countries, overcome obstacles, taste of the most distant pleasures."*

I will dress him and feed him and call him George. Having kids is the best revenge.

Growing up, Charles Bovary was a bit of a dolt. Bullies *loved* him. Well, they loved harassing him. Same diff. It might've been OK had he been a smarty-pants, but no. ~~Prince~~ Charles was boring and not very bright. Lethal combo.

He becomes a doctor—barely—then marries an old widow who croaks soon after. Inheritance, here we come! Or not. The old broad stiffed him. Damn. Before the ball-and-chain croaks, though, Charlie chats up a neighboring farmer and beholds Emma Rouault. So young, so pretty. So young. Once his wife is dead, he waits a respectable time before putting the moves on Emma. Ten minutes should be good, don't you think? OK, fine, an hour?

A sweet little thing, Emma had an excellent education—in a convent. Not really a lot to do in one—certainly limited flirtation prospects—so Emma spent most of her time daydreaming about one thing. Care to take a guess? If you say "deep spiritual contemplation," you're fired.

Charlie proposes to Emma, her dad says sure, so they get married. Yay! OK, now what? In Emma's romance novels, the women are always worshipped and live elegant, wealthy lives. One problem, sweetie. You married a country doctor. Not a very good one, either. So you and the fancy lifestyle? Not happening.

Emma: Ugh, life is *soooo* boring. Why won't you entertain me? *(whine whine)*

She gets pregnant and has a little girl. That'll keep her busy and happy, right? Nope. Emma's not too fond of the motherhood thing, either. So when she meets Léon, a young, intelligent law student, she crushes on him hardcore. He has the hots for her, too, but she is oh so virtuous and doesn't give in . . . because she's an idiot. Dude gives up and heads to Paris. Buh-bye.

Life is back to boring . . . until a rich, gorgeous, did I say rich? landowner stops by the doctor's office for a servant and spies Emma, ripe for the picking. Rodolphe seduces her, and they get freaky for a good four years. Emma's so in love, and he's so rich, and they're going to run away together . . . except not really. Dude bails last minute by sending a note in the bottom of a basket of apricots. Seriously? First of all, who thinks to look underneath a pile of fruit? And really? That might even be worse than breaking up by text. Not cool.

Poor heartbroken Emma almost dies. Once she starts to recover, Charlie takes her to zee opera. And who should she see but Léon! They have the sex every week while Charlie thinks she's taking piano lessons. Someone's certainly tinkling the ivories, if you know what I mean. But soon both she and Léon get bored with each other. Rodolphe was just so much more dashing. *Le sigh.*

All the while, Ems is buying so much awesome stuff to feel oh so rich and special. Unfortunately, it's all on credit, and she drags Charlie down the debt hole with her. When it comes time to cough up, she begs her lovers for money, but they're like, "Yeah right. Piss off, whore." Woe is she, so she chugs a bottle of arsenic. That whole romantic suicide thing where the heroine perishes so elegantly? Total lie. Poisoning yourself with arsenic is incredibly painful, and you suffer. A lot.

A widower again, Charlie doesn't know what to do with himself. So he basically wastes away, living off what he makes from selling all his stuff that wasn't already repossessed because of Emma's spendy ways. Wait, didn't they have a daughter or something? Oh yeah, the kid. She gets shipped off to relatives, who ship her off to work in a cotton mill. Lovely.

Gustave Flaubert wasn't terribly fond of the middle class and their "morals," and he was a tad bitter after his trial (shocker). He didn't much like romance novels, either, with their unattainable desires impressed upon naive young girls who think Prince Charming on his white horse will save the day. So he wrote depressingly realistic books instead. Yay?

The Metamorphosis
by Franz Kafka

Published: 1915
Category: novella
Banned for: The Czech government didn't like Kafka because he only wrote in German, even though he grew up in Prague, so they banned his books. The Nazi government didn't like Kafka because he was a Jew. They didn't like him so much that they didn't just ban his books—years after his death, they confiscated all of Kafka's papers and letters to his girlfriend. The Russians banned Kafka's books because they were too depressing. Um, what? Communist Russia is the definition of depressing. Maybe they worried it would be overkill.

"One morning, as Gregor Samsa was waking up from anxious dreams, he discovered that in bed he had been changed into a monstrous verminous bug."

Don't you just hate when that happens?

Last night, I had this really weird dream that I turned into a ginormous cockroach. I was so grossed out I tried to squish myself.

Oh, wait. That wasn't me. It was Gregor Samsa, who actually *did* turn into a giant bug, which he figured out when he tried to get out of bed one morning and couldn't roll over because he was stuck on his back. ("Oy vey! I'm an insect and I can't get up!") Should have slept on his side—reduces pressure points and is so much better for the spine . . . except he doesn't have one anymore, so, uh, never mind.

As roach-Gregor lies in bed, he ponders a bug's life: He has no money. He hates his job. He's still living with his parents. Basically, his life sucks, and now he's a giant insect-monster. Man, can't a bug get a break?

He's usually on time for work, but he already missed his train, so Mom comes to wake him. He's flopping about, trying to roll over, his spindly little legs kicking frenetically in the air.

Mom: Greggie, stop shlepping around, you're late for work!

Gregor: Gimme a minute, ma!

Mom hears: *screech scritch chitter chitter*.

Something's wrong, so the whole family gathers outside his bedroom: Dad, Mom, sister Grete, and his boss. Wait, his *boss*? Oy. Mad boss threatens to ~~flush~~ fire the poor bug, but Gregor finally flips himself, then opens the door with his mouth.

Shhurprishe!

For some odd reason, the Samsas aren't terribly fond of surprises. Everyone runs, screaming, and Boss Man hauls tuches from the apartment. Gregor tries to catch up and explain, but Dad blocks the way with a rolled-up newspaper and his cane. *Whap! Whap!* Back, you beast! *Whap!*

Gregor scuttles back to his room to avoid the blows, but his klutzy new body isn't any help, as he injures himself trying to get through the doorway. Poor bug. Why don't you take a little nap, see if life doesn't go back to normal while you're unconscious?

At this point, you might be asking, "How exactly did he turn into a giant bug in the first place?" No one knows, and that's NOT THE POINT. The point, all you literal-minded readers, is—honestly I'm not sure there is a point yet.

Gregor wakes to find that (a) he's still a bug, (b) someone left some milk in a bowl for him, and (c) his buggy self doesn't like milk. Which is horrible because it used to be his absolute favoritest thing *evar*, so he hides under the couch in his room. Yes, hiding from your problems will make everything better. Next morning, Grete replaces the milk with rotten table scraps. Once she leaves, he chows down. Yum!

They get into a bit of a routine: Grete feeds and cleans up after him while he hides under the couch so she won't freak out if she sees him. Probably a good idea. Pretty soon, though, Gregor starts exploring his room in his new body. Climbing the walls and crawling on the ceiling is fun!

Grete soon realizes what all the little scufflings mean, so she decides to take some furniture out of his room to give him more space to, um, play.

But Gregor doesn't like that. Nuh uh. He tries to grab a framed photograph, but when Ma sees her roach-child hanging off the wall, she faints.

He runs into the kitchen, where Dad drives him off by chucking apples at him. Back in his room, Gregor realizes that one of the apples got stuck in his back, badly injuring him. Even better, it stays there and begins to rot. That's gotta smart.

Eventually, the family can't take it anymore, so they discuss what to do. He overhears their kvetching, where they agree that Gregor should just go away so they can move on with their lives. So Gregorbug goes back to his room and dies. *Finally*. They can be a normal family again. Well, without him of course, but still—no more giant insect!

Admit it; you're not really sad about Gregor's tragic fate. After all, he was a nasty cockroachy thing, and all creepy-crawlies *must die*.

Now, if you'll excuse me for a moment, I've got to take a Silkwood shower and pop over to the store for some roach motels. Kind of gives new meaning to the Hotel California, doesn't it? He could check out any time he liked, but he could never leave.

Franz Kafka was a Czech-born German Jew with daddy issues. What does that have to do with a bizarro book about a man turning into a bug? Plenty. Oh, you want me to explain? Ugh, *fine*. (1) He didn't really fit in anywhere. (2) His dad made him feel like an unwanted insect. There's probably a lot more to it than that, but I don't think either of us wants to dive into that man's twisted psyche any more than we already have. *Next!*

Middlemarch by George Eliot

Published: 1870
Category: novel (serialized)

"Marriage drinks up all of our power of giving or getting any blessedness in that sort of love. I know it may be very dear—but it murders our marriage—and then the marriage stays with us like a murder—and everything else is gone."

Bitter, party of one, your table is ready.

In the quaint little English town of Middlemarch lives the wealthy but idealistic Dorothea, along with her sister Celia and Uncle Brooke. *Zzzzt . . .* oh, sorry, where was I? Dorothea's basically odd, as she's more interested in spirituality and charity than romance. If you say so. She ends up marrying Mr. Casaubon, a crabby old man with nasty moles all over. Hawt.

She's quite the hottie, though, so her choice confuddles anyone with eyes. But she's determined to do IMPORTANT WORK with her life. Except not really because she's a woman of the gentry, expected to sit and look pretty while the menfolk do all their thinking for them. Dorothea does her own thinking—thank heavens—but that only gets her so far as helping hubby with *his* IMPORTANT WORK. So close, and yet so far. Hubby doesn't want her help because he's a man. Dorothea thinks: He's such an amazing guy. *Sigh.* As his wife I can find fulfillment through his dreams and aspirations. Casaubon thinks: Dorothea would be the perfect wife. She actually pays attention to me, and I do need a secretary . . . Plus it's so *cute* how she thinks she could actually help a man with his magnum opus. Hah!

She doesn't realize Casaubon's a self-centered jerk until they're on their honeymoon in Rome. So many wonderful sites to see—by herself of course because hubby is spending the entire trip working in Italian libraries. Screw the libraries, you just got married, dude. There are other, more important things to do. *Nudge nudge, wink wink?* No?

Hopeless. While sightseeing solo, Dorothea runs into Casaubon's painter cousin, Will Ladislaw. Cas doesn't like the kid because he's artistic, which means he's a dreamer with no ambitions or hope for the future. Even in Rome, cause it's not like that city is known for its art, or . . . nevermind. But she and Will hit it off, so she's not completely bored out of her skull. Worst. Honeymoon. Ever.

Back in Middlemarch, self-proclaimed princess Rosamond is going on a hunt—a man hunt. Tertius Lydgate, the new doc in town, is more interested in doctor stuff than the ladies at the moment. His experiments are totally important, so he'll just enjoy the view for now. But he's not getting away so easily. Rosamond thinks: He's so dashing and handsome, and his family are aristocrats, so we'll be rich and have a beautiful house. I deserve the best of everything because I'm a princess, *tee hee.* Lydgate thinks: She's so pretty . . . but I'm not getting married any time soon. I have too much work at the hospital . . . but she's so pretty.

Then there's Fred, Rosamond's good-for-nothing gambling brother. He's got the hots for local girl Mary. Unfortunately, she's known him her whole life. Mary thinks: I love Fred, but if that punk doesn't get his butt in gear and actually do something, ain't no way I'ma marry him. Fred thinks: Mary's swell. She doesn't like it when I gamble, but . . . pair o' sixes, that's all I need. Another pair of sixes, and I'll—crap.

Eventually, Rosamond uses her wily feminine ways to manipulate Lydgate into marrying her. Must be the tears. She busts out the water-works whenever she wants something. Ah, wedded bliss. It's just so . . . miserable. Yup, they quickly realize they're not compatible. So to keep her happy, Lydgate spends lots of money that he doesn't have. Boys, this is what happens when you don't think with your brain.

Dorothea and Casaubon return from Rome, and someone's a little jealous. Can you blame him? His cousin is young, gorgeous, charming, artistic . . . did it suddenly get hot in here? Dorothea is oblivious to Ladislaw's puppy love and Casaubon's raging jealousy, so when Cass tells her that Will isn't welcome to visit because it'll distract him from his work . . . there goes any hope of actual conversation or, you know, anything other than absolute boredom. So Uncle Brooke invites Will to stay with him instead. That's a good plan. No wrong can come from this.

Then Casaubon croaks. Darn. Crotchety old man is out of the way. Now Dorothea has a fortune and independence. But bitter old hubby has plans for that—he included a clause in his will that Dorothea gets nada if she marries Ladislaw. Haha! Revenge! Or not, if the widow had never considered dating the sexy artist. But now that you mention it . . .

The next time they meet, they have a super-hawt makeout session in her library. Thanks to dead hubby for setting things in motion. So Dorothea and Ladislaw get married. Fred shapes up and marries Mary. Rosamond and Lydgate bolt when a scandal breaks and they go broke. There's a whole lot more in this eight-hundred-page monster, but this is all you get. Seriously, eight hundred pages condensed to around eight hundred words? I want a medal.

FYI: **George Eliot** wasn't a dude. Let's get that out of the way. Her name was actually Mary Anne Evans, and she wrote using a male pseudonym because she didn't want to get stuck writing sappy chick-lit, which is all women were allowed to write then (kind of like the Brontë sisters, pages 108 and 268). People *lurved* Eliot's books—even Queen Victoria was a huge fangirl, but it took awhile to get her to read them on account of Eliot's illicit behavior. She lived openly with a married man—with permission from his wife, of course. Well sure, so long as she's cool with it. Sister-wives 4evar!

Jules ROUFF et C°, éditeurs, 14, Cloître Saint-Honoré, PARIS.

Les Misérables by Victor Hugo

Published: 1862
Category: novel (historical, serialized)
Banned for: prostitution, murder, portraying the Church as unimportant, glorifying the French Revolution (during the Second Empire), and making *les royaux* look bad.

> *"The poor little despairing thing could not help crying: 'Oh my God! Oh God!' At that moment she suddenly felt that the weight of the bucket was gone. A hand, which seemed enormous to her, had just caught the handle, and was carrying it easily."*

Might be coming on a bit strong there, Valjean. Now's probably not the best time to ask, "Who's your daddy?"

Jean Valjean has been in prison a long-ass time—nineteen years—so he must be some horrible criminal. Not quite: He stole a loaf of bread to feed his sister's starving family. (Well, that and he tried to escape a couple times. So it's partially his fault, which people like to forget. Details.) But, still. What's the punishment for stealing a croissant?

As Valjean stumbles around trying to find work or food, a saintly bishop takes him in for the night. Valjean repays the kindness by yoinking the dude's silver quiet-like when everyone is sleeping. Except he gets caught.

Officer: Dude stole your stuff.

Bishop: No, he didn't. I gave it to him.

Officer and Valjean: Really?

Bishop: Yep. He's going to use it to become a good man. (Not so subtle hint.)

Valjean: Uh, thanks. *<bolts>*

Meanwhile, young Fantine has already fallen in love, had a baby, and been abandoned by her lover without a centime. But she has a brilliant idea: I'll go home, and everything will be fine. Because that always works. On the way back to her small (minded) town, she realizes, hey, showing up as a single mother might not be the best thing for my kid. Goodbye, respectability and any chance for a decent life. So a few towns before home, Fantine spots a woman playing lovingly with her kids. Jackpot.

Fantine: You're a great mom. Would you raise my kid if I pay you?

Madame Thénardier: Did you say money?

Valjean pulled himself up by the bootstraps and has taken on a new identity as Monsieur Madeleine. Everybody loves him because he ~~is a super-tasty sponge cake~~ has a big factory and is nice to people. They even elect him mayor. One of his new employees? Fantine. That's so great helping out an unwe—oh, we're not supposed to know that. But someone finds out, and the factory gossips make sure the foreman fires her for being a slut.

The Thénardiers are asking for more moola so they can continue to ~~rip off Fantine~~ care for Cosette . . . who is, um, sick *(cough cough)*. What's a single mom to do? Well, first she sells her two front teeth. Let's hope the Tooth Fairy cut her some slack and gave her a good deal. Then it's her hair, and finally—you guessed it—her body.

Fantine finally snaps when some jerk heckles her. She launches into him, slashing at his face, but she's not doing so great at the biting wifout her two fwunt teef. Then *(cue sinister music)* Inspector Javert shows up. He's about to send her to the clink when the mayor intervenes. Madeleine gets Fantine off, but Javert recognizes him. Naw, couldn't be Valjean. That guy's going on trial this week to get hauled back to prison.

We'll skip all the moral agonizing and go directly to court, where Madeleine shouts "Objection!" during the other Valjean's trial and turns himself in. Sort of. Everyone's so stunned, they let him walk. He races back to see Fantine, who has a nasty fever. Javert rushes into the hospital, twirling his evil mustachios, to arrest the real Valjean—which scares Fantine to death. Literally.

Let's take an intermission here as Hugo describes in *excruciatingly long-winded detail* the history of the Battle of Waterloo. Go ahead, take a potty break; I know you've been holding it. No need to hurry. We're going to be here for a while. Seriously, it's, like, *three hundred* pages long, and only the last couple of pages of it matter to the story.

Valjean goes back to prison but later escapes. He finds Cosette and buys her from the nasty Thénardiers. He takes her to Paris, but Javert tracks them down, so they flee. They find a new place inside a convent—clever!—where Cosette goes to school and Valjean works as a gardener.

Fast forward a bit. Marius is strolling along when he sees Cosette in the convent gardens, and it's OMG <3 4ever. He dabbles in stalkery before he works up the nerve to speak to her, but by then it's too late. Papa Valjean don't want no boys messing around with his baby girl, so *poof!* they disappear. Poor Marius is heartbroken. Kid, Cosette's cute and all, but there are plenty more ladies out there you can instalove. Get over it.

But then he sees her again when she and Daddy Warbucks stop by his neighbor's house. After they leave, Marius oh so casually stops by for a chat about a certain girl. He finds out that his neighbors, the Thénardiers, are planning to attack Daddy Warbucks and rob him. So

Marius calls the police, specifically Inspector Javert. It's basically the worst high school and family reunion ever . . . combined.

Valjean escapes with Cosette again. But then Eponine Thénardier, who is in love with Marius, tracks down Cosette for him. We should really introduce her to Sydney Milk Carton (page 217).

Valjean finds out about Cosette's little romance with Marius and is ready to skedaddle again, this time to England. Marius mopes. OK, kid, we get it. Every time she vanishes the world ends, but do you have to throw yourself into the revolution your friends are plotting? Better to die than to move on with your life? Got it.

At the barricade, breathlessly waiting for the fighting to begin, they all . . . burst into song? Seriously? Oh Broadway. As the fighting starts, they realize one of their recruits is a spy—none other than Javert. Dun dun *dunnnn*. Valjean shows up and says he'll take care of killing the traitor, but then he lets his arch-nemesis go. But what's Valjean doing there in the first place? Saving the man his daughter loves. Oy. Kids these days and their drama.

When Marius gets shot, Valjean carries him away from the fight, and then Javert tries to arrest Valjean. Crap timing, dude. Valjean convinces Javert to let them go, to save the kid's life, obv. Javert agrees, triggering a moral dilemma alert. He just let a criminal go free. So he throws himself into the Seine and drowns. A tad extreme, but, hey, do what you gotta do.

And so we come to our happy ending: Marius survives. Yay! He and Cosette marry. Double yay! Then Marius slowly estranges Cosette from her papa. Tr— what? That's not happy. Yeah, apparently Marius can't forgive a man for stealing *a loaf of bread* thirty years ago. But when he finds out that Valjean saved him from the fighting, well, that changes everything. Welcome to the fam—oh, your dad's dying because I took you away from him. My bad. And Valjean dies.

He might have taken *forever* to tell the story, but no one can say that **Victor Hugo** didn't practice what he preached. He became a politician and fought for social change. A politician with public morals? *Sacré bleu!* He even left 50,000 francs to the poor when he died.

Moby-Dick by Herman Melville

Published: 1851
Category: doorstop in the form of a novel
Banned for: perceived homosexual overtones. Honestly, bestiality's probably a better bet with how obsessed our dear Captain Ahab is with the great white whale.

"Look sharp, all of ye! There are whales here-abouts! If ye see a white one, split your lungs for him!"

Or, you know, just shout, "Hey, there's a white one!"
That works, too.

Let's get the big spoiler out of the way: EVERYONE DIES. Except Ishmael . . . and the whale. But everyone else? Deadski.

Surprisingly, there's really not a lot to this story if you cut out those huge, boring chunks of text blubber describing the whaling industry in nineteenth-century America. I know, you were *so* looking forward to hearing about that, but you'll live. Ahab won't, but there you go. Our narrator stops at an inn on the Massachusetts coast. He's on a bit of a downer, so he figures a job on a whaling ship in the middle of the ocean will perk him right up. For now, though, he just wants a good night's sleep. *Yawn.* Imagine his surprise later when a very large tattooed man climbs into bed with him. Hello, nurse. But it's all good. The inn was full, and he agreed to ~~give birth in the manger~~ share his bed with a man he'd never met before. So Ish spends a lovely night spooning with Queequeg, a Polynesian harpooner #notametaphor. They share some pillow talk and realize, hey, we should totally be BFFs. Let's find a ship we can work on together.

Next day, they set out to find the perfect ship. Bee tee dubs, isn't it so much fun having a new bestie? Then they see the *Pequod*.

This is no ordinary ship. No, this one looks like it was decorated by a witch doctor, with whalebones and teeth festooned all over it. Fabulous! Let's choose this one, honey. *(Lowers voice)* I mean, yeah, this'll do.

While signing up, they get an earful about the colorful captain. Ahab is . . . well, complicated. You could say he's an ungodly, god-like man. Cappy's still recovering from a whale biting off one of his legs during the last trip. But don't worry, he'll be ready to go when the ship sails. Wait, what happened? Bit *off* one of his legs? Hmm. Oh, what the heck. Let's do it.

Turns out, Ahab's totally crushing. On a sperm whale. Named Moby-Dick. I really don't want to know what kind of twisted stuff he's into, but he drags the entire ship's crew—including the first mate barista named Starbuck—into his maniacal search for vengeance. He even brought his own special team of harpooners along, including a creepy prophet who rants about hearses and dying. Can we make sure he only gets decaf?

They don't actually see Ahab until they're well away from port, but once they do it's like he's a rock star. Must be that new smexy leg made out of a whale's jawbone, and that scar running down his face—some say the rest of his body—that give him such a bad-boy vibe. Then he speaks. *(Cue dramatic lighting. Something something rousing speech. Triumphant call to action. Thunderous applause. Cut aaaand scene!)*

Actually, Ahab goes off on some crazypants tirade about some great white whale that has a vendetta against him—and the sailors totally buy it. The wicked beast savages ships and men because it likes to be evil. Yeah, or, you know, he could just be trying to save himself and his whale buddies.

Soon First Mate ~~Mocha Latte~~ Starbuck isn't the only one bamboozled by the charismatic Cap'n-Crunch-for-brains. The rest of the crew realizes that the middle of the ocean is probably not the best place to realize that your leader is a stark raving lunatic. There's no way to stop the ride at that point. Please keep your hands and feet inside the ship at all times, and enjoy the ride!

According to Ahab, the voyage's only purpose is to hunt down the wretched beast. In the meantime, they harpoon a few whales and, you know, do what they're being paid to do. Sometimes they come across other whaling ships, but Ahab's not down with chitchat. After a few weeks, they finally spot him: Moby-Dick ahoy!

They jump in their whaling boats, Ahab giddy as a school-girl. The big mean whale destroys one of the boats. They spot him again the next day, and this time they harpoon him, but he smashes another boat and carries away the weird prophet dude, attached to the harpoon rope.

Just let it go, Ahab. It's OK. Talk to Captain Hook (page 177) about vendettas against large aquatic animals. It never ends well. Nor will the world end if a large, man-eating whale terrorizes the ocean. You can get a job at Red Lobster or Long John Silver's. Wait, strike that. Johnny Silver is almost as cuckoo for Cocoa Puffs as the cap'n (page 237). Just put the harpoon down, and everything will be all right.

Nope. We're going after the whale again. Well, frak. Can someone "accidentally" harpoon the captain so we can get out of here in one piece? First Mate Frappuccino considers it at one point, but he's a Quaker, so not so much with the violence against humans. Whales are fine, though. Which is too bad because you're gonna regret it later. Like tomorrow, which is when they spot the whale again.

They attack. People die. Moby rams the ship and sinks it, which creates a whirlpool as it sucks the ship and men down into the sea with it. Sluuuuurp! Except Ishmael, who was thrown from the boat, like, ages ago and chills in a coffin-turned-liferaft until another ship floats by a couple days later.

Herman Melville liked to take inspiration from current events. Who doesn't? Much easier that way—especially when the newspaper offers up gems like Mocha Dick, an albino sperm whale killed off the coast of Chile that reportedly had twenty harpoons in its back and enjoyed ramming whaling ships.

Moll Flanders by Daniel Defoe

Published: 1722
Category: novel
Banned for: sex—*all* of it—and what a variety from which to choose: adultery, incest . . . you name it and Moll's done it. Funny thing is, Defoe actually left out the *really* naughty bits to stay out of jail.

> *"I was now the most unhappy of all women in the world. Oh! had the story never been told me, all had been well; it had been no crime to have lain with my husband, since as to his being my relation I had known nothing of it."*

How do you "accidentally" marry your own brother? Even if you had no clue that you were related, what are the chances? Brain bleach, please.

Defoe liked his book titles long. The complete title for this one is: *The Fortunes and Misfortunes of the Famous Moll Flanders, Etc. Who was born in Newgate, and during a life of continu'd Variety for Three-score Years, besides her Childhood, was Twelve Year a Whore, five times a Wife (whereof once to her own brother), Twelve Year a Thief, Eight Year a Transported Felon in Virginia, at last grew Rich, liv'd Honest and died a Penitent. Written from her own Memorandums.*

Our dear Moll Flanders started life in a rather, um, foreboding manner. Her mum was sentenced to death, but with Moll a'coming the jailers held off the execution. Eventually they just shipped mummy dearest off to America and sent Moll to a nice foster home. Oh, Moll isn't actually her name. She never reveals her real name. She clearly doesn't want to tarnish her upstanding image within the community.

Heh. Her last name changed with each new husband she acquired anyway. How many of those did she have? Let's see . . . husbands: five (including one brother); lovers: three-plus; children: twelve (all of whom she abandons).

Once Moll hits her teens, she becomes a servant in a house with a lovely family that has two fine-looking sons, both of whom are in love with her. She's in love with the first, so when he says, "Let's get our groove on," she says, "OK!" thinking they'll eventually get married. *Bzzzt!* Wrong answer. Lover #1 pawns her off on his younger brother, who is still all gaga for her. So she marries the younger brother.

He's not nearly as hot as the older one, but he's got money, so . . . eh. Plus, he dies a few years later anyway. So she pawns the kids off on the in-laws, and now she's out on her own. Such a caring mother you are, Moll. She pretends to be rich to land a rich husband, which goes well—until the hubby she acquires goes bankrupt and leaves her penniless. Thanks. Love you, too.

Next it turns out that the charming man with whom she falls in love and joins in America *is* too good to be true. She has a nice convo with her mother-in-law one day about how MIL was actually in prison when she gave birth to a girl before being shipped off to the Americas with other prisoners. *Ding ding ding!* We have a match. Mother-in-law is also long lost mother, which means Moll is married to her brother and has been having his kids for *years* without realizing it. YUCK.

Still, he's her half-brother, and it's not like she *knew* that he was her bro or even that her mom was still alive. But still: vom. Once she found out, it would've been totally understandable for her to ditch the glitch and pray her children didn't turn into mutants, yet she sticks around for a bit longer—though sex is totally off the table. So to speak.

She heads back to England and meets a nice guy, whose wife has gone a bit batshit. Everything's going well—until lover boy gets all religious and ditches Moll out of guilt.

Next, a still-married banker proposes to her. She says yes—if he can get a divorce—but travels to Lancashire in the meantime, where she marries some guy she thinks is rich. But he thinks she's rich. When they both figure out that neither of them have any money, they split. She goes back to the banker, who finally divorced his wife, so he becomes her fifth husband—and then dies soon after.

Again? Great. Out on her butt, Moll lands on hard times. She doesn't do "poor" very well, so she stumbles into a new career: thievery. A life of crime suits her, and she does a dang good job of it—until she gets caught a few years later and tossed in the jail where she was born. Talk about coming full circle. While there, she runs into Richie Not-sorich from Lancashire. They hit it off again while in the slammer and decide to get married again, convincing the law people to reduce their sentences and send them to the colonies instead. When they arrive in America as prisoners, Moll uses her super-wily ways to convince the officials to not mark them as convicts. Hey, use it if you've got it. The pair buy a plantation and live happily for a good long while.

At the end, Moll meets her son/nephew, all growed up now. Eventually she and hubby #4/6 (were you keeping track?) move back to England and do good to make up for all the bad they did earlier. Because that makes it all OK. Deathbed repentance wins again.

Daniel Defoe had something of a chip on his shoulder. He was lower middle class and Puritan, so the wealthy Anglican literary club of the day totally snubbed him. Rude.

Le Morte d'Arthur
by Sir Thomas Malory

Published: 1485
Category: prose
Banned for: being junk—according to at least one parent, who challenged the book at a school in the UK. Better switch off *Merlin* and all those other shows about Arthur, then, because those really are junk compared to *this* junk.

"Yet some men say in many parts of England that King Arthur is not dead, but had by the will of our Lord Jesu into another place; and men say that he shall come again, and he shall win the holy cross."

Arthur's not dead because he's really Jesus? So what about the part where he has a kid with his sister? You know what?—never mind. Don't want to know.

For those who don't speak French, *morte* means death. Which pretty much spoils the whole story. Thanks, Mal. I mean, what's the point in reading it since we know how it ends? #ironyalert.

So King Arthur. If you haven't heard of him before, he's kind of a big deal. He pulls a sword named Excalibur from a stone, which means he's king, yadda, yadda, and then he dies. There's a little more to it, but you can read about the first bit over at *The Once and Future King* (page 170)—except the weird Robin Hood and fairies part; ignore that. This book is similar to OAFK, but this one came first by almost five hundred years, and it's more a collection of short stories while the other is an actual, you know, novel. Well, four of them, but let's not get persnickety.

Let's jump in when Arthur gets hitched to a hot babe named Genevere. If you haven't noticed, she can't decide how to spell her name, so she changes it constantly in just about every book she appears in. Such a prima donna. Anyway, her dad is so proud that his little pumpkin head is getting married that he gets the new couple a table—a big round one that seats 150 people. "Gee . . . thanks, Dad. Where do you think we should put it, sweetie?" "How about up your—*ahem.*"

Genevere likes to sit in on her husband's business meetings. Makes her feel important, plus it gives her more men to nag on a regular basis. "It's called chivalry, guys. Is it really so hard? You hold the door open for her. Also, helping townspeople with their spring cleaning does not include raping and pillaging. Got it?" (To see what happens when a knight needs punishing and Gen steps in, take a look at the Wife of Bath's story on page 31.)

Skipping to the next interesting part—skipping, skipping—and we arrive in, um, Rome? Wait, did we skip *too* far ahead? Nope. After Art gets hitched, he and his knights are spoiling for a fight, so they choose the Romans. Well, the Romans might have started it by demanding taxes when Art's peeps were all, No taxation without representation! Anyone fancy a cuppa tea? Then it all descends into a pissing match in which Art and Emperor Lucius argue over who conquered whom first. Does it really matter, guys? Everyone has conquered everyone up to this point, so whatevs.

The Round Table gang sets out to fight the Romans, but then when they get to France, they run into a giant that murders, rapes, and eats, well, *everything*. So they have to take on that dude first. By the time they're done, it's a bloody mess, and taking down the Romans is a cakewalk.

Next we hop, skip, and jump back to Camelot, where the drama's about to get interesting. If you think spray-tanned housewives are catty meltdowns waiting to happen, wait until you see these men in shining armor. Launcelot du Lac is totes perfect. He and Gen fall in love and have their fun. But then he gets tricked into becoming a papa with Elayne. He eventually sparks the downfall of Camelot and dies far from Gen. No happily ever after here.

The knight Tristam falls in love with this chick Isode, which sounds a lot like Tristan and Isolde, that legend/opera/James Franco bomb. Yeah, that one. Tristam fights Launcelot and they become besties.

Galahad is Launce's kid, and he is the most virginest guy ever. Which he's advertising? Let's be honest, kid. You're not having much luck with the ladies, are ya? Don't worry, when your voice drops and you grow some chest hair, all the girls will start chasing you—literally—so invest in a fast horse. Wait, being a pure virgin makes him the only knight worthy enough to search for the Holy Grail? Interesting.

It all goes to hell when evil Mordred steals the kingdom and takes step-mom Gen as queen. Ew. During their epic last battle, Art kills Mordred but sustains fatal wounds as well. Then Gen and Launce get sick and die not too long after. Great. There aren't any other heirs around, so do we have to go through the whole sword-in-rock mess again? Nope, because Constantine becomes king. Wait, who's Constantine? Oh, if you hear of anyone looking for a huge round table that'll seat an army, send 'em to the posting on Craigslist.

You can thank **Sir Thomas Malory** for all those unrealistic romantic ~~clichés~~ expectations. You know: knights in shining armor spouting poetry and ~~holding doors open~~ saving damsels. He took the traditional Arthurian legends, which had been around for ages, and wrote them down. Ugh. Thanks, Tommy.

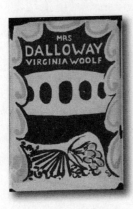

Mrs. Dalloway by Virginia Woolf

Published: 1925
Category: novel
Banned for: Our dear Mrs. Dalloway has been banned on numerous occasions because she kissed a girl when she was in her teens. And she *liked* it. Not only that, but Septimus has a really *really* good friend named Evans. Just how good is up to debate as Woolfie kept things vague. . . .

"For Heaven only knows why one loves it so, how one sees it so, making it up, building it round one, tumbling it, creating it every moment afresh; but the veriest frumps, the most dejected of miseries sitting on doorsteps (drink their downfall) do the same; can't be dealt with, she felt positive, by Acts of Parliament for that very reason: they love life."

I . . . wait, what? She lost me at "veriest frumps." What say we can this and get back to the party, yes? Anyone here know how to translate Woolf?

It's a June day in 1923, in the posh Westminster area of London, and we're experiencing a day in the life of Clarissa Dalloway. That's pretty much it. Really. Clarissa is a bored housewife. Septimus Smith is a vet of the Great War, who brought back a nasty case of PTSD. They never meet each other and only connect in one really random place at the end of the book. What can I say? Woolf was a little off her rocker.

Much of the book concerns itself with the characters' thoughts, the use of free indirect discourse meaning that we get to breast-stroke our way through a stream-of-consciousness head-hop throughout one novel-length day. The story often flashes back to each character's "continuous present." What does that mean? Nothing—and it makes the whole story *crazy* complicated. Clarissa's present-whatever-thingie focuses on her happy youth in Bourton. For Septimus, it's back to the foxholes during the war. *Incoming!*

Early that morning: *Yaaaawn.* Good morning, Mrs. Dalloway. Rise and shine because today is a very special day. She's throwing a party! To get ready, she goes shopping for flowers on a busy London street. She'd best get those home before her mind starts to wander. . . . Oh, wait, too late. Dammit . . .

11:00 a.m.: Clarissa returns to find ex-boyfriend Peter Walsh chilling on her couch. Oh Peter, you've got to get over your obsession with Clarissa. I mean, she's not all that special. I should know; I've already spent the better part of a morning inside her head. Yes, she rejected your proposal all those years ago, but seriously, dude, she's married and has a kid old enough to start thinking marriage herself. Let. It. Go.

11:30 a.m.: Clarissa finally gets Pete out of the house, so he meanders through Regent's Park . . . *Hey, Septimus! How've you been? Mmm, not so good, huh?* Looks like Seven is still shell-shocked from the Great War. Really, it wasn't all that "great" considering Sep has a case of the crazies. He used to be a poet, with feelings and such, but the war depressed him so much that it didn't even faze him when his best bud, Evans, died. Yikes.

Noon: Time for Septimus's appointment with his shrink, Sir William Bradshaw. Yay. Those doctor people already know everything about Septimus, so there's no point in listening to him or trying to figure out what the real problem is. They'll just toss him in an asylum, tearing him away from his wife—the only person who truly makes poor Septimus happy—and it'll all fix itself. Excellent plan, sir.

1:30 p.m.: Richard Dalloway comes back from lunch with highty-toighty society folk and brings Clarissa a big bouquet of roses. *Awww!* He wants to tell her that he loves her, but he can't because it's been too long since he said it last. Way to chicken out of that one, Dick. Clarissa ponders privacy and loneliness.

Late afternoon: Septimus and his wife spend the afternoon together in their peaceful apartment. How lovely . . .

6:00 p.m.: . . . until his doc shows up to take him away to the funny farm. He says no deal and leaps out the window instead. As Peter Walsh is walking back to Clarissa's for the party, he hears the siren of an ambulance on the way to collect the Septimus pancake.

Early evening: When guests arrive, the talk of the night turns to Sir William, who will be late to the party because of some unfortunate business with a client. It's a terrible inconvenience. All kinds of head-aches with traffic and whatnot. And the mess . . . *tut tut.*

Clarissa sneaks off to think some more—*because she clearly hasn't done enough of that today.* This time, she ponders the poor soul who went bungee jumping sans cord. What a brave man for not caving to society and its pressures! Er, OK. Also, it's her fault that he jumped, because she's a high-society hostess and is responsible for every person disaffected by modern life. Someone's a bit self-involved now, isn't she?

Now for the big finish: Clarissa goes back to the party! Yep, that's all, folks.

One person, however, gets a tad excited by her return. A certain jilted ex, who offers up a silent toast. Here's to you, Mrs. Dalloway.

Who's afraid of the big bad **Virginia Woolf**? Non-lit majors, that's for sure. Plus many of Woolf's contemporaries, especially those in "proper" literary circles. Women weren't allowed to attend university then, so she and her siblings had to make do by hosting salons in their home each week. No, they did not give each other makeovers—they had art parties. Sounds riveting, doesn't it? They discussed all kinds of taboo subjects, like religion, the arts, and sex—even homosexuality!

This book would have been a lot more interesting, however, if they had discussed *how to write good fiction.*

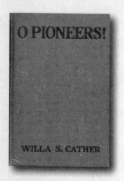

O Pioneers! by Willa Cather

Published: 1913
Category: novel
Banned for: being un-American. Seems Cather was too sympathetic toward adulterers and murderers in her story.

> *"There are only two or three human stories, and they go on repeating themselves as fiercely as if they had never happened before; like the larks in this country, that have been singing the same five notes over for thousands of years."*

Don't you just hate it when you get an earworm song stuck in your head for thousands of years?

Alex's family has a nice little farm along a stretch of the Nebraska plains called the Divide. Daddy is dying, though, so he tells his fam that he's leaving the farm to Alex. But Alex is short for Alexandra—she's a girl! Women can't be strong men; women don't lead. Except she does because she's more determined and forward-thinking than her brawny brothers.

She proves her mettle when everyone else decides to sell their farms because of depression and drought, and Alexandra convinces her brothers to take out a new mortgage so they can buy more land. She also convinces them to try some newfangled farming techniques that they're resisting. Old ways are good enough, *grumblegrumble.*

Fast forward sixteen years. Alexandra's farm is the most successful in the area. *Nyah nyah!* She proved them wrong, and each of her brothers has his own farm, as well as a family. In fact, they're so successful that younger brother Emil can go off to college. After traveling for several years, Alexandra's longtime friend Carl comes back to visit. Her bros don't like it when Alexandra gets close to Carl again, though, and they run him off so nothing will stand in the way of their kids inheriting Alexandra's farm.

Emil comes back from college and falls in love with his old friend Marie. Unfortunately, she's already unhappily married, so Emil takes off for Mexico to forget about her, but it doesn't help. (Should've asked Robert how well that works, Em—page 18.) He returns even more in love with her than ever. They make out at the fair.

He plans to take off again, but then a friend unexpectedly dies. A few days later, he enters a state of rapture in the church—um, what?—and decides to bid Marie bye-bye forever. When he goes to see her at home, she's enraptured, too. Out in the apple orchard. Huh. What are the odds. He lies down next to her, and her jealous husband shoots them both from behind the bushes.

Hubby goes to jail for ten years, and Alexandra's pretty exhausted by life at that point. She's sad over the murder of her bro and friend, so she lobbies to have the murderer pardoned. I mean, it's nice that you're so . . . *nice*, but he's not even getting the electric chair. He could probably stand a few more years in the pokey for that. One day she comes back from visiting the murderer to find Carl waiting for her. He left Alaska the moment he heard about Emil's death. Now he's back to comfort her, so it shouldn't be too surprising that they get married. Because nothing can kill true love—except Marie's husband.

Willa Cather grew up and went to college in Nebraska, but once she moved east after graduating she never lived out west again. Oh, I see how it is. Well, fine. At least she wrote about the midwest. Not too many writers did back then, which is probably why critics hailed her as a uniquely American writer without a whole lot of European influence.

The Odyssey by Homer

Published: 700 BC, give or take a century
Category: epic poem

> *"Just as I*
> *have come from afar, creating pain for many—*
> *men and women across the good green earth—*
> *so let his name be Odysseus . . .*
> *the Son of Pain, a name he'll earn in full."*

It's one thing to call your kid a pain, but actually naming him that?
Ouch.

The boys of Greece have ridden their big horsey through the gates of Troy, grabbed Helen, and are ready to sail home. (To see what happens to the other team, check out Aeneas's story on page 6.) Unfortunately for them, some of the gods are grumpy, which may or may not have something to due with Odysseus's men going all pirate and ransacking an island. Arrrrgh! The gods blow Odysseus's twelve ships the wrong way—hey, that's our exit!—and what starts out bad gets worse as they wander the sea for ten years. Sounds like someone got driving directions from Moses.

First they land on the island of the Cyclopes, really big one-eyed creatures that like humans . . . for dinner. They escape after blinding Polyphemus, the Cyclops who holds them captive. Unfortunately, they messed with the wrong cyclops. Polyphemus turns out to be Poseidon's son. Water god gets seriously pissed when he learns what happened, so it's no surprise when he does his best to drown them.

Odie and his guys get some good luck when Aeolus, ruler of the winds, gives them a wind bag—literally—to guide them home. It's smooth sailing . . . until the men get greedy and, thinking the bag has gold in it, open it. They can see their home island, Ithaca, but the wind bag blows them back the way they came—and onto an island of cannibals.

Twelve ships become one as the cannibals sink and nom them. The remaining ship makes landfall on the island of the sorceress Circe.

Western lit's first feminist, she has a little fun by turning Odie's men into pigs, but he eventually negotiates their return to human form. They spend the next year in relative luxury, as Odysseus canoodles with Circe until his men convince him that, hey, ticktock, party's over. They really should be going home now.

They visit the land of the dead to get directions home—because they have extra-special GPS?—and they're off again. They make it safely past the Sirens but not so safely past a six-headed monster, losing one man to each head. <*chomp!*>

Needing a break, they chill out for a hot second on the island of the sun god. Barbecuing one of Helios's prize cows = probably not the brightest idea. Helios threatens to drive the sun into the Underworld (bright light, bright light!) unless Zeus punishes the men. Another shipwreck later, Odie lands on Calypso's island, the sole survivor. She keeps him there as her lover amid festive steel drum music until Zeus makes her release him seven years later. Someone's obviously not in a rush to get back home.

Meanwhile, back in Ithaca, everyone thinks Odie is dead, so a bunch of bachelors show up wanting to marry the widow. Penelope puts off giving them an answer—"Lemme just finish weaving this, uh, tapestry," which she unpicks every night—so they stick around for ages, cavorting with the servants and eating all the food.

Odysseus's son, Telemachus, sets out to find papa with the help of Athena, who is the goddess president of Odysseus's fan club since he's a smartypants and a warrior, which is *totally* her type. She helps him out here and there along the way without, you know, actually guiding him safely home after he set sail from Troy. Minor details. Anyway, Athena disguises Odie, who *finally* makes it back to Ithaca, as a beggar so he can scope out the party scene back home. He meets up with his now-teenage son, and they kill all the bachelors mucking up the palace.

Homer ~~Simpson~~ lived around, say, 700 BC, give or take a few hundred years, except he might not have been real. Some scholarly types think he's just a made-up combination of a bunch of poets over the centuries who recited this windbag of a story from memory. And you thought it sucked when you had to memorize "The Raven" in high school.

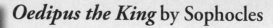

Oedipus the King by Sophocles

Published: 429 BC
Category: play (tragedy)

> *"It was my fate that I would marry*
> *my own mother and shed my father's blood*
> *with my own hands. That's why, many years ago,*
> *I left my home in Corinth. Things turned out well . . ."*

You call this turning out well? I'd hate to see what a bad family reunion looks like. <shudder>

King Laius of Thebes and his queen, Jocasta, are having a baby. Awww, how cute. An oracle comes for a visit and tells the proud parents: Your little bundle of joy is going to kill his father. What's a dad to do? Make his wife kill the brat, obviously. But she can't do it, so she hands the *enfant terrible* to a servant, who gives the kid to a shepherd in Corinth.

The shepherd offers the little murderer to the childless king and queen of Corinth, who adopt him. When Oedipus is all growed up, someone lets it slip that he's not really the king's son. Teh oops. So off he trots to Delphi, where the oracle says: Lots of doom! Oh, and you'll murder your dad and marry your mom.

Oedipus runs away (1) because he loves his parents and (2) gross. While on the lam, he runs into some jerk. Well, they're not so much on a baby sheep as they are stuck in the road because neither jackwaggon will move his chariot. They fight, and, you guessed it, Oed kills Laius without realizing he is (a) king of Thebes, and (b) dear ol' dad.

Well, that's just great. Without a king, Thebes falls victim to the Sphinx: a bird-cat beasty that rips apart anyone who can't solve some weirdo riddle. Oed's totally got this one, so he trots along and meets up with the bird-cat, solving the riddle and saving the day. Sort of. For defeating the Sphinx, he wins Queen Jocasta for a bride. They get it on, and he winds up siring his own siblings. (You don't even want to know what happens to the sibs. Someone get TLC on the phone. These people deserve their own reality show: *Living with the Rexes*. Tune in next week for *Antigone,* where the brother-sons kill each other and sister-daughter hangs herself. This family is seriously screwed.) And now we start the play! Yes, that was all back story.

Because the gods are awesome, they set up this whole drama with nasty little prophecies, then make sure they happen, and finally punish Oedipus and his family because he did what they said he was going to do even though he tried to get out of it. Worst party game ever.

Once the sibling-children are nearly grown, it's time for daddy to get spanked—and not in a good way. Punishment #1: Plague! Oed sends his bruncle-in-law, Creon, to Delphi to figure out what the Hades is going on.

Creon comes back and says there's bad mojo in the kingdom because King Laius's murderer was never caught. So now Oedipus has to figure out who killed King Laius. (Hint: YOU.) He sends for the blind prophet Tiresias to help him find the murderer. The prophet knows what's up and tells him, "You can't handle the truth!" Oed gets mad and says, "Tell me now, or I kill you!" So Tiresias does, but Oedipus won't believe him. Traitor!

It all goes downhill from there, but eventually the truth comes to light: Not only did he do the nasty with his own mom, but he spawned some of Sigmund Freud's choicest fantasies. (You can keep your third leg, thankyouverymuch.) Jocasta hangs herself because ew. When Oedipus finds his mom-wife, he takes her body down and uses her dress pins to stab out his own eyes. Which means the last thing he sees before he goes blind is his dead wife-mom's naked body, and that makes everything better.

Sophocles was the king of tragedy in his day. Dude had mad skills—with more than 123 plays under his belt . . . but only seven of them survive in full. Then again, maybe we should be grateful. Can you imagine what else Sophocles had up his toga?

Of Mice and Men
by John Steinbeck

Published: 1937
Category: novella
Banned for: *Booyah!* Steinbeck wins another game of Banned Bingo with double points for being challenged by the KKK *and* a black power group. Plus some warm fuzzies for being unpatriotic and anti-business. Johnny boy gets all the best ones.

> *"Guys like us, that work on ranches, are the loneliest guys in the world. They got no family. They don't belong no place. . . . With us it ain't like that. We got a future. We got somebody to talk to that gives a damn about us. We don't have to sit in no bar room blowin' in our jack jus' because we got no place else to go. If them other guys gets in jail they can rot for all anybody gives a damn. But not us."*

Aw, how tender.

George and Lennie travel California together getting odd jobs during the Depression as farm hands. They're bestest pals even though they're polar opposites. George is short and shrewd while Lennie is a husky boy and thick in the head. So most of the time George takes care of Lennie, which Lennie likes just fine.

Sitting under a tree by a nice little pond, they camp out for the night before heading to a new farm for work the next day. George sees Lennie tightly holding something. Oh. Lovely. A dead mouse. Seems Lennie accidentally killed it by petting too hard. Tough love? Naw, Lennie's love is the killing kind.

In addition to animals, Lennie tends to have problems interacting with other folk. He likes touching pretty things, for example a woman's red dress, but usually the woman is still wearing the dress. For some reason, women don't like it when he does that so they cry rape, and their menfolk come running. Last time that happened on a farm where they worked, Lennie nearly got lynched. *Eep.* George's life would be so much easier without having to watch out for Lennie, but he cares for the big lug. Aw.

Before they go to sleep, George tells Lennie—yet. again.—about their shared dream of owning a farm together. They'll build a nice farmhouse set on ten acres with a rabbit hutch out back. It's a good thing that rabbits breed like, well, rabbits; Lennie will have plenty of pets to love to death. They'll have an orchard filled with apple trees, a windmill nearby, plus a chicken coop and a smokehouse for the pigs. That's the life. But Lennie has a tendency to stumble into trouble. So George tells him that if it happens again to head back to the pond nearby and hide in the brush so George can find him. That's a good Lennie. Now go to sleep.

Their new farm has lots of politics and easily bruised egos. Which sounds like the perfect place to take a manchild. The boss's son Curley doesn't like big guys, so he acts like a jerk to Lennie. Curley's wife likes to flirt with all the farmhands, and he likes to fly into jealous rages when she does. But it's always the fault of the farm workers. Obviously.

A while later, farm supervisor Slim gives Lennie a puppy from the litter his dog just had. Aww, how nice. Lennie will take such good care of it. But he keeps getting in trouble for playing with all the puppies and taking them away from their mother.

George is telling Lennie about their farm again one day when an old one-handed worker asks if he can get in on the deal. He has a bunch of money stashed away. Pooling their savings, they can actually afford it, rabbit hutch and all. Yay! Nothing can go wrong now that they're so close to realizing their dream. They decide to work until the end of the month, then take their earnings and buy their own place. No foreshadowing or suspenseful music here. Nope.

Curley accuses Slim of flirting with his wife but later apologizes. He's in a fighting mood, though, so when he sees Lennie and his oblivious perma-grin, Curley starts hitting him for laughing. That doesn't go so well when Lennie crushes Curley's hand. But the guy wouldn't quit hitting him, so he had to make it stop. I totally understand, big guy. Not his fault. He's just so . . . big. Poor lug doesn't know his own strength. After things blow over, he's out in the barn petting his cute widdle puppy, petting it and petting it until he cuddles it to death.

But then Curley's wife finds him in the barn. Sad wifey is sad, too. She'll never become a Hollywood starlet, which is why she constantly flirts with the farm workers: to stroke her ego. When she finds out that Lennie likes to touch soft things, she lets him stroke her hair. Unfortunately, Lennie still hasn't realized how strong he is, and he accidentally breaks her neck. Ruh roh! Run and hide!

When George hears what happened, he dashes off to the brush near the pond to find his gentle giant hiding under the designated tree. With a lynch mob hot on their trail, the other hands rush after George. They find them soon after they hear a shot fired. George took care of his friend so well that he shot him in the back of the head to protect him from the angry mob. Right before he did, though, he went over his dream with Lennie one more time so his best friend would die a happy man.

Sniffle.

John Steinbeck grew up in rural NorCal and spent summers working as a farm hand on nearby ranches. He studied at Stanford but never graduated. Unlike some hoighty-toighty Ivy League students back east, Steinbeck respected his humble neighbors and wrote about them with dignity and regard. What a weirdo.

The Old Man and the Sea
by Ernest Hemingway

Published: 1952
Category: novella

"You did not kill the fish only to keep alive and to sell for food, he thought. You killed him for pride and because you are a fisherman. You loved him when he was alive and you loved him after. If you love him, it is not a sin to kill him. Or is it more?"

Depends on whether you loved him with some lemon juice and a nice white wine.

An old man sails his boat into the sea and tries to catch a fish. That's the entire plot. Really. But the story stretches on for one hundred pages. Talk about filler. Still, it's a guppy compared to *Moby-Dick* (page 149).

Old Santiago's had a bad streak lately: eighty-four days without catching a single fish. Perhaps it's time to start thinking about retirement. Dude has such bad luck that the parents of his apprentice make the kid find a luckier boat to fish on. But the kid is loyal, so every night he helps the old man bring in his gear, cook his dinner, and discuss American baseball. Golly gee, that Joe DiMaggio is one swell ballplayer.

Tired of ~~being a loser~~ his losing streak, Santiago takes his little boat out farther than ever before. He drops his line down one hundred fathoms. If you can't fathom what a fathom is, it's a long way down, six hundred feet to be precise. But one hundred fathoms sounds cooler, especially for an old dude.

Here, fishie fishie fishie!

Santiago hooks a fish immediately. Way to go, old man! He tries to reel it up, but the fish is having none of that. This ain't no ordinary fish, either; it's a marlin! What, you ask, is a marlin, and why is it so special? It's a big fish—not as big as a shark, but big. The fish makes a run for it, tugging Santiago's little boat behind it. *Wheeeee!*

Marlin drags the poor old man around—holding on for dear life—for two whole days. Why didn't he just let the fish go? Well, he's an old man, and being stubborn is what they do. That and complain about their bad backs and how much everything costs these days. Anyhow, as Marlin tows him for days, he ponders how alike they both are: strong, noble . . . and scaly? That's great, Iago. Maybe it's time to consider letting go for some food or water so the hallucinations abate.

On day three, he *finally* gets the monster fish close enough to harpoon it. Which means Santiago wins. GOAL!

But wait, the adventure's not over yet. A shiver of sharks—seriously, that's what it's called—assails the little boat. Turns out that tying a ginormous fish carcass to the side of your boat, leaving a trail of blood in the water, is the *perfect* way to attract sharks. Who knew? Didn't quite think that one through, now did we, Santiago? He's so far out that there's no way he can get home in time to save his poor fishie corpse. He fights off the sharks as best he can, but eventually they get a nice dinner, tied up nice and tidy for them to nom.

Santiago makes it to shore and collapses into bed, exhausted. A crowd gathers around his boat, muttering in awe about the shark skeleton tied to it. Which is really a marlin skeleton, duh. The apprentice is overjoyed to find Santiago passed out in his hut. Old man, big sea. You do the math.

Good gravy, are we done yet?

Almost. The boy tells Santiago the baseball scores, and they agree to become fishing buddies again. Then the old man goes back to sleep, and you fall asleep realizing that the only thing more boring than fishing is reading about it.

Ernest Hemingway was a man's man: rough and tumble. *Rawr!* No wonder most of his books revolve around manly sports: bullfighting, boxing, big game hunting, and, you guessed it, fishing.

The Once and Future King by T. H. White

Published: 1958
Category: novel (fantasy)

"Might does not make right! Right makes right!"

Got it. What does that make left?

The Once and Future King is actually a series of four books usually squished together in a single volume. They tell of the life and not-so-fun times of King Arthur and his Round Table. Well, the knights too, but we'll get to them later. Plus there's another volume, *The Book of Merlyn*, published posthumously, which fittingly deals with the wizard's last lessons for Arthur before he kicked the bucket—but people tend to ignore that one. Sorry, Merlyn, you were ~~ahead of~~ behind your times.

The Sword in the Stone

You might have heard about this one in some cartoonish manner. Let's just say that no one in this story gets a happily ever after.

This kid called The Wart lives with Sir Ector, his foster father, and his foster brother, Kay. Yes, Kay is male. Wart is a runt, but Kay still has jealousy issues. Merlyn might have something to do with that, because he offers to tutor Wart, and turns the kid into various animals and teaches him lots of cool stuff. He also teaches him how to be just and kind, which = zzzzz.

Since the Wart is a good kid, he asks Merlyn to turn Kay into an animal, too, just for funsies. The magician won't, but he does tell them where to go on an adventure. So Wart and Kay wander off into the forest, where they meet Robin *Wood*. Not a typo. They go off adventuring and rescue Friar Tuck from a naughty band of fairies that live in a castle made entirely of food. Wait, when did we teleport into a Grimm tale?

A couple years later, Kay is preparing to become a knight, and the Wart will be his squire. By that time, Merlyn's taken off for who knows when (kinda difficult to pin him down when he lives through time backward). Then the news that King Uther Pendragon has croaked hits town. Without an heir, the next king will be decided by pulling a sword stuck in an anvil and a stone below. Only the rightful king can yoink it from the rock, blah blah blah.

Which means it's tournament time! It's the hottest event of the year, and *everyone* will be there. Dudes keep trying to pull the friggin' sword from that friggin' rock, but nothing doing, so they host a tourney to get more men in to have a go with the bloody sword. Kay pulls up to the tourney and realizes, crap!, he forgot his sword. So he sends Wart to get it for him, but the inn where they're staying is closed. Whatever will poor Wart do? But then—*dun dunnuNAH!*—he sees a sword sticking out of some random rock. He'll totes put it back later because he's only borrowing it. So he yanks that sucker out and Wart becomes King Arthur. W00t, w00t!

The Queen of Air and Darkness

Turns out that Arthur was actually the son of Uther Pendragon, so he's ~~too~~ legit if anyone asks why a runt is king. Merlyn shows up again to help the kid out, and boy does he need it. The nation's constantly at war with the different people living there: Normans (like Papa Pendragon), Saxons, and Gaels. They all like to fight. A lot.

So Merlyn teaches the dim-witted Arthur that war is bad. We should *stop* the wars, not keep at it. Which means nobles pimped out in armor astride their one-horsepower vehicles shouldn't be out quashing peasants. That's *bad*, Wart. Bad. We don't use people like kids' little tin soldiers because real soldiers don't just fall over; they bleed and die.

Arthur: So war isn't fun?
Merlyn: Correct.
Arthur: But what about—
Merlyn: NO.
Arthur: But I—
Merlyn: *(stern glare)*
Arthur: Fine. Whatever. War is stupid.

So Art figures out a new way to wage war that will make it *un*fun for all the nobles. Instead of scooting soldiers about fields, now the knights have to fight for their own lives. Dudes, y'all got pwned! Well, except the hot witch Morgause, who seduces the young king by using magic and pwns *him*. The ick factor is high on this one, kids, but not because she's a witch. She's actually his half-sister, even though he doesn't know it. Doesn't matter—still *gross*. Even better? She gets preggers and has the bastard Mordred, who turns out to be *more* ~~dread~~ than just an illegitimate child.

The Ill-Made Knight

You might have heard something about this knight named Lancelot. He's Arthur's BFF. They're tight, but then Lance totally crushes on Art's lady, Guenever, and Camelot goes to pot because of it. That's one mighty fling, I tell ya.

Lance realizes it's not ideal to be in love with the queen, so he takes off for a few years, does good stuff to help people, and comes back a hero. But first, he gets tricked into sleeping with Elaine, which makes the queen jealous. Arthur realizes his girl and his bestie are getting it on, but he doesn't want to lose either of them, so he pretends they're just really good friends. Uh huh. Not just a river in Egypt. When you're the queen, an affair means treason and death. Yikes. Meanwhile, Camelot's not looking so hot, so Arthur sends his knights off to find the ~~wild goose~~ Holy Grail.

The Candle in the Wind

Sing it, Sir Elton! Art's son/nephew Mordred is a bit angry, so he plots Uncle Daddy's downfall. Mordred forces Art to admit that Guen and Lance are doing the nasty, which means the king has to put them on trial for treason and condemn his wife to die. Family counseling obviously didn't work.

Lancelot rides in all knight-in-shining-armor and saves Guenever from burning at the stake, Art goes to war against Lance, and Mordred sneaks up on Uncle Daddy and steals his throne. Technically he *is* next in line, but it's usually courteous to wait until the previous king dies. The story ends with Arthur ready to attack his own castle (!), realizing that he's probably gonna die the next day.

T. H. White wrote about one of the greatest romances ever, and yet he never had a lasting romantic relationship of his own. Let's just say Terence had mommy issues. ~~Mrs. Bates~~ White was über-clingy and demanded that he love her most of all and always. Except he sort of hated her for it. Not too surprising, then, that women didn't really do it for him when he got older. So he jousted for the other side, if you know what I'm sayin'.

Paradise Lost by John Milton

Published: 1667
Category: epic poem
Banned for: being written by Milton, who landed himself on the Catholic Church's official list of banned books. Perhaps he shouldn't have called Rome a modern Babylon and bishops Egyptian taskmasters.

"Better to reign in Hell than serve in Heaven."

A big fish in a small pond still makes for good fish sticks.

Satan: Yaaawn. Ssstretch. Good morn— uh, where the hell are we?

Big Guy: Oh yeah. Forgot to mention that I banished you to a hot little resort called hell. You've got a great piece of land right next to the lake of fire. It's the hottest new place in town. Have fun! Toodles.

Satan's a bit steamed over the new digs, even after they spruce up the place into a new capitol: Pandemonium. So he gathers his fallen angel buddies for a chat.

Satan: This totally bites, but don't give up, guys. We can still rock the boat from down here. We just need a good plan.

Moloch: Time for WAR! Booyah!

Belial: Eh, I'm good. Just bring me a hot toddy and a good book, and I'll settle in just fine.

Mammon: There's plenty of ~~cool~~ hot stuff going on, so we can, you know, make do with what we've got.

Satan *(sighs)*: Not helping. Bel and Mam, you're both fired. Anyone have a brilliant idea? Beelzebub, you're good at devilish little plots. What should we do?

Beelzebub: Mayhem is good and all, but I'm a big fan of subversion. We'll get back at God by . . . messing with his precious little mankind. He'll never see it coming.

Satan: Excellent idea. Suit up, boys. Time to partay!

Meanwhile, behind some clouds, God rolls his eyes.

God: Do they really think I can't see what they're up to? Morons. They'll have their fun corrupting men, but I've got an ace up my sleeve that they'll never trump: Jesus.

Angel fangirls cheer Him on.

God: All right, calm down. Show's about to start. Who wants popcorn?

Down in hell, Satan meets up with his children, Sin and Death.

Satan: Ready to have some fun, kids? Remember: Break all the rules and corrupt anything and everything possible. Let's go!

They fly out the gates of hell and zero in on Earth.

Satan: Breaker, breaker, do you read me? We've got Earth in sight.

Chaos: Copy that, Lucifer. You are cleared for landing. Over.

Down on Earth, Adam and Eve are frolicking through the Garden of Eden.

Angel Gabriel: Now Adam, you'll want to watch out. There's a wild and dangerous Satan lurking round these parts.

Adam: A Satan? What's that? *(gazes at flower petals)*

Gabe: Don't worry about that; just run from anyone you don't know and yell out "Stranger Danger!" We'll come take care of it.

Adam: Oh. OK. *(chases a goat)*

Gabe: And don't forget—no eating fruit from the Tree of Knowledge! You know what that'll do to your sugar levels.

Later, Gabe sits Adam and Eve down for a chat about the War in Heaven and the Creation of the Earth. The condensed version: Lucifer (a.k.a. Satan) got jealous of the Son (a.k.a. Jesus), so he picked a fight. He sweet-talked about a third of all the angels into following him. That's when the real fighting began. (Hey! Leave that mountain alone. Seriously? You just gouged the Earth. What are we supposed to call it now, the Grand Canyon? Whatevs.) The fighting is wrecking the scenery, so God sent the Son to stop the shenanigans and herd the troublemakers into hell.

Son: And stay there!

Lucifer: *(blows raspberry)*

Then Gabe describes how Adam was made from dirt and all that fun stuff you already know. If not, find a Bible because I'm so not condensing that thing. Way too much. The night ends with Adam getting all mushy and romantic.

Adam: Eve is the most beautifulest woman to ever walk the Earth . . .

Eve: Really? Did you just hear yourself? I'm the *only* woman to have walked the Earth. You want some happy fun times, you're going to have to try harder than that.

A few days later . . .

Adam: Let's work together today, honey.

Eve: Dude, I need some space. I know I came from your rib and all, but you're really starting to smother me.

Adam: But darling—

Eve: Sit! Now stay . . . stay!

Adam: *(whimpers and watches her leave with sad eyes)*

Satan sneaks into Eden and sees Eve wander off alone. Excellent. So he turns into a snake and slithers up to her.

Satan: You musssst be ssssso tired, working sssssso hard like you are. Would you like ssssome fruit? An apple, perhapssssss?

Eve: I sure am, Mister . . . uh, I didn't catch your name. But hey, I can't eat that.

Satan: Why not? It'sss tassssssty. Come on. Everyone'ssss doing it. It won't hurt, jussst thisss once.

Eve: Oh fine. *(chomp)* Mmm . . . tasty.

Satan: Wait for it . . .

Eve: Oh $#!%, what did I just do? I've got to hide before Adam sees what I've done.

Adam: Hey, honey. Did you find something for lunch? Looks yummy.

He grabs the apple and takes a big ol' bite.

Adam: Yummm . . . wait a second. What the %&#! did you just make me eat?

Eve: What did I—hey, what's that hanging there on your . . . well, *hello*.

They grab each other and dash into the woods.

Satan: My work here is done.

Satan returns to hell and stands triumphantly at his throne . . . where everyone boos him. Wait, why would they boo when he just caused the fall of man? *Pop!* All of the devils turn into snakes.

Back on Earth, Adam and Eve are doing the worst walk of shame ever—right past the gates of Eden as the Archangel Michael shoos them out. But first, the Son pronounces their sentence: "Life will suck, but it'll be worth it. Don't worry, I'll come back later and fix everything. But next time obey the rules. Now go off and have lots of babies. You've got a world to populate!"

Eve apologizes, Adam forgives her, and the rest is in the Bible.

The life of a writer is tough. I mean, we spend long hours in front of the computer every day and when we don't get bored we get hand cramps. Can't complain too much, though, considering **John Milton** wrote all of *Paradise Lost* while BLIND, dictating the verse to one of his aides. That's dedication, I tell you.

Peter Pan by J. M. Barrie

Published: 1904
Category: play (children's)
Banned for: a stereotypical portrayal of ~~Indians~~, ~~American Indians~~, Native Americans, which doesn't sit right with some people, despite those characters—especially Tiger Lily—coming off as noble and good. Let's also not forget that some of the book's early illustrations depict mermaids *with boobies!*

"To die will be an awfully big adventure."

That's great, Peter, but let's stick to adventures where we get to stay alive, please.

You can blame the whole missing-shadow thing on Mrs. Darling. She saw the lost boy Peter Pan playing Peeping Tom outside her children's bedroom window and made a grab for him. Peter dashed off, but she nabbed his shadow, so she rolled it up and put it in a drawer. Because shadows work like that. Hey, it's on Wikipedia, so it must be true.

When Peeping Peter goes from voyeurism to breaking and entering one night while the 'rents are out, Wendy catches him. He was crying because his shadow wouldn't cooperate, so really it wasn't hard. Wendy sews the shadow back on and proves herself a paragon of Victorian prudery by offering Peter a thimble as a kiss.

Peter invites the kids to Neverland—no, not the ranch, so we don't need to worry about the kids. I think. Tinkerbell sprinkles them with her pixie dust, which allows them to fly. OK, maybe we should worry. Wendy plays mother to the gang of Lost Boys, and they go on all sorts of adventures. Some of those adventures involve a beautiful Indian princess named Tiger Lily, and some half-nekkid mermaids splashing in the lagoon. Boys really *don't* have to grow up in this world.

Wendy starts to fall in love with Peter, but he only wants her as a mother. How's that for the world's worst rejection? As Wendy is telling the boys a story one day, she remembers her parents and decides to break up the party. Time to go home. But, dun dun *dunnn*, Captain Hook captures her and the Lost Boys, holding them all prisoner on his pirate ship, where Hook plans to make Wendy the pirates' mother and kill the Lost Boys. You don't remember just how creepy this story is, do you? Don't worry. Blocking out things is just the brain's way of coping with early childhood trauma.

Peter wakes up—who *sleeps* through his friends' kidnapping?—and hears the terrible news from Tinkerbell. Being the good troublemaker that he is, Peter remembers to take his medicine before flying off to rescue everyone, but Hook has poisoned it. Tink drinks it instead and starts to die. The only way to save her? Clapping. Really. Come on, start clapping. I said *clap, dammit!* We can't move on until Tink is back and all buzzy and annoying again, and this story is skeeving me out, so let's get it over with, please.

After a round of applause from a mysterious audience of raucous children—who are totally breaking the fourth wall, Barrie—Pete flies off to the pirate ship to save everyone. On his way, he finds a crocodile that ticks like a clock, the croc that *ate* Hook's hand, though of course Pan doesn't know it. Petey pirates the idea and goes around making ticking noises to scare off other creatures. He keeps it up when he reaches the ship, which freaks Hook out.

Peter and Hook fight it out, which ends with Peter kicking Hook off the ship and into the hungry croc's mouth. Before becoming a croc snack, Hook pouts: Bad form, Peter! Because somehow a grown man hijacking a kid's pretend mother to be his own is good form. Right.

Wendy and the crew are done with the whole Lost Boy, stay-a-kid-forever thing, thankfully, so they fly the pirate ship back to London. How steampunk of them. The Lost Boys decide to stay, and Mrs. Darling adopts the lot of them. Apparently, Wendy isn't the first Darling to fall for Peter's charms. So, wait . . . ew? Either way, it helps when explaining to your parents why you arrived on a flying pirate ship with a herd of wild boys.

Mrs. Darling offers to adopt Peter as well—double ew—but he won't be tamed. He'd rather stay a boy forever. Which is what most men do anyway. Oh, the irony.

J. M. Barrie never really quit tinkering around with Peter Pan. Peter first appeared in the adult novel *The Little White Bird*. He got his own story as star of the 1904 play *Peter Pan; or, the Boy Who Wouldn't Grow Up* (working title: *The Boy Who Hated Mothers*—seriously), later rewritten into the 1911 book *Peter and Wendy*. Even after the play had a good long run, Barrie kept fiddling with it. Also, dude should have Freud on speed dial.

The Picture of Dorian Gray by Oscar Wilde

Published: 1890
Category: novel
Banned for: veiled references to homosexuality, etc. Or in the original (uncut) version, homoerotica for all!

"There is no such thing as a moral or an immoral book. Books are well written, or badly written. That is all."

Yeah, try telling that to the Nazis and the New York Times Book Review.

Painter Basil Hallward takes Dorian Gray as his muse (in more ways than one, if you read the uncensored version finally published in 2011). Lord Henry ~~wanton~~ Wotton enjoys lobbing quips and spoiling himself more than doing anything productive. Don't we all. He loves to sensationalize his views on life in order to shock his friends, so when he meets impressionable pretty boy Dorian, he convinces him that the most important things in life are youth and beauty. Well duh. Traumatized, Dory calls up Faustie's old friend (page 68). "If you make the painting get old and ugly instead of me, I'll totes give you my soul. It'll just get in the way of my vanity anyway." Deal.

Like a cute widdle puppy dog, Dorian drools on Wotton's every word. All you need in life is the physical pleasure. You know, the good stuff, like sex, drugs, rock 'n' roll, booze . . . even though Wilde never actually mentions anything *specific*. Letting *our* sick and twisted minds do all the work? That's cheating! But the libertine life isn't all that great. Says who? Perhaps Dorian's first ~~obsession~~ love interest. He thinks he's in lurve with the actress Sibyl. Yeah, you and every other hornball. When she stops performing because she's experiencing real love for the first time, *yawn*, Dorian gets bored and casts her off like a worn Jimmy Choo.

He gets home and sees that the painting changed: now it's sneering. You mean pictures can move? Someone should get a patent on that. They'll make *thousands*. Well, at least we know Dory has some snark mixed in with all that pretty paint. But the sneer is kinda ugly, so Dorian figures he'll fix it by begging forgiveness. But—drama queen alert—she already chug-a-lugged some acid. Too late now. Oh, well. On with the party! Then the portrait really heads to hangover central, so Dory hides it where only he can see it.

Fast forward eighteen years. Dorian still has his gorgeous baby face, but the painting is butt ugly and getting worse by the day. Come on, guys. Really funny. Put back Dorian's pic and get rid of the Keith Richards one. Dorian sure has gotten his debauch on. He's sorta proud of all his conquests, though, so when Basil stops by to call an intervention—it took him *eighteen years* to realize something was up?—dude shows him the painting. Basil is horrified. "It's not possible! I can't be that bad of an artist." Dorian's not up for the guilt trip—preaching to the crypt, anyone?—so he knifes the painter. *Wah wah.*

Not to worry. Murder's just another vice on the ~~menu~~ portrait. Dorian blackmails someone into disposing of Basil's body by dissolving it with acids—hey kids, time for some science experiment fun!—then he's off to an opium den. Good times. When Sibyl's brother sees Dorian there, he recognizes him as the dude who stiffed his sister—literally—but that guy should be ~~old and wrinkly~~ middle-aged by now. Unless . . . *nah*. Couldn't be him.

Dorian bolts for his place in the country, where he resolves to change, but the vengeful bro catches up with him just in time to get accidentally shot by game hunters. "But he wasn't wearing an orange vest!" "Because it's a fashion crime, duh." Well isn't that convenient. Dorian's being a good boy now, so he sneaks a peek at the painting to see how nice and perfect it is again—but *ahhhhhh* ohmygoshmakeitstop! Somehow his faux repenting didn't take and the painting is even rat nastier than before.

So he stabs the painting with the knife he used to kill Hallward—because that will make it look better. Someone needs to go back to art class—and magically kills himself. He starts screaming like a girl, so his servants come a'runnin' and find the boss man dead on the floor, a ~~Republican~~ vile, shriveled old man. The only way they even know it's him is by the rings he's wearing. The painting, on the other hand, is back to its original glory. Dun dun *dunnnn.*

Oscar Wilde, a notoriously flamboyant man, always wore the most fashionable ensembles. Although married, he preferred the company of gentlemen—a *man's* man, if you get my drift—which tragically led to a soul-crushing two-year imprisonment for committing indecent acts. The unnamed but not so subtle acts of immorality in *Dorian Gray* certainly didn't help on that count. Whoops.

The Pilgrim's Progress
by John Bunyan

Published: 1678
Category: epic poem

"Here is a poor burdened sinner. I come from the City of Destruction, but am going to Mount Zion, that I may be delivered from the Wrath to come; I would therefore, Sir, since I am informed that by this Gate is the Way thither, know if you are willing to let me in?"

Dude, just knock. He doesn't need to hear your life story first.

Here, you're going to need this helmet. Why? Because you're about to be bashed over the head repeatedly with symbolism. It's painful. Everything in this book has *deep* and *philosophical* meaning, but they can be hard to see coming, so watch out for symbols crashing into your skull.

Let's meet our main man, Christian. He's a *Christian*—if you can believe it—and a pilgrim. Sadly, he doesn't hunt turkeys or eat their roasted carcasses with gravy, stuffing, and pumpkin pie. Mmmm, pie. A shame, really. Those pilgrims were a lot more interesting. Christian leaves the City of Destruction to find the Celestial City (*choirs of angels sing*). He tries to bring the fam, but they're total sinners and don't want to wander aimlessly to find some mythical city run by an invisible honcho. Fine, have fun in hell. Say hi to Virgil for me? Kthxbai.

Christian is walking along, *walkwalkwalk,* when, oh no! He falls into the Bog of Eternal Stench. No wait, it's actually the Slough of

Despond, but it probably stinks, too. Eventually he pulls himself out of the muck. Hey, look, it's Worldly Wiseman (not Jewish, I checked). Dude looks fine with all his cool clothes and [insert latest Apple product here].

WW: Life is *awesome*. You totes don't need religion. Really, it's fun over here on the Dark Side. We have cookies. Also, you reek.

Christian: No way, man. I am CHRISTIAN. *(Superhero cape flaps in the wind.)*

WW: Whatevs. *(pulls out his smartphone to text a friend)* "Up 4 munchies? Dude just shot me down. Need ice cream & guy talk."

Chris crashes at Goodwill's crib for a bit until WW "suggests" that Chris visit his friend. "Interpreter's a great guy. You'll love him. *(mutters to self)* Get out of my freakin' house! Ugh." Unfortunately, Interpreter's a bit of a know-it-all and insists on telling Christian all about faith. "Uh, thanks for . . . stuff. I gotta scram!" He goes on his merry way and runs into the Shining Ones, who are the latest prepackaged boy band handing out tickets to get into Celestial City. Wait, is this a city or an amusement park? Eh, who cares. Race you to the log ride!

Excited, Chris falls asleep. *(dreams)* "Sweet rollercoaster. Cotton candy. Omnomnom." *(drools on pillow)* When he wakes up, his ticket is gone! No bumper cars for you, bud. He goes back down the trail and eventually finds it. Sigh of relief. Now he *really* wants to get there—and fast.

He keeps going, *walkwalkwalk,* until he comes to Palace Beautiful, where four hot chicks give him food and a nice bed. Before he leaves, they suit him up and give him a sword. What is he supposed to do with a sword? They're not gonna let him take that on the Ferris wheel.

Next day, he's off again and reaches the Valley of Humiliation. "*Stupid, stupid.* How could I spill the soup all over myself and the nice lady next to me at dinner last night? I'm just a clumsy oaf." *(hangs head in shame)* Huh, what's that up ahead? Oh, just the monster Apollyon, who is not a Greek god (again, I checked). Wait, did you say "*monster*"? Christian tries to run, but his armor's too heavy. *Stabbity stab stab*, and Apollyon goes down for the count.

Good grief, are we there yet? Not quite. Just have to get through the Valley of the Shadow of Death and then through the city of Vanity and its world-renowned fair filled with more than enough debauching to satisfy every addiction. It won't hurt to take a little peek. Hey, isn't that Dorian Gray? (See page 179) What's he doing to the . . . oh my. Chris and his homeboy Faithful, who shows up for no apparent reason, resist all the shiny temptations, but the fairgoers are like, "Weirdos. They didn't debauch even a little." So the city's lovely denizens won't let Chris and Faithful leave. Instead, they chuck Chris in prison and execute Faithful.

Chris escapes and finds a new travel buddy, Hopeful. GET IT? They *walkwalkwalk* into even more adventures. *Yawn.* I don't know how much more of this I can take. Why don't we speed things up a bit? They walk through the plain of Ease, then reach the Doubting Castle, where they're tortured. But they have the magic key of Promise that unlocks ALL THE DOORS. So they escape.

Along the way they meet Ignorance Smurf, Flatterer Smurf, Atheist Smurf, and Babe the Blue Ox. They reach the Delectable Mountains— because they've walked all the way onto the Candy Land board by now—and then pass into the Enchanted Meadow, which makes them sleepy. To stay awake, they chug some Red Bull and discuss Hopeful's many sins. Fun?

And then . . . they're at the gates of Celestial City. Oh. No, wait. They have to cross a river before they can get there. Someone should really build a bridge because Christian almost drowns trying to get across. The gates open, and they are welcomed in. *(The crowd cheers.)*

The end . . . of book 1.

What? Noooo! Fine, the super-abbreviated version of the sequel: Christian's wife, Christiana, (GET IT?) and their daughter finally come to their senses and travel to Celestial City.

~~Paul~~ **John Bunyan** was a criminal. Really. He wrote *Pilgrim* while in prison for a dozen years. His crime? Preaching. At the time, it was illegal to be a Puritan in England. That's it? I was hoping for something a bit more exciting. Not even trespassing? Huh. *Boring.*

The Portrait of a Lady by Henry James

Published: 1881
Category: novel (serialized)

"Under certain circumstances there are few hours in life more agreeable than the hour dedicated to the ceremony known as afternoon tea."

Uh, yeah, tea is nice, but I can think of a much better way to kill an hour—if you know what I'm saying.

Isabel Archer's daddy just died. But then her aunt takes her to Europe to meet her Uncle Touchett and cousin Ralph, who win the Worst Names Ever Award. When she gets there, she meets her great family members, plus some fancy noblemen like Lord Warburton, who falls in love with her. Some girls have all the luck.

But Isabel doesn't want to get married because chick's got plans, which include travel and not becoming a good little wife popping out babies. Sing it, sista! Then her friend Henrietta shows up in England and tells Isabel that the guy from back home who's in love with her is *oming-cay* to *isit-vay*. So Caspar Goodwood—new contender for worst name!—pops by. "Hey, girl. Missed you. Mwah, mwah."

He wants her to marry him; forget the Warburton dude. Um, no. Not until she puts on her big-girl panties and travels the world a bit. Then, in two years or so, you can bring it up again. But no guarantees. He (reluctantly) agrees to go back to America and wait for her. Dude, she's got you whipped. *Wha-psh!*

She's in London when she hears that her uncle is ~~sick~~ dying. First daddy, now uncle. She's not going to have any men in her life left— especially if she holds out on getting married. At uncle's place, she meets another house guest named Madame Merle. Who told HJ these names were OK? Oof. Anyway, Isabel and MM become besties as they wait for Uncle Touchett to kick the bucket.

Cousin Ralph knows his papa plans to leave him a nice chunk of change, but turns out that Ralphie is dying, too, so he doesn't really need the spendy cash. He convinces dear dad to leave some of the inheritance to cousin Isabel. Once uncle bucks the kick-it, Isabel becomes a super-hot heiress, and all the guys want to drink her milkshake. So to speak. Not because of her new fortune. No, they like her sparkling personality and vivacious wit. Wait, what's her name again?

Isabel travels on with her auntie to the family's villa in Florence. Guess who tags along . . . Madame Merle! So much fun. Oh, here's a nice man you should ~~marry~~ meet, Merle's old friend Gilbert Osmond. Wonder of wonders, soon Isabel thinks she's in love. Italy—they must put something in the water. (See page 200)

Isabel: I lurve him soooo, but I'm still an independent woman, so I won't listen to common sense or any reason that my concerned friends and family might offer up.

Everyone who actually cares about her: Don't do it. You're being stupid. Wh— *(door in face)*

Isabel: I'm getting married!

Everyone else: *(bang head repeatedly against the wall)*

Darlin', he ain't nothin' but a gold digger. Probably should've listened when people were talking sense because now you're stuck with the jerk. Hope you enjoy the ride! A few years later . . .

Isabel: So I might have been a tad brash in marrying that jackass man.

Everyone else: WE TOLD YOU SO.

Isabel: *(sobs)*

That ~~Donny~~ Osmond boy was more interested in her money than her. Shocking, I know. He already had a daughter, so it's not much of a stretch for him to expect his young bride to behave just like her: passive, obedient, etc. He pretty much wants to break her spirit. If that doesn't make for a happy marriage, I don't know what does. But then Isabel discovers that cousin Ralph is dying, so she wants to go visit. Which is somehow improper . . . why?

You know what really isn't proper? Osmond having an illegitimate daughter with . . . anyone want to take a guess? . . . Madame Merle! Wait a minute, so her dear friend set her up with her lover so they could both tap her assets? Er, that came out wrong. But, yes, they're both after your booty. Dammit. I mean loot.

After that icebreaker, Isabel ignores Gil's wishes and goes to England anyway and admits that she messed up big time. Then she runs into Caspar—who, if you'll remember, dear, waited two years for you—who tells her she should ditch the sitch and marry him. But marriage entered into on false pretenses in an effort to break a woman's spirit and then control her money is a sacred institution. Besides, she has to help the bastard's daughter so her monster of a father doesn't crush the girl's soul. Eh, I guess. So she goes back to her hubby. Give him hell, dear.

Henry James loved Europe, which shouldn't surprise you since Isabel spent so much time there. But the American writer, who'd been living in England since 1876, became a British subject to protest America not entering World War I soon enough. That's one way to put your money where your mouth is.

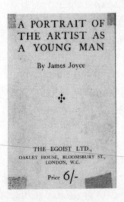

A Portrait of the Artist as a Young Man by James Joyce
Published: 1916
Category: novel (serialized)

"Once upon a time and a very good time it was there was a moocow coming down along the road and this moocow that was coming down along the road met a nicens little boy named baby tuckoo."

If widdle Stevie wants to hear a story before beddie-bye, wet's get him in his jimmyjams and get him a gwass of warm cough syrup to knock him out.

There's a good reason for not letting a three-year-old write a book: It comes out as gibberish. Jimmy Joyce should have recognized that when he started writing a book about *moocows*. For the record, gibberish at three does not equate to an artistic temperament. It means he's a toddler. But those aren't scribbles; they're avant-garde expressions of who the hell knows what. Right.

Joyce should have stopped before he started. Dude sired stream-of-consciousness writing, and we all know how fun that is to read. If you don't, take a peek at one of the more impossible texts to get through, like *The Sound and the Fury* (page 208), or Joyce's disasterpiece, *Ulysses* (page 243), and try to read a few actual pages from the book. Then, my friends, you shall appreciate the genius of *The Faker's Guide*: stream-of-crap translated for general consumption. You're welcome.

But now back to the moocows . . . oh, wait, never mind. We're already moving to Stephen Dedalus's school years at Clongowes Wood College, one of those super-fun boarding schools run by Jesuit priests. Yay for regular beatings and one-on-one time with the priests. Ahem. When a bully pushes him into a cesspool, he gets sick. No surprise there, really—anyone would after accidentally doing the backstroke in a slurry pond. In that moment, SD decides he's an outsider. Hate to break it to you, kid, but it's probably because you smell like crap. No, no, but it's *more* than that, he's . . . *different*. Well, that's nice. Go hose off again. You reek.

His next riveting memory is from Christmas when he was about six. For the first time ever, he gets to sit at the adult table for dinner! Too bad he didn't realize that the kiddie table is so much better; you can still play volcano with your mashed potatoes and not get yelled at. Instead, at the grownup table, you have to listen to crabby, opinionated adults badger each other about how the world is going to hell and why the other [religion / political party / football team] is responsible. Did I mention that the fam is Irish Catholic in Dublin right about the time of the Easter Rising? No? Well, there's that.

Back at school, Stevie breaks his glasses and gets in trouble because he can't do his homework. Then the big mean prefect of studies mocks him. Wait a sec. A student gets teased for not getting his schoolwork done? That *never* happens. So he tattles on the prefect to the school rector. Justice! Triumph brings a new respect from his classmates. Wow, David, you sure got your Goliath good. Or it got you out of trouble in one minor incident. Whatever floats your goat.

Then it's back home for summer vacation, where he learns that—*horror!*—his family is now poor and can't afford to send him to a fancy boarding school anymore. Now he must attend the regular day school run by Jesuits. It turns out all right, though, because a smaller pond makes him a bigger fish. He gets loads of attention for writing essays and—another gold star for you—lots of good reviews for acting in the school play. Even though he's doing well, Stevie just doesn't feel like he fits in and starts to question his faith. Hey, kid, you're probably in the majority there. You just haven't realized that most people don't admit to being holiday Catholics.

But his sensitive-artistic temperament really doesn't quite jibe with his classmates. That's a tough one, kid. You'll totally get bullied for that. Poets just don't get the street cred they used to. Been downhill ever since Byron. Sad, really.

Stevie's confused, so he wanders Dublin in some existential crisis. Gosh, it's like he's the first teenager ever to feel disillusioned by church, family, and society. So he ends up at a brothel—just the place to go when deluged by inner turmoil. Now he can add some healthy Catholic guilt about having humped a hooker into the mix. He likes it so much that, mixed with his sexually repressed upbringing, it explodes into a debauched bender of sin.

OK, so he might have taken it a bit too far. Moderation and all that. No? Oh boy, looks like we're swinging to the other extreme and going über-religious: attending a three-day spiritual retreat, confessing on a regular basis, praying all day long, and going to church all the time. Whoa, kid. Chill.

The priests notice how devoted he has become to religion, so they say, hey, you should become a priest. Hmm . . . probably not the best idea. This religion bender's gonna swing back the other direction any minute now. Even though he's fascinated by life in the priesthood, SD realizes that he likes the carnal stuff too much and decides against the priesthood. Whew. Bullet dodged, Steve-o.

When he hears that the fam is moving yet again because they have no money, he goes for a walk on the beach. A hot girl is wading in the ocean when he realizes that he likes beautiful things. No, not just girls. He likes the beauty of the world in art and literature. After this epiphany, he decides to head to college and tries to formulate his own blend of spirituality and sensuality without the extreme benders. Excellent move, I must say. Probably helps that the puberty hormones are calming down.

He's still odd at university, though—introspective and avoiding religious and political discussions—so he goes abroad to figure out what he believes and who he is as a person and an artist. Well, that's not so bad. Had us worried about you for a bit with all that disconcerting talk of moocows. Looks like you might turn out OK. Just don't mention the *tuckoo* again. Still weird.

For even more Dedalus-y fun, tune in next time to *Ulysses* (page 243).

James Joyce grew up in an Irish Catholic family in Dublin. They were poor, he went to Jesuit school, and this sounds oddly familiar. Maybe because the entire book is about Joyce until he left Ireland to travel abroad. So, what, change a couple of names and dates and—*bam!*—best-selling novel? *Note to self . . .*

PRIDE AND PREJUDICE

Pride and Prejudice
by Jane Austen

Published: 1813
Category: novel
Banned for: to control the female population in Iran. No romance! Ever!

"It is a truth universally acknowledged, that a single man in possession of a good fortune, must be in want of a wife."

Is this irony or reverse psychology? I can't tell. Wait, is there a difference? Anybody want to play whist?

Disclaimer: No matter how much anyone jokes about P&P, I have yet to meet a woman who doesn't swoon over (a) Mr. Darcy, (b) Colin Firth, or (c) Mr. Darcy played by Colin Firth. However, there is still some debate over (d) Matthew Macfayden as Mr. Darcy.

Now, heads up, ladies. We're going on a MAN HUNT . . . says Mama Bennett. So when Mr. Bingley moves to town with a cool £5,000 a year—a.k.a. *loaded*—the ladies are ready and waiting. It's love at first sight for Mr. Bingley and Jane Bennett, and by the end of the ball where they meet, Mama Bennett has the wedding planned. But Bingley isn't the only hot rich thing to attend the ball that night. He brings along his even richer friend Mr. Darcy, and boy do the ladies like the look of him—until he insults our sharp-tongued heroine, Lizzie, and then everyone hates the arrogant prick.

Darcy quickly realizes that he spoke too quickly when the hard-to-catch Lizzie snags his interest. But by then—magpie alert—Lizzie has set her sights on the dashing officer Mr. Wickam, who was Darcy's childhood friend. They both vie for Lizzie's attention, but Wickam's sweet words earworm their way into Lizzie's ~~heart~~ strong sense of justice. The rogue Darcy, says Wickam with his ol' big puppy dog eyes, left him destitute. Liz believes him instantly because such a handsome man would *never* lie to manipulate others' opinions of him. Pretty people never fib. Fact.

In the meantime, the Bennetts' smarmy preacher cousin, Mr. Collins, comes to pick a wife from among his cousins. Um, ew. Mama Bennett pushes him toward Lizzie, but she's all, "Sha! Yeah, right!" Papa Bennett finds the whole thing hilarious. Not willing to go home empty-handed, Mr. Collins marries Lizzie's best friend instead. So . . . everyone's happy? But then Bingley *et al.* unexpectedly scram for London, leaving behind a heartbroken Jane. Sad face.

Lizzie goes to visit her BFF Mrs. Collins. Everything's hunky dory . . . until Mr. Darcy appears and proposes. But again Liz is like, "Sha! Yeah, right!" She heads home, then takes off on another trip with her aunt and uncle to visit . . . Mr. Darcy's hometown? Gee, it's almost like some ~~author~~ supernatural force is propelling her toward him.

Darcy's not home, so they do some light trespassing, which they call sightseeing, at his estate when . . . he comes home early. No! How is this possible? It's just too perfect. He's not supposed to show up at his own house. It's clearly meant to be! Darcy smooves on the charm, and Lizzie rethinks her prejudice against Darcy's pride. Ohhhhh. *Got it.* Anyway, all is going splendidly . . . when they receive word that the wicked Wickam absconded with the youngest Bennett girl. The girls are all ruined because obviously you should be judged solely by the actions of your relatives. (*whistles* ~~nervously~~ *innocently*)

Unbeknownst to Lizzie, though, Darcy plays dashing knight by finding the illicit couple, forcing them to marry, and keeping it all hushed up. So . . . good? Kind of hard to tell. Then he convinces Bingley to marry Jane, proposes to Lizzie *one more time*, and she finally caves. In the end, the poor girls get the rich men because love conquers all ~~and rich guys have mush for brains~~. *Sigh.* This, gentlemen, is why you will never measure up to fictional characters. You probably shouldn't bother trying—except you totally should. Got it?

Jane Austen might now be considered the epitome of romance writing, but by her death at age forty-two she was pretty much just an old maid. The best romantic writer ever never had any of her own. Unless she did, but then her family burned pretty much all of her correspondence—which was pretty routine back then to protect people's privacy. Yeah, I don't know what that is either. Man, those guys were PR geniuses.

Remembrance of Things Past by Marcel Proust

Published: 1913–27
Category: novels—seven of them in nine endless volumes
Banned for: homosexual comings and goings. The Nazis probably saw a nine-volume story and thought they could really get their bonfires burning. Innuendo not intended. Maybe.

> *"She sent out for one of those short, plump little cakes called 'petites madeleines,' which look as though they had been moulded in the fluted scallop of a pilgrim's shell. And soon, mechanically, weary after a dull day with the prospect of a depressing morrow, I raised to my lips a spoonful of the tea in which I had soaked a morsel of the cake. No sooner had the warm liquid, and the crumbs with it, touched my palate than a shudder ran through my whole body, and I stopped, intent upon the extraordinary changes that were taking place."*

Um, wow. Anybody know where I can get one of those cookies? What exactly is in them? Wait. Alice, is that you? (page 10)

It's gonna get crazy up in here. Why? For starters, there are seven—that's right, SEVEN—books to whip through, two of them so long they were split into two volumes. Then there's the narrator, Marcel, a "fictional" character based on the author. Plus we've got some inter-crossing stories from a smorgasbord of characters, which makes this whole damn book SO. MUCH. FUN. Don't you worry, though. We're gonna whip through this one so fast you'll only have to suffer a few minutes. Also, we have Herr Doktor Freud on standby. Trust me, we're gonna need him.

Volume 1: *Swann's Way*
Marcel eats a cookie, which makes him happy. Yay cookies! Nomnom-nom. Marcel used to eat these cookies as a kid, so they make him flash back to his childhood. Usually those kinds of cookies are called pot brownies. Heh, I kid. They're actually little spongy cake cookies called petite madeleines, shaped like seashells. Mmm . . . cookies.

OK, vacay in Cambray! Marcel and the 'rents are visiting his gramps in the northern French town, which is so dang gorgeous that Marcel is gonna be a writer so he can describe it. During a walk with the fam, he runs into a friend of gramps, Charles Swann; his wife, Odette; and their daughter, Gilberte. Right there Cupid flings an arrow at Marcel's heart. He's in *lurve*. Gilberte is perfect with the bluest eyes (black actually).

Flash back fifteen years to a different boy's obsession: Charles Swann falls for the courtesan (meaning: high-class hooker) Odette, thereby ruining the suspense because we know they get married even though she's not his type (meaning: total hottie). They have an affair (probably because he doesn't realize that she usually gets paid for gettin' it on). She gets bored and finds more interesting company. He gets upset that she cheats on him. So they break up, and Swanny boy realizes he wasted the love of his lifetime on a hooker who wasn't even pretty. The horror!

Volume 2: Within a Budding Grove
Marcel, now a teen, is living in Paris, where he hangs with writers who know his parents. He shows one writer a story he penned, and he's basically told it's crap. He spends a lot of time with Gilberte, but they get in a fight and he decides to never see her again, so he starts hanging around her mom instead. I thought Odette was supposed to be a swan, not a cougar. Anyway, Marcel eventually stops fawning over mama swan as well, and then crushes on every girl he sees. So basically he's a normal hornball teenage boy. While on vacay with his grandma at the beach, he sees a group of girls and falls in love with them. Yep, all of 'em—but especially Albertine, who rejects him. Cue violin.

Volume 3: The Guermantes Way (published in two volumes)
Our boy has social aspirations now. His family lives in Paris next to the duke and duchess of Guermantes. Marcel wants access to their inner circle, so he befriends their cousin and eventually slithers his way in. There he meets Baron de Charlus, who takes him on as a protégé. (Innuendo somewhat intended.)

Volume 4: Cities of the Plain (En français: Sodome et Gomorrhe, published in two volumes)
Marcel figures out that Charlus is gay after watching him sneak off with various guys. So the narrator spends time with Albertine, and then he realizes she likes the guys *and* the ladies. Almost all at once

he becomes: (a) bored with Albertine, and (b) jealous of her and her lesbian friends. So he convinces her to run off to Paris with him. Of course he does.

Volume 5: The Captive
Albertine's lesbian tendencies fascinate yet repulse Marcel, so he's pretty much a guy and has no clue what he wants. Problem is, he becomes crazy controlling jealous with Albertine and treats her like a prisoner. They fight, and he decides to break things off when he learns that she already left him, which throws him into anguish. Cue cello.

Volume 6: The Fugitive
Dude is still upset that Albertine leaves. They argue via letter when he gets a telegram that Albertine is dead. Nooooo! It's always after the guy has been a total ass to the woman he loves that he realizes he actually loved her. Couldn't have come to that conclusion before she died, could he? Men.

Volume 7: The Past Recaptured
Years later, he runs into many of the characters from throughout the series. He'd taken a short break at a Paris sanitarium—guilty conscience, perhaps?—but finds out that most of them either died, got married, or became gay. But they all got old. Including himself.

Blah blah blah. I want a cookie, but can we make it a macaron instead? Proust totally would have written about macarons had they existed then. It's just like heaven in a cookie, bliss in the form of meringue and sugar. *Cue flashback . . .*

Even though he wrote openly about homosexuality, **Marcel Proust** never came out. As a writer, he wins the prize for longest. book. EVAR: about 3,200 pages, give or take a few thousand. And you thought *War and Peace* (page 256) was bad. Proust eventually had to stop writing because he died. We owe the Grim Reaper for that one. Thanks, bro.

Robinson Crusoe
by Daniel Defoe

Published: 1719
Category: novel (epistolary, confessional)
Banned for: being racist, sexist, and imperialist by London public schools in 1985. Poor Peter Rabbit and Benjamin Bunny got the boot at the same time for being (middle) classist. I wish I were kidding.

> *"'O drug!' said I aloud, 'what art thou good for? Thou art not worth to me, no, not the taking off of the ground; one of those knives is worth all this heap; I have no manner of use for thee; e'en remain where thou art and go to the bottom as a creature whose life is not worth saving.' However, upon second thoughts, I took it away. . . ."*

I don't know what you do with your gold and treasure, but I'm certainly not sniffing or smoking mine.

First of all, the full title of this one is actually *The Life and Strange Surprizing Adventures of Robinson Crusoe, of York, Mariner: Who lived Eight and Twenty Years, all alone in an un-inhabited Island on the Coast of America, near the Mouth of the Great River of Oroonoque; Having been cast on Shore by Shipwreck, wherein all the Men perished but himself. With An Account how he was at last as strangely deliver'd by Pirates*—but we couldn't get that to fit in the header, so we abreeved it. OK, now the story.

Papa tells young Robinson to study and get a job (sha na na na), but our adventurous rascal will have none of that. He's off to be a . . . merchant. His first trip is a success, so he figures, hey, I can totally do this. But on the next trip, Moorish pirates attack and drag him off to slavery in North Africa. Yeah, that wasn't supposed to happen.

He and another young slave escape and sail off along the African coast, where they meet a Portuguese ship. The captain buys the slave from Robinson—wait, they were *both* slaves; I smell a double standard—and drops Robby off in Brazil. Robby buys a plantation that turns out to be pretty successful. Still not good enough for our Rob, though, who decides to get his fingers in the African slave trade.

One word: karma, and it's going to bite you in the derriere real soon, which happens rather quickly when he shipwrecks near the coast of Trinidad. He's the only survivor and scavenges what he can from the wreckage. On shore, he builds a nice little shelter and finds a friendly little herd of goats to have ~~over~~ for lunch. *Maaaaahhh!*

A year passes, and one day he gets sick and hallucinates angels telling him to repent. I'll say. Do unto others sound familiar? Right after that, he gets soused on tobacco-infused rum—*blarf*—and has a rapturous experience in which he's forgiven of his sins. Sure he was. He decides to do some exploring and discovers he's actually on a deserted island. Wait, it took him a *year* to realize that? Really? #islandfail. Big time.

Out exploring, he finds a valley filled with grapes. Sweet! ~~Fresh fruit makes a man healthy and strong~~. Alcohol fixins! He builds a nice little shack with plenty of shade. He's feeling a bit better now, so he declares himself king of the island. He also finds a parrot that he trains to speak and stumbles on a random colony of penguins. Yes, in the tropics. They exist; look it up.

About fifteen years into his sojourn, Crucifix notices a footprint on the beach. Must be the Devil. Yeah, because that's the most logical explanation. Idjit. Turns out, the neighbors from the mainland came for a visit—to eat the survivors of a Spanish shipwreck. Ladies and gentlemen, we have cannibals!

Crusoe saves one of the cannibals' captives, who becomes his bestie forever. He names him after the day that he saved him, and he quickly becomes Crusoe's servant. He teaches Friday some basic English and converts him to Christianity. Later, Friday spots a ship nearby, and men come ashore with three captives tied up. Turns out there was a mutiny, which Crusoe resolves.

Then he heads back to England, where he finds out that all but two of his sisters are dead. But he sells his plantations in Brazil, and he's rich. Then he gets all itchy to sail again—there's an OTC cream for that, I'm sure—but he's afraid of being shipwrecked.

Never fear, late bloomers. **Daniel Defoe** didn't start writing fiction until he was sixty years old. Pretty impressive, considering he penned another great classic: *Moll Flanders* (page 152). Before becoming a world-famous author? Yeah, he was a traveling hosiery salesman. Back then, men's pants were considered hosiery, but still.

"ROMEO & JULIET."

Romeo and Juliet
by William Shakespeare

Published: 1595 or so
Category: play (tragedy)
Banned for: teaching kids to disobey their parents. Oh, and teaching them about sex and suicide and drugs. You know, all the good stuff. (Minus the suicide.)

*"What's in a name? That which we call a rose
by any other name would smell as sweet."*

Maybe. But would you really consider giving your crush a bouquet of slut blossoms?

Wait, you don't know the story of *Romeo and Juliet*? Uh, where have you been . . . ever? It's the greatest love story ever told. Well, it isn't so much a love story as it is a freaky tale of gang warfare, teen hankering, and tag-team suicide over a relationship less than a week old. And you thought your last relationship was a mess.

The Capulets (Juliet's peeps) and the Montagues (Romeo's clan) hate each other. Why? Not important. They just do—so they kill players from the opposing team whenever possible. They're also the top families in Verona and rule the roost . . . or at least opposite ends of it.

Recently dumped, Romeo's moping and being all emo, so his cousin Mercutio says, "Hey, let's go crash the Capulet party!" Because crashing your arch-nemesis's party can only end well. Don't these kids read *Batman*?

Anyway, it's a costume party, so they mix and mingle. But then Romeo spots Juliet, and it's all over. He's ass-over-tea-kettle in love. They make out, but when someone realizes The Enemy is frolicking among them, Romeo & co. bolt. Except Romeo doesn't really leave. He goes all stalkarazzi and watches Juliet babbling to herself through her open bedroom window. Crazy girls are hot? Needless to say, our peeping tom goes all hornball and climbs her trellis. Not a metaphor . . . except kinda. So some rando voyeur she *just* met climbs into her bedroom? How romantic.

Since their instantaneous and baseless love will obviously last *for all time*, they get engaged before Romeo takes off that night and then get married in secret the next day.

What Claire Danes didn't tell Leonardo DiCaprio, *ahem*, is that her parents are trying to foist her off on some rich guy named Paris. Oops. Then there's this duel that Romeo won't fight in, so his cousin does instead, and several people end up dead because Romeo and his crew crashed the Capulet party. That's some pretty serious bouncing. The one dude Romeo killed during the whole fight turns out to be Juliet's cousin. Uh oh. Worse? A whole bunch of witnesses saw him do it, so Romeo skips town, banished forever.

Meanwhile, Juliet gets a serious case of the frowny faces when she learns that her perfect new hubby murdered one of her relatives—he started it!—but she's even sadder when she realizes that she's being married to Paris polygamously, and Romeo's gone for good. (Cue break up music.)

Or is he? She devises a secret plan with the friar who married them. She'll fake her own death, then after the funeral Romeo will sneak in and steal her away. Excellent plan—unless the guy never gets the letter explaining the complicated plot and thinks she's really dead. Why didn't they just text? So much simpler.

So here's how it plays out: Juliet pretends to die, and Romeo jaunts back to Verona, poison in hand. When Romeo catches up with her, she looks and feels dead, so she must be ~~a witch~~ dead. He gurgles the poison, dies, and falls on top of her. (Sex = death.) She wakes up with a corpse on top of her and wigs out—but not because her boyfriend killed himself on top of her. No, she loses it because her tru luv 4ever doesn't exist anymore. So she stabs herself in the heart because she's a drama queen and Romeo used all the poison.

As anyone who has ever been a teenaged hormonal nutjob or dated one knows romance is some tricky shizz. Strangely, until **William Shakespeare** wrote *R+J*, romance wasn't considered tragic enough for dramatic works. Can you imagine? I mean, what were they doing?

A Room with a View by E. M. Forster

Published: 1908
Category: novel

"This desire to govern a woman—it lies very deep, and men and women must fight it together. . . . But I do love you surely in a better way than he does. Yes—really in a better way. I want you to have your own thoughts even when I hold you in my arms."

Only a gay dude would (have a straight guy) say this to a woman. Oh well. Swoon.

Lucy Honeychurch is vacationing in glorious Florence with her neurotic spinster cousin, Charlotte. If that doesn't sound like a recipe for fun, I don't know what does. When they arrive at the pension where they'll be staying, their rooms have a view of the courtyard instead of the river. I mean, really. Charlotte makes a big fuss, and when another guest overhears her hullabaloo, he offers to switch with the ladies.

How rude! Doesn't he know that being straightforward is a crime against British society? Despite the effrontery, Charlotte agrees.

Lucy goes sightseeing with another woman staying at the hotel, but they get lost and finally the woman gets distracted and abandons Lucy. Fortunately, Lulu runs into Mr. Emerson and his son, George—hottie alert! Even though he is a bit emo. They tour a church, zzzzzz, and then Charlotte finally finds Lucy unchaperoned in the company of two men. The skank.

The next day, rebellious Lucy, bored because nothing interesting ever happens to her, goes on a walk by herself. She decides to buy some postcards—because that's exciting—when she sees two Italian men fighting. One of them stabs the other in the back, and blood gushes everywhere. Innocent, sheltered Lucy faints—right into the arms of George, who totally wasn't stalking her or anything. Anyway, Lucy comes to in his arms, embarrassed, and he walks her back to the hotel.

On a trip to the countryside with several people from the hotel, she wanders around for a bit before running into George on a terrace covered in flowers because he's still totally not following her. He's surprised to see her but recovers quickly and kisses her . . . just as Charlotte walks in. Of course. She convinces Lucy to keep it a secret.

The next day, the ladies take off for Rome to meet up with some family friends. Lucy meets the fiendishly named Cecil Vyse, who decides to woo her as well. On paper, he's the better choice: He has wealth, charm, and connections. But he's also an arrogant schmuck, so . . . not so much. He proposes to Lucy twice, and, smart girl, she rejects him both times. Then he proposes again after they return to England, and she caves. I mean, who needs happiness? Love is overrated anyway.

Cecil enjoys mocking her backward family and friends, and when he finds out that there's a house in the area for rent, he tells some bumpkins he met at a museum in London that they should move in. Isn't that funny? Poor people are so entertaining! Then the Emersons move in. Of course.

When George finds out she's engaged to Cecil, he declares his love for her and tells her to dump the shnook. She does, but she still won't marry George. Instead, she'll never marry anyone and plans a trip to Greece with some old biddies she met in Italy. *(raises eyebrow)*

Everyone is sad until Papa Emerson straight up tells her that she loves George but just won't admit it. Which is true? Lucy elopes with George—the good guy wins, for once!—and the book ends at the pension in Florence where they first met. Sigh. So romantic.

E. M. Forster lived forever, watching the buttoned-up Victorian era give way to the loose days of the Jazz Age . . . and then some. He even lived long enough to see the start of the gay liberation movement, even though he never came out. Ironic, really, considering the focus in his work on personal freedom.

The Scarlet Letter
by Nathaniel Hawthorne

Published: 1850
Category: novel
Banned for: Hawthorne had a best seller on his hands with this one. Sweet! But that also means his very vocal critics were extra loud when it became über-popular. One guy, Reverend Arthur Coxe, took it so far as to nearly cause a riot in Salem, which forced Hawth and his fam to flee their home. Yikes. Sounds like a certain reverend doth protest too much.

"Come up hither, Hester, thou and little Pearl. . . . Ye have both been here before, but I was not with you. Come up hither once again, and we will stand all three together!"

Sing it, preacher man! It's about time you 'fessed up.

Hester Prynne is an *adulteress*. There, I said it. Oh, the depravity.

Town leaders skillfully deduce Hester's crime with a key piece of evidence: her baby bump. Since it's obviously the responsibility of the public to condemn people for private actions between consenting adults, they drag her to the town scaffold with a crimson "A" blazoned on her chest. No, children, "A" is *not* for Apple. A is for adultery, B is for bigamy, C is for cuckold, D is for damnation. . . .

Oh, that evil woman, getting preggers outside marriage. Why, it's shocking! I mean, no *man* would ever . . . do . . . such a . . . wait a second, guys, who got her pregnant? Had to have been someone in town since her husband is lost at sea. Technically that makes her more of a widow than an adulteress, but that's not the point. The point is that Hester is a *sinner!* So of course she and her innocent child must suffer for it.

They boot her out and make her wear that flaming letter on her breast forever and ever. Because getting more people to stare at her bazoombas will make things better. But that's not the point. The point is to mock and shame her, so really the big red letter just keeps townsfolk from getting soft and treating her like a normal human being instead of a *she-devil*. Coldhearted gossip just isn't enough to keep Hester humiliated. Damn that woman!

So Hester embroiders her new red logo onto her dresses all pretty-like with gold thread—the latest in illicit high fashion. Think of it as hooker chic.

The good townsfolk demand to know the name of her baby daddy, but her lips are sealed (this time). So she and Pearl bear the punishment alone. They move into a small cottage on the edge of the woods where Hester works as a seamstress. Since wicked women also tend to be crafty, she uses her punishment—and tatas—as a prime advertising space for her sewing skills.

Unlike the townsfolk, Hester is charitable and, you know, spends a lot of her time helping others. (What's that, hypocrisy? You'll have to speak a little louder.) As a single mom working full-time without child support, she does her best, but Pearl still grows into a wild child who refuses to obey everyone, including her mother. Rules, schmules.

The story takes a twist for the worse when an outwardly nice but inwardly evil doctor overdramatically named Chillingworth moves to town. Doc watches from the sidelines a bit before revealing his true identity to Hester: He's her (supposedly) dead husband. Except really he's alive and planning his revenge on her for stepping out on him and making him look bad in front of the guys. *Bwahahaha!*

He becomes instant BFFs with the local minister, Arthur Dimmesdale, whose health is going down the chute. Eventually, Chill moves in with preacher man Dimmy. How kind-hearted! Except not so much. Doc suspects the preacher is Pearl's papa. The pastor? Impossible. But evil doc is right, so he has a little fun with bestie before moving into full vengeance mode. The preferred method of punishment? Emotional agony via guilt, of course.

One night, Hester and Pearl go for a midnight walk and see preacher daddy standing on the scaffold. They join him, the three holding hands as a sinful little family. But preacher daddy still won't tell people that Pearl is his daughter. What will they think? The next day, a meteor streaks across the sky, leaving a nice long red tail in the form of the letter "A." How is that meteorologically possible, you ask? That's not the point. Now shut up and let me finish.

Hester and pastor secretly meet in the forest, where she tells him all about his doctor buddy. Sensing the impending hammer of doom, they decide to sneak off as a family aboard a ship leaving for Europe in four days. Aw, how sweet. He gets the family but still doesn't have to admit the guilt. Setting such a great example there, preacher man. Unfortunately, the doc decides to tag along and books his own passage on the ship. On day three, Dimmy delivers the most amazing sermon ever, captivating the crowd. *<tears>* Isn't he such a good man? Then he walks to the scaffold and confesses, Maury-style: "I'm the daddy!"

Dimmy tears open his shirt to reveal his own red "A," but this one is burned into his chest. Seriously, dude, no wonder you didn't feel so hot. Then he falls over dead. *(Stunned silence.)*

Furious that he didn't get to do the outing, Chill dies a sad little man a year later. Hester and Pearl vamoose for Europe, though Hester eventually comes back to her cottage and continues to be all nice and charitable—still wearing her special red logo. Self-flagellation, much? By then, Pearl has married an aristocrat and is raising her own kid, which goes to show that while people can't stand adultery, bastards are totally fine. Who wants to bet that Pearl told her new hubby something other than the whole truth?

Nathaniel Hawthorne descended from a dude central to another case of the masses casting unfair judgment upon women in colonial Massachusetts: John Hathorne, a friendly judge and executioner during the Salem Witch Trials. (You can see his handiwork in action in *The Crucible,* page 50.) The *very* humpy Nathaniel was somewhat ashamed of his ancestor, which couldn't possibly have influenced this blasting portrayal of hypocritical Puritan behavior.

Sense and Sensibility by Jane Austen

Published: 1811
Category: novel
Banned for: not being sufficiently Islamic. When the Iranian Revolution forced women back into their hijabs, they banned everything by Jane Austen, which is even sadder than Mr. Willoughby dumping Marianne for an heiress.

"I think very highly of him—that I greatly esteem him."

Wow. That's one sizzling romance. Can't you just see the heat, the passion, the matching table settings?

Daddy Dashwood dies. John, the son from his first marriage, inherits *everything*, even though he's already rich, but there's never too much money for his wife, Fanny—who is one—and who convinces him to boot his step-mom and half-sisters from the only home the girls have ever known. Buh-bye!

While the Dashwood women are house hunting, they get to live as guests in their own home. Yeah, I'm pretty sure their wound already has enough salt in it. Fanny starts inviting her family to visit, but it turns out that her brother, Edward Ferrars, is actually a nice guy. Who knew? He takes a liking to eldest daughter Elinor, who's a smitten kitten in return.

The ladies find a house that fits their budget, is in a nice part of the countryside, and is near relatives. Can someone put me in touch with the ladies' real estate agent? I need some new digs. But the budding romance between Ferrari and Elinor fizzles. Could it have something to do with his secret engagement to another girl, whom Elinor doesn't know anything about yet. Naw. Farewell, marriage prospects. Hello, spinsterhood.

The Dashwood women set up home in a pitiable little cottage bigger than your apartment. Yeah, poor them. They meet some of the neighbors, get annoyed by their cousins, and then get set up with old bachelors. When the youngest sister, who is not important enough to be named, teases Elinor about Eddie, it earns El a reprieve from the matchmakers. Hallelujah. So middle-daughter Marianne becomes the target for old busybodies trying to marry off their *mature* friend Colonel Brandon.

Life's not bad per se, but Ed never visits like he promised. <sob> Middle-daughter Marianne meets the love of her life while out walking, because that totally happens. She sprains her ankle in the process, but she's more than happy to play damsel in distress to handsome Mr.

Willoughby, heir to his aunt's extensive property and fortune. *Cha-ching!* They fall in love, but the dream crumbles into a bajillion pieces when he abandons Marianne, who does a remarkable impression of Niagara Falls. His aunt disinherited him, and boy wants cash in his pocket, so he's off to London and quickly engaged to a woman with a huge . . . dowry. Sensing a pattern here? Marianne finds out at the best possible moment: when she's in London and sees him dancing at a ball with the other woman. Marianne makes a scene, declares her love for him, and turns into that crazy drunk girl at the party. Someone take her home, please.

Elinor's off having a romantic drama of her own. Apparently, one of the "friends" staying with her in London is secretly engaged to Ed, which is why he didn't make a move on Elinor earlier. When Edward's mother finds out about the engagement—from the fiancée's own mouth, because that was bright—she disinherits him and forbids the marriage. Ed, too noble to dump the girl after years of stringing her along, keeps the engagement even though he's now in love with Elinor.

London *sucked*, so the girls head home. They make a stop at a friend's house first, where zombie Marianne wanders off during a rainstorm, catches a fever, and nearly dies of a broken heart. Yeah, that and not the fever. But, hey, look at that Colonel Brandon, who rescued you when you collapsed in the rain and got sick. Yes, he's ancient, but such a gentleman . . .

Elinor sends for mom, while the doctor bleeds Marianne to get rid of her fever. That's one way to keep kids from faking illness to stay home from school. She survives—barely. Back to Barton, and who should show up but Edward looking for ~~Bella~~ Elinor? Seems his secret fiancée ditched him for his elder brother, whom Mother Ferrari doesn't disinherit even though big bro is marrying the same girl who caused the mess in the first place. Well that's totally fair.

Brandon's not dashing, handsome, young, or . . . whatever, but who cares? It's always better to settle than become an old maid. Then we learn that Willoughby got Colonel Brandon's young ward preggers, which is why auntie kicked him out and he dashed off to London to find a wealthy bride. I'm not saying he's a gold digger, but . . .

Marianne marries ~~Snape~~ Colonel Brandon. Elinor marries Edward, who becomes a preacher, and everyone is happy. Except Willoughby and his ~~money~~ wife.

Jane Austen is one of the most celebrated female authors in the English language *now*. But back then people thought only men could write perfectly feminine romantic stories. Her novels appeared anonymously, and no one even knew her name until after she died at the young age of forty-two. Also, for someone so completely obsessed about getting hitched, she never did. Oh, the irony.

The Sound and the Fury
by William Faulkner

Published: 1929
Category: novel
Banned for: being a radically experimental artistic endeavor that contained even a hint of sexuality or vulgarity. The New York Society for the Suppression of Vice liked to shout slogans like: "Morals not Art and Literature!" and "Books are feeders for brothels!" so it shouldn't come as much of a surprise that they took special note of this one. Or, you know, anything ever printed on paper. I'd hate to know what they did for entertainment. "Is the paint done drying yet? Can we do another coat?"

"A man is the sum of his misfortunes. One day you'd think misfortune would get tired but then time is your misfortune."

Sounds like someone needs to re-up his scrip. CVS has a twenty-four-hour pharmacy, you know.

The Compsons used to be rather hoighty-toighty in their part of Mississippi: the county of—and this one's a doozy—Yoknapatawpha. (No one could possibly make up such a bizarre name, except Faulkner did. Take it as a warning for what's to come.) So there are three brothers: Benjy, Quentin, and Jason. They each get their own section in the book, which follows their thoughts around like puppy dogs. Aw, puppies are cute. Look, shiny! Oh, plus a random fourth part because you can't neglect the Omniscient Narrator. If you did, it would hurt its feelings. If you haven't guessed already, this one's another lovely stream-of-consciousness . . . wait, what was I saying? I saw a squirrel.

The Compson boys have a sister, Candace, but she's not a man, so she doesn't get her own section. Or anything, really, because she's a slut, and slutty girls don't get anything but scorn.

April 7, 1928: Benjy
Life started out a tad rough for Benjy. His parents figured out by the time he was five that his mental faculties were, um, not there. Sorry, kiddo, you're too retarded—and we mean that literally—to be named after your illustrious uncle Maury ~~Povich~~. So now you're Benjy. Feel free to screw up that name as much as you like. We're still deciding whether to take away your last name, too, and whether to leave you on the church steps because you're not normal. Better luck next time.

Hey, Compsons, ever wonder why your family's not so special anymore? Yeah, this. Since Benjy is autistic, his section jumps around in time, and his thoughts tend toward the primitive and literal. Benjy loves: fire, the golf course, and his sister. The last because Caddy was the only person in the family who was actually nice to him. Her name connects to the golf course next door, where he hears people yell out, "Caddie!" all the time. Which is . . . yeah. Anyway, in no sequential order—because it doesn't have one—Benjy's disjointed narrative:

This one time when he was three his sister climbed a tree to spy on their grandmother's funeral, which the adults neglected to tell the kids about. When he and his brothers looked up, she had mud all over her panties. Thus begins an entire novel about three brothers obsessing over their sister's sexuality. Healthy.

He thinks about when Caddy wears perfume—she normally smells like trees, apparently—then later gives up her V-card. That didn't go so well, as Caddy gets preggers and then married real quick—which ends in divorce once hubby realizes the kid isn't his. Oops. Minor detail. Benjy also remembers how his brother Quentin committed suicide—hey! We haven't made it to his section yet.

Another time, Benjy gets castrated. *What the—?* What is wrong with you people? Since that's obviously a painful memory, we jump to dead Quentin's section.

June 2, 1910: Quentin

Today is special. It's the day Quentin is going to off himself. Lovely.

Quentin is a student at Hahvud, but he's not doing so hot in the actual going to class, completing assignments, and studying department. Possibly because he's so obsessed with the ideal of southern gentility, which pretty much went to pot after the Civil War. Dude, it's been fifty years. Get over it. So he's stuck with antiquated ideas of sexuality—specifically that women can't have it—rather than evolving new ones. Darwin says: You lose.

He also has a hard time focusing because Caddy gets preggers as an unwed teen. To fix the problem, he tells his dad that he slept with his sister. Because incest is obviously better than sleeping around. That boy has one twisted mind. It's nice that he wants to help his sister out, but she'd do better without it, thankyouverymuch. Dad (fortunately) realizes it's a total lie, and Caddy ends up marrying real quick to cover that she was a bit free with her party favors, but when hubby finds out the kid isn't his, he boots them both out. Sound familiar?

This section is a total pleasure to read as Quentin's mental state deteriorates kinda quick before his permanent swim it gets to the point where there's no actual punctuation or grammar or sentences really have fun with that one

Let's cut to Jason now because Quentin just took a long walk off a short bridge. *Glug.*

Good Friday, April 6, 1928: Jason

Jason pretty much embodies the redneck white-trash stereotype. You can toss in thief, misogynist, and sadist, too. In Jason's section we learn that:

Caddy got divorced. (OMG, we *know*!) She named her daughter Quentin. Which . . . yikes. She also got banished from the family home, so she's living in a nearby county where she works to send money back home for her daughter's care. The extra special fun part about that one? Mama Compson won't take any of her money, so she burns the checks, but ~~upstanding citizen~~ money-grubbing Jason forges a copy of the check, which he gives to Mom for kindling, and then cashes the real one and keeps it all for himself. That? Oh, that's just my head banging against the wall.

By the present, though, Jason has become the main breadwinner because Papa Compson has died. So the money kind of goes toward Quentin's stuff but not completely. Then she figures out what he's doing and takes off with $7,000 of ~~his~~ her money. It's not stealing if it was supposed to be hers anyway, right? Except she takes all the rest of his money too and runs away with some carney dude.

Easter Sunday, April 8, 1928

Because the rest of the book is so rational, this section mainly follows the Compsons' black servant, Dilsey, who spends her time at church thinking about how far the family has fallen. Which is pretty darn far by this point.

In the end, Jason and Benjy go for a ride in their craptastic horse-drawn wagon (probably because Jason's too cheap to spring for a car). But instead of going the right way through for their drive, Dilsey's son directs the horses on another path, which sends Benjy into fits. Uh oh. Someone messed up Benjy's routine, so Jason has to calm him down. Once they start going the right way again, Benjy pretty much forgets it ever happened—and Jason's fine with it, too.

William Faulkner originally wanted the book to appear in fourteen different colors of ink to help translate Benjy's section as it jumps back and forth and all over the place in time. Super cost inefficient, so Faulkner just used italics . . . and critics wonder why most people can't get through the book? The Folio Society did finally print an edition with colored ink, which is supposedly easier to read and look at all the pretty colors.

The Strange Case of Dr. Jekyll and Mr. Hyde
by Robert Louis Stevenson

Published: 1886
Category: novella
Banned for: freaking out RLS's wife. She made him burn the first draft.

"There is something wrong with his appearance; something displeasing, something downright detestable."

Yeah, but who doesn't love a good bad boy. Didn't you know that stalking a girl and watching her while she sleeps is sexy?
Oh baby.

Dr. Henry Jekyll's a nice enough man—when he isn't a maniacal sadistic *lunatic*. But everyone has faults, you know? We should probably cut him some slack, considering he does try to keep the crazy in the bottle. Then again, he should probably try harder . . .

When the lawyer Mr. Utterson hears gossip about a woman trampled by some butt-ugly dude on a London street, he's a tad curious. Especially when it's said that the dude went into an abandoned building then emerged with a check signed by a respectable gentleman to pay off the girl's family. Doesn't take him long to guess that beastman is Mr. Hyde and the ~~beauty~~ gentleman is Dr. Jekyll. He also recently heard that Jekyll had created a new will giving everything to—wait for it—Mr. Hyde. Utterson suspects blackmail, so he visits a mutual friend, Dr. Lanyon. But the two docs are sort of on the outsies because of Jekyll's "unscientific balderdash." Um, OK. Utterson plays detective and follows Hyde to the same building where Jekyll has his laboratory. When he finally meets Hyde face-to-hideously-deformed-face, he gets the guy's address. You know, in case they want to chillax later. Jekyll tells Utterson to ignore Hyde. "He's just some *(mumblemumble)*, but I got it covered." Uh huh, sure you do.

A year later, Hyde beats some guy to death. Unfortunately, it would appear that he went Hulktastic on a member of Parliament. Let's applaud his effort to rid the earth of politicians, but people tend to pay attention when powerful guys get beat down. Utterson takes the police to Hyde's place, but Hyde oh-so-surprisingly has gone on the run. So Utterson talks to Jekyll who oh-so-conveniently has a note written by Hyde apologizing for being a psychopath and promising to disappear forever. Huh. Look at that. Hyde has similar handwriting to Jekyll's. It's like, I don't know, Jekyll wrote the letter and pretended it was Hyde. Still, it's a wonder they can read the handwriting at all. Jekyll is a doctor, after all.

For a couple months Jekyll is friendly with everyone, and life is hunky-dory. But then he goes antisocial again, and Doc Lanyon dies soon after. Before he croaks, Lanyon gives Utterson a letter but makes him promise not to open it until Jekyll is dead. Because that's not ominous at all. Utterson doesn't open the letter. Which is nice, I guess, but who respects a dead guy's wishes when there are juicy secrets to be learned?

Then one day, Jekyll's butler comes running to Utterson. They dash off to Jekyll's lab, where he's locked himself in the past two weeks, and beat down the door. They find Hyde's corpse wearing Jekyll's duds. Totes bizarre. Plus, there's a suicide note. So Utterson heads home, utterly confused, to do some light reading.

First up is Lanyon's letter: Basically, Lanyon wigged when he saw Jekyll transform into Hyde. As in, he freaked so hard he died. (Note to self: Disinvite from Halloween party.) Jekyll's letter describes how he figured out how to separate the good and bad halves of himself using a funky potion. (Good thing Alice Liddell didn't get a hold of it—page 10 —can you imagine?) Thus Hyde was born: a monster of a man lacking conscience who reveled in the dark, carnal side of life so Jekyll could live guilt-free the rest of the time. Jekyll transformed into beasty Hyde, partied for a bit, then went back to being a prim and proper Victorian gentleman come morning. (A titillating line from the burned first draft of the story: "From an early age, however, I became in secret the slave of certain appetites.") Fun!

But Hyde started coming out to play when not invited, usually while Jekyll slept. So Jekyll stopped with the potion mumbo jumbo because Hyde was giving even *him* the heebie-jeebies, but after a while the cravings got so bad that he caved and let Hyde out again. Who promptly murdered someone. Oops.

Hyde, um, hid, but then went to Lanyon for help. Lanyon got some change-back potion for him, then lost his shiz when Hyde did his mighty morphing . . . and died not long after. The sitch went from *reallybad* to *couldn'tbeworse* rather quickly, with Hyde showing up uninvited pretty much all the time. So Jekyll chugged all the changey juice, wrote his byebye note, and completely disappears into Hyde, who then commits suicide. *Wah wah.*

Robert Louis Stevenson was ill much of his life, but that didn't stop him from doing what he wanted, like traveling from Europe to California to be with the woman he lurved even though it almost killed him. Like, several times. Not really one to keep a hold on strong urges, that one.

The Stranger by Albert Camus

Published: 1942
Category: novella

*"She asked me if I loved her.
I told her it didn't mean anything
but I didn't think so."*

Famous last words.

Everything about Meursault is meh. His mom dies, but he doesn't cry. He gets engaged, but he doesn't care about the woman he'll marry. He murders a man, but he can't be bothered to feel guilty for it. Dude has issues. Let's start viss his muzzah . . .

He gets a telegram about her death, so he asks his boss for time off to attend the funeral. Bossman makes him feel guilty for asking but lets him go. (Just to be clear: he feels bad about missing work but not that his mother died. Now we know when Vulcans came to Earth.) Bored stiff at the funeral, he won't talk to anyone. He takes off immediately after because he wants to get a full night's sleep in his own bed. It's the simple pleasures, ya know?

Next day he heads for some fun and sun on the beach, not a care in the world. He runs into a former co-worker, Marie, and they see a movie. Then they go back to his place for some horizontal hokey pokey. When Meursault wakes up the next morning, Marie's gone. Whatevs. So he goes back to sleep until noon. He sits on his balcony and people-watches the rest of the day, and angsty teens everywhere learn why no one has ever made a movie of this action-packed story. Except some Italian, and a Turkish guy, but no one cares about them.

When he wakes up again, he's got a case of the Mondays, so he goes to work. People ask about his mom, and he's like, "Whatever. I've got work to do." On his way home that night, he chats with a neighbor, and they have dinner. Everyone says Raymond is a pimp, but he claims to be a warehouse guard. Whatever, Pimp. Rayray asks if Meursault wants to be friends, and he's all, "Meh. Sure." Rayray says that he had a "mistress" who cheated on him, so he beat her up. Then he fought with her brother. He's still mad that she cheated, so he wants Meh to write her a letter to lure her back so he can beat her up again. Meh agrees—natch.

The next Saturday, he and Marie go to the beach, but they get horny, so they rush home to do the nasty. They hear arguing next door and find Ray beating his mistress again. The police come and literally bitch-slap Rayray, who has Meh tell the police that the mistress was cheating on him, which somehow makes it *totally OK* for him to beat her to a bloody pulp.

Next week while they're chilling at a friend's beach house, Marie asks Meh if he wants to get married. He says—you're never gonna guess—"Whatever," so they're getting married. Yay?

Another week on, they run into the mistress's brother, who stabs Rayray. Ray gets stitched back up—and then gets his gun. Meursault follows along but convinces Ray to cool it and give him the gun. They go back to the house, then Meh goes back to the beach and shoots the dude himself. *Whahuh?* He even pauses for a moment to consider what he's done, then unloads the rest of the clip into the guy. For funsies.

When his lawyer comes, he asks why Meh didn't shed a single tear at his mom's funeral. Apparently he's being tried for being an ass. Makes total sense. When Meh goes before the magistrate, he says that he *might* have loved his mom, but he doesn't believe in God. So the official dubs him Monsieur Antichrist and tosses him in the clink for a year as the investigation continues. Jail sucks because he can't go swimming, smoke, or have sex. He gets over it, though, and life returns to meh. People say lots of good and bad about him, but ultimately he's an indifferent weirdo whom people hate, so he's sent on his way by our friend Madame Guillotine. Before his execution, though, Meursault decides that he just wants an angry crowd to scream at him because that would be . . . interesting.

Scaramouche, scaramouche. Can you do the fandango?

Growing up impoverished in French-controlled Algeria and surviving in German-occupied France can make a man think that life is basically one big rando nightmare and doubt that the universe has reason. Who knew? **Albert Camus** derived his absurdist philosophy from watching masochistic a-holes massacre innocents while running the world. Also, wear your seatbelt.

A Tale of Two Cities by Charles Dickens

Published: 1859
Category: novel (historical)

"It was the best of times, it was the worst of times, it was the age of wisdom, it was the age of foolishness, it was the epoch of belief, it was the epoch of incredulity, it was the season of Light, it was the season of Darkness, it was the spring of hope, it was the winter of despair . . ."

It. was. the. longest. sentence. ever.

Ah, the French and their lovely revolutions. We've got belle Paris on one side and stately London on the other. When a cask of wine breaks in the streets of Paris, you don't slurp it from the ground—unless you're dirt poor and a fan of earthy wine. But they certainly had reasons to get drunk and forget their problems, including evil aristocrats who throw people in prison for eighteen years without trial.

Doctor Manette, just back from an extended vacation at the Bastille Resort and Spa, is hiding at the Defarges' wine shop, just upstairs from all the dirty drunks, where he is (re)introduced to the beautiful orphaned Lucy—who's not an orphan anymore 'cause Daddy's alive! But speak quietly and call him ~~24601~~ 105 North Tower. He's got a little PTSD, but don't worry. Just keep the shoe-making bench handy and ignore that he has no idea who you are. You two are going to have a great time once you get to London.

Five years later, the froggie Charles Darnay is on trial in London for treason (instead of espionage), accused of passing British secrets to France (like, say, a spy would). But his lawyer has a secret weapon: a doppelganger. No, really. His name is Sydney Carton, and he's a douche canoe compared to Darnay, but whatcha gonna do? The two men are so identical that even witnesses can't tell them apart, so neither of them could have done it. Logic fail, but the lawyer gets points for getting Darnay acquitted, right?

Elsewhere in London, Doctor Manette is back to working as a doctor, though he's still holding onto that shoe bench. Good plan. If not being crazy doesn't work out, French shoes are always in demand.

Speaking of France, the evil Marquis Evrémonde is speeding through a Paris street in his carriage when—*thump thump!*—he runs over a little boy. The angry mob gets even mobbier when the Marquis tosses a coin to the dead boy's father so he can go buy a new one. Back at the castle, his stupidly idealistic nephew is waiting for him, blathering about how he doesn't want to be marquis when the old guy croaks. Who does this Charles Darnay think he is? You know, other than the heir to the Evrémonde title, lands, and fortune. Marquis Mark is tired, so he says they'll speak in the morning . . . and wakes up dead. Turns out the Marquis shouldn't have ticked off those peasants. During the night, the speed bump's father put a note over Evrémonde's heart and then stuck it in place with a dagger.

"What did the note say?" you ask. "Drive him fast to his tomb. XOXO." (Note to self: Always disinherit relatives *before* going to bed.)

A year later, Darnay asks the doc if he can marry Lucy. Manette's like, "Sure, just don't tell me about your secret past because it'll probably traumatize me." But Darnay's not the only one with the hots for Lucy. Milk Carton's all: "I love you, Lucy, but I don't deserve you because I'm a bad man. But you make me want to be a better man, so there's that. I'll do anything for you. Just don't tell anyone, and I'll stop being creepy." On the day of his wedding to Lucy, Darnay finally tells his doc-in-law who he really is. Not a good idea. Doc whips out the cray-cray—again with the shoes—but wakes up all better a few days later. "Crazy? Who went crazy?"

Fast forward a few years. The Darnays have a daughter and are good pals with Doppelganger Milk Carton. Wealthy Frenchmen are moving their money and themselves over to England because it's not safe in France anymore. How so? *Revolution!* Storm the Bastille! Kill people! Oh look, it's our friends the Defarges. While releasing prisoners and murdering guards, they mosey up to 105 North Tower and discover a secret.

When Darnay hears that someone back in France is in trouble because of the Evrémondes, he goes to help. Smart move, Charlie. He's captured (duh) but acquitted after telling a sob story about leaving France because he had nothing left after renouncing his title.

Aaaaand then he's arrested again on new charges. The accuser? Doctor Manette! Actually, it was a letter that Manette wrote—describing why he took an all-expenses paid trip to the Bastille Resort and Spa—that Defarge found in the tower. Some nobleman saw a pretty girl he wanted to poke. Her hubby wasn't so much into the sharing, so the nobleman had him killed and then violently raped the girl. Ah, Paris, the city of lovers. Her younger brother tried to get revenge but got stabbed instead. Doc Manette attended the siblings. Neither survived, but he heard the whole story, which earned him that petite vacation in the Bastille.

"Who was this evil nobleman?" I hear you say (and seriously cool it with all the questions). Why, it was none other than Marquis Evrémonde! But wasn't he murdered in revenge for the death of a speed bump? Well, yes, *technically*—but Darnay is related to him, so obviously he's guilty, too. Off with his head!

So Milk Carton decides to do a little spying on the Defarges at their wine shop. Madame Defarge is actually the sister of the woman who was raped and wants everyone associated with the Marquis to die. Selfless doppelganger to the rescue, Milk Carton concocts a cunning plan to save Darnay: Bribe guards, drug Darnay, switch clothes, and have Darnay carried out to the Manettes so they can all vamoose from Paris . . . except for Carton (SadTrombone.com).

Madame Defarge goes to arrest the Manettes, but they've already, uh, moosed. Peeved that they've escaped, she tries to go after them but scuffles with the maid and accidentally shoots herself in the process. *Le oops.*

As Darnay and fam drive off into the sunset, Carton stands in line with a couple dozen other prisoners, eagerly awaiting their turn on the guillotine. You must be this tall—uh, *this* tall to ride this ride. Step right up! *Chop.* Next! *Chop.*

Charles Dickens stumbled on the idea for this book while acting in a play by his friend Wilkie Collins (page 262). *The Frozen Deep* features a love triangle in which two dudes fight for the same lady, but one guy ends up sacrificing his life for the other. Awww. But in case you thought Dickens was a romantic at heart, he picked up his mistress, Ellen Tiernan, a fellow actor in the play, during the show and then basically turned his back on his wife and ten kids.

Tess of the d'Urbervilles
by Thomas Hardy

Published: 1891
Category: novel (serialized)
Banned for: Tess got censored before the book even published, but that still wasn't enough for some ~~prudes~~ people. Hardy cut out quite a few scenes deemed too racy for publication before it was serialized in

The Graphic newspaper. You'd think with a name like that, he'd have gotten away with a lot more. So does anyone have a copy of the "original" version of *Tess*? Purely for research, I swear.

> *"You, and those like you, take your fill of pleasure on earth by making the*
> *life of such as me bitter and black with sorrow; and then it is a fine thing,*
> *when you have had enough of that, to think of securing your pleasure in*
> *heaven by becoming converted!"*

Yes. Tragically, last-minute repentance totally works, as Faust
figured out (page 68).

Tess's family aren't what you'd call contributing members of society. Think more Thenardier than Valjean (page 145), if you get my drift. Get one of those leeches stuck on you, and you'll never get them off. So when Mr. Durbeyfield finds out that he's descended from the so amazingly awesome d'Urberville family, he's more than happy to profit from the news. He sends Tess off to ~~beg~~ get money from the d'Urbervilles living nearby. Family ties and all that.

But wouldn't you know it? They're not actually d'Urbervilles. They just changed their name to make themselves look cooler. (Because that always works. Just ask Sean Puff the Diddy Daddy Dragon Combs.) Son, Alec, is a slimeball, but he takes a shine to pretty Tess. He gets her a job out of the goodness of his heart. Yep, that's gotta be it. One night after a big party, he "escorts" her home, in the sense that he drags her out to the woods where no one can hear her scream. Isn't he such a dreamboat?

That Tess sure is a hussy. Such a shame that she can't keep her legs together when a guy is forcing himself on her. She's not what you'd call a strong woman, so she continues as Alec's booty call for a bit—until she finds out that she's got one in the oven. Then it's back home with the fam, where she gives birth to a son she names Sorrow. Yeah, seriously. Except he won't have to worry about playground taunts for long. Sorrow gets sick, but Tess's daddy's been at the bottle and wouldn't let the pastor in to cause the family more shame, so she baptizes the baby herself before he dies. The Church doesn't buy it, though, so Sorrow is condemned to the corner of the churchyard where witches, suicides, and other unbaptized babies are buried. Harsh.

Surprisingly, there aren't any jobs available for unchaste women in her town, so she takes off to find work, ending up at Talbothays Dairy, where she meets a man with the awful name of Angel Clare. (Someone's trying too Hardy.) They fall in love, and he proposes. She accepts but feels guilty, so she writes him a letter detailing her past—instead of just telling him—but it gets stuck under the carpet when she slides it beneath his door. Yeah, the *carpet* is a plot device in this one. We're really scraping the bottom of the . . . never mind.

They get married, which means it's time to air the dirty laundry. He had an affair with an older woman in London. She was raped and gave birth to a child that died. She forgives him, but angelic Angel tosses her out. He figures that, since Tess slept with Alec and had his kid, he's basically her husband, because that's totally how it works. He can screw around, but rape equals marriage. Besides, it wasn't *rape* rape. Totally not the same if she already knows the guy.

Angel takes off for Brazil, thinking that distance will help him work through his issues and maybe someday he'll forgive her. Such a gentleman. With nowhere else to go, Tess ends up back home, but then Daddy Durbeyfield dies, and they get booted from their home. So she has to find work to support the family—again. Then she runs into rapey Alec, who's now a traveling *preacher,* of all things. He also blames Tess for tempting him, because now we're in medieval Saudi Arabia.

He abandons his ministry to take up with Tess (shocker). She needs the money to help her family, so she agrees. Plus, Alec convinces her that Angel will never come back for her. When Angel shows up begging for her forgiveness—of *course*—she's devastated and tells him he's too late. So devastated, in fact, that she stabs Alec. The landlady figures out what happened when the ceiling starts bleeding. Gross.

Tess and Angel flee but get cornered at Stonehenge, which isn't an overly dramatic setting for something big about to happen at all. She begs Angel to take care of her sister by marrying her. (Two sisters for the price of one!) In the morning, after sleeping on the sacrificial altar—METAPHOR ALERT—she gets dragged off to stand trial for murder. She swings, neck first, as Angel and her sister walk away, hand in hand. In the sequel, Tess and Hester Prynne (page 202) start a support group, and Madame Bovary (page 137) thinks about joining.

Insincere repentance: 2. Being good: 0.

Thomas Hardy couldn't win. I mean, he also couldn't write a happy story to save his friggin' life, but this time the public outcry centered on the portrayal of a "fallen woman" in a sympathetic light. Slut-shaming a rape victim? Pretty low, even for the Victorians.

The Three Musketeers by **Alexandre Dumas**

Published: 1844
Category: novel (serialized, historical)
Banned for: pissing off the Roman Catholic Church. His books weren't all saucy and smexy; no, Dumas's literary crime was turning clergy into bad guys, kind of like Cardinal Richelieu. Makes you long for the days when the worst thing that wicked priests did was try to take over the world but left the choirboys alone.

"All for one, one for all."

Kinky.

OK, kids. We've got a fun day ahead in the happiest place on Earth. No, not Disneyland Paris, though "musketeers" is easy to mix up with "mouseketeers"—except for the stabby part, and that's just the theme park. No, we're talking the City of Lights circa 1625, during the reign of Louis XIII (that's three Louises before Madame Guillotine crashed the party, in case you're counting).

Young, dirt-poor d'Artagnan needs to cool his hot little head before he can play with the big boys. He has a letter that his dad wrote to his old friend in charge of the musketeers saying he should be a musketeer, too. When an older guy laughs at d'Artagnan's poor horse, kid gets all up in arms and challenges the guy, then gets his rump handed to him on a plate and his letter stolen. Lesson learned? Not so much.

He reaches Paris, but without the letter d'Art can't get into the musketeers. But then he sees the guy who stole his letter walking down the street. So he races to catch up with the guy and in the process pisses off three other musketeers. Smoove, kid.

They meet up later to duel, and d'Art realizes that his opponents are bestest buds: Athos, Porthos, and Aramis, a.k.a. the Three Muske-teers. Like you didn't see that coming. But Cardinal Richelieu's guard breaks up the illegal duel. Fine, whatever. But when Rich-man's men try to arrest all four of them, it's time to wipe the ground with the guards' smug faces. The musket boys are totally outnumbered, but that's fine because it'll make them look better after they win. It doesn't help the kid's ego when the king hears of the fight and how well d'Art did and gives him a position with the special guards. He and the boys are cool, though, so d'Artagnan becomes their ~~third~~ fourth wheel.

D'Art's landlord is an ancient man with a hot young wife. Guy's not rich, so use your imagination. Wifey has other problems to worry about, though, because she's just been kidnapped. She works as the queen's maid, which means she's the perfect person to ~~torture~~ ask about the queen's secretest secrets. The cardinal wants to take the queen down, because she rejected him . . . and *someone* took it personally.

Musketeers plus one to the rescue! They find the wife, Constance, and bring her back safe. D'Art falls in <3 with her. So when he sees her walking on a bridge with a strange dude, he ~~stalks them~~ stops for a chat. Dude is actually a duke—a British one, from Buckingham—which means THE ENEMY. But the queen is working on improving foreign relations . . . Bucky is also her super-secret lover. Earlier that night, the queen gave her noble boy toy an awesome gift: twelve diamond tags (jewelry something or other) in a rosewood box. It's a re-gift, though, since she just got them from the king. Why is it that the rich ones are so cheap?

When Richi finds out that she gave them away, he tells the king to have a huge fancy ball—and command the queen to wear the diamonds. Because that specific a request isn't odd at all. So now we're in freak-out mode since there aren't any modes of transportation faster than horse or boat. Tick tock on the steam engine, guys. Just saying.

So d'Art and friends dash off to England to save the queen from her own stupidity. Spies and assassins waylay all but the kid, but we're going to skip to the part where Cardy's super-sexy secret spy Milady (not her real name, which is actually Clarick, but if you had a name like that you'd grasp onto something better, too) is snipping a couple of the diamond tags off the ornamental thingie that the Duke is wearing. She makes sure to send those to the cardinal so that he can use them in a blackmail scheme. *Bwahaha.*

When d'Art finally arrives in London, he goes immediately to see Bucky, who realizes that, wait, there are only ten tags. That means— eep! Call the jeweler! Bucky's personal jeweler churns out two exact replicas and fixes the tags up all nice and pretty like they'd never been touched. Talk about tight deadlines.

D'Art races back to France on some awesome horses that the duke has ready along the way so the jewels will arrive in twelve hours, even though the Chunnel is much faster. He gets back in time, much to Richi's surprise, and the queen is wearing the complete set of tags. Drat. Foiled!

The queen gives d'Art a huge diamond ring for his good work. Um, you might want to check and make sure that no one recently gave her that because we really don't have time to go through all this again. Constance is oh so grateful for d'Art helping the queen that she sets up a time to, uh, thank him personally—but then she's kidnapped. Again.

When d'Art sees Milady, he wants some of that. He's a smart kid, so he pretends to be the guy she's in love with and gets his boogie on. They bicker back and forth over the next few weeks, attempting murder and rolling in the hay. You know, your average hookup. But when her nightgown tears, boy wonder sees that she has the brand of a criminal on her arm . . . which surely he should have seen by now. Clearly they're doing it wrong. Also, that mark will get her executed.

More adventures, secrets, and murder attempts, blah blah blah, and then Milady is captured and put in an English prison . . . where she escapes by using her feminine wiles against the ~~helpless~~ idiot guard. Work it, honey.

Back in France and pissed at d'Art, she locates the convent where Constance has been staying, which was supposed to protect her from people like Milady. Oops. They become BFFs, but when d'Artagnan and friends are just about to save Constance, Milady poisons her, and she dies while Milady escapes. Not cool. So they track down Milady—again—and this time make sure she's executed. Flashback: Turns out that she was actually married to Athos, but when he discovered her cramp stamp, he thought she only married him for his money, so he literally hanged her from a tree. Wha? She (obviously) survived.

In the end, d'Artagnan gets a prestigious new gig in the musketeers from none other than zee cardinal heemself. Can't say the Rich-man isn't a good sport. D'Artagnan actually earns a higher rank than his more experienced buddies, which I'm sure they all loved.

Alexandre Dumas, père, was quite the baby daddy. He wasn't what you'd call faithful to his wife with his forty-plus affairs. It's surprising he had any bedpost left to notch after all that. It's a wonder he even had time to write.

The Time Machine
by H. G. Wells

Published: 1895
Category: novella (science fiction)
Banned for: royally pissing off the Nazis. They didn't just burn it. Oh no, Mr. H.G. peeved the goose-steppers so much that they added him to the list of intellectuals to be hunted down and executed once Germany conquered England.

"If Time is really only a fourth dimension of Space, why is it, and why has it always been, regarded as something different? And why cannot we move in Time as we move about in the other dimensions of Space?"

Nice try, Captain Kirk, but I'd like to introduce you to a friend of mine named Einstein.

Narrator is a guest at a dinner party hosted by brilliant inventor Time Traveler. (Names have been changed to protect identities. Also, Author probably didn't feel like bothering.) At dinner, discussion turns to time travel. Traveler postulates that time is the fourth dimension. With the right geometric calculations of wibbly wobbly timey wimey crap, he can move through time as easily as through physical space.

None of the guests believes it possible, but they're nice enough to wait until the party's over before mocking him. Yeah, yeah. That T.T. is such a funny guy, as in "funny farm" funny, but he serves great wine, so eh. The following week, however, Traveler fumbles down the stairs, fashionably late for his own party, except his clothes and appearance are in shambles.

Seems our fearless Traveler took a little jaunt into the future. Not too far . . . just *AD 802701.* There he met a childlike race called the Eloi, which isn't Aramaic for "My God" in case you wanted to know. They're cute, sweet, and lazy, without any attention span or curiosity. Just like puppies. Aw, I want a pet Eloi! I'll hug him and pet him and name him George.

Ahem. So the Eloi's high-tech buildings are starting to crumble. What? *High tech* to T.T., silly, which means they're, like, totally old school for the too-cool Eloi. But they don't have to work for food or pretty much anything, so it's . . . paradise?

After a quick peek around, he heads back to the time machine—but it's gone! Dude, where's my time machine? It's got to be around here somewhere. It was by the tall tree next to the . . . Traveler follows drag-marks in the dirt to a locked building that looks like a sphinx. Nice garage, guys, but I sorta need to get inside. Guys?

All of a sudden, a bunch of hairy ape-things called Morlocks attack him. These are the yang to the Eloi's ying: big scaries that live underground and do all the work for the spoiled Eloi. Have you spotted the political message yet?—because I don't think Wells could find a bigger hammer to hit you over the head. Oh, that's OK then. We don't usually pay attention to what the help look like anyway, so ugly monsters are totes workable. Just . . . disappear . . . when guests are around, 'kay?

Traveler hightails it to safety, then rescues an Eloi from drowning, even though her peeps were chilling not far away. What? Someone's drowning? Call the cabana boy. He'll deal with that. Weena (feminine version of . . . uh, never mind) becomes Traveler's friend in a "my dog is my friend" sense. She follows him around and leads him to some ancient ruins, which turn out to be a museum—of stuff from his day! Shocker. He grabs some matches and makes a weapon from what he finds there. (I sure hope he found some duct tape.) Now they're ready to rumble!

They head back as night falls, which is always the best time to wander through enemy territory. Then—surprise!—Morlocks catch them. Seems the hairy beasts have developed a taste for plump little Eloi. (They're especially great sautéed in a nice wine sauce with root vegetables and mushrooms. Delish!) Traveler starts a fire to scare the beasts away, but it turns into a forest fire that kills the Morlocks *and* Weena. Oops, MY BAD. In a last-ditch effort to ensnare our wary Traveler, they use his time contraption as bait. So, um, they just gave him access to his getaway car.

Traveler is off, zoom zooming thirty million years in the future, where he meets a big crab-thing, one of the last living creatures on Earth. Which is . . . unfortunate. He escapes and keeps hopping forward until he gets to the dying planet. The sun is now a gargantuan red orb, the only sign of life a humongo black blob. Lovely. What's old is new again, I guess?

Ready to head home, Traveler pops back to three hours after he left. It's always nice to cut down on long commute times. And then he stumbles down the stairs and chows down on a hunk of meat as he tells the dinner guests of his adventures. Whoa, déjà vu. The guests enjoy his tall tales. Sadly, his only proof is two strange flowers from the Eloi's world. So the next day, he's off on another jaunt to get some hard evidence. He gets back in the Delorean, goes back to the future. Remember: pics or it didn't happen. And no one ever hears from him again. Maybe he just found a nice little Eloi to settle down with and raised a family of baby crab things. And they lived happily ever after?

As a science teacher and Darwinist, it wasn't too much of a stretch for **H. G. Wells** to ponder impossibly far-out-there ideas like time travel and alien invasions. I bet he built a time machine of his own, because he successfully predicted the start of World War II, give or take a few months. Did he tell fortunes as well? 'Cause mama needs a best seller.

To Kill a Mockingbird by Harper Lee

Published: 1960
Category: novel
Banned for: racism. White, black, take your pick. Everyone is more than happy to get offended.

"You never really understand a person until you consider things from his point of view . . . until you climb into his skin and walk around in it."

It's like she's wearing someone as a suit. A Boo Radley suit—wait, wrong movie . . .

Scout Finch is a precocious child. Along with her older brother, Jem, and their friend ~~Truman Capote~~ Dill they make up scary stories about the unfortunately nicknamed recluse "Boo" Radley. Apparently Boo (a) eats cats and squirrels *(Road kill. Yum!)*, (b) stabs relatives with scissors *(Careful! You'll poke an eye out)*, and (c) is completely nuts *(see a and b)*. Such a vivid imagination Scout has.

While the kids are stalking poor Boo, they start finding little surprises in a tree near Boo's house. Oh, how nice. There couldn't possibly be a problem with accepting gifts from an unknown person near their big, bad, scary neighbor's house.

Everything's wonderful, *tra la la*, and then . . . oh, it's too horrible to tell! Scout's dad, Atticus, is appointed to defend a black man accused of raping a white woman. Even worse, Atticus *accepts* and will do his best to prove the man's innocence. *Scandalous!*

Well, the townspeople know how to fix this problem. Get a rope! Too bad those men didn't reckon on feisty little Scout and her friends crashing the lynching party just as it was about to get interesting. They would have gotten away with it, too, if it wasn't for those meddlesome kids! Oops, wrong channel.

In court, Atticus puts the smackdown on the prosecution. Turns out the "victim" and her father were lying. You don't say. But really, what's a drunk yet oblivious father to do when he catches his daughter chasing after a black guy? If you're a racist white man in the 1950s, you blame the black man, of course. Problem solved. Doesn't matter if he's innocent. Minor detail.

Yay! Tom didn't do it! He's sure to be acquitted. Aaaaand no. Who cares about truth or justice in a court of law? Pshaw, certainly not the all-white jury. Tom knows he's a dead man either way, so he tries to escape from jail and is shot down like a mockingbird.

Always the sore winner, Papa Ewel hates that Atticus caught him in his lies, so he attacks Scout and Jem. Way to prove yourself a man there, Ewel. Get an innocent man convicted of raping your daughter, then try to murder the defense attorney's kids. Foolproof.

Boo fights off Ewel but stabs the bad, bad man in the process. Sheriff isn't keen on seeing another innocent man convicted, so he says Ewel died falling on his own knife.

So let's review: A bad man lies, so an innocent one dies. Then a good man lies to protect an innocent because the bad man dies. Justice, you have been miscarried. But what does any of this have to do with shooting birds? Nothing, obviously.

After Boo saves Scout, she realizes that she misjudged him. Took you long enough, kid. I thought they said you were smart. Sheesh.

How do you follow up a work of literary genius that won the Pulitzer and earned its author a Presidential Medal of Freedom? If you're **Harper Lee,** you become a curmudgeonly old recluse and never publish another book. Ever. "I have said what I wanted to say and I will not say it again." So it had nothing to do with those two later books you started writing but then abandoned? Yeah, uh huh.

To the Lighthouse by Virginia Woolf

Published: 1927
Category: novel

"The Lighthouse was then a silvery, misty-looking tower with a yellow eye, that opened suddenly, and softly in the evening. Now—James looked at the Lighthouse. He could see the white-washed rocks; the tower, stark and straight; he could see that it was barred with black and white; he could see windows in it; he could even see washing spread on the rocks to dry. So that was the Lighthouse, was it?"

Yep, kid, that was the lighthouse. In related news, if you build something up too much you'll surely be disappointed. That's life.

Buckle up, kids. It's going to be a long ride. We've got stream of consciousness up ahead, and you know how fun that is. It's gonna take us a good ten years to actually get to the lighthouse, so everyone go to the bathroom before we leave because we're not stopping for breaks until lunch—and no arguing. Don't make me turn this thing around. (Seriously. Please. Don't. It's too much.)

At the family vacation home in the Hebrides Islands, west of Scotland, Mr. and Mrs. Ramsay spend the summer with their *eight* kids. Yeesh, poor Mrs. Ramsay. But the Great War is looming on the horizon, so she might be glad to have that many in case she loses a couple. Never can be too prepared, you know.

Eight-year-old James sees a lighthouse across the way and wants to visit. Dad says: *(grumble grumble)* Weather'll be terrible. *(Grumbles some more.)* What James hears: Dad hates us kids, and wants to make us all miserable. I hate him! Mrs. Ramsay has to pacify both her boys. "Daddy's not mean. He just flies off the handle at the stupidest things." "You're a great philosopher, dear. Of course you are."

The Ramsays host a dinner party that night, inviting a smorgasbord of friends: Mr. Tansay, who admires Mr. Ramsay's philosophical work but thinks women can't paint or write; Lily Briscoe, a young painter who thinks Mr. Tansay is a chauvinistic prick and has decided to remain single forever; Augustus Carmichael, a starving poet who asks for seconds on the soup but is slapped down by Mr. Ramsay. Everyone has fun anyway. "Of course it was a lovely evening. Just don't invite me to the next one. No reason."

But at the end of the night, Mrs. Ramsay reflects that the happiness can't last. Which is what you get for marrying a metaphysical philosopher, lady. Drums the happiness right out of living. When she stops by the parlor to chat with Mr. Ramsay after all the guests have left, she has to coddle him *again* as he starts getting all insecure. Him: "Butbutbut you have to tell me you love me all the time because I'm insecure and have a horrible temper. How can I possibly know you love me if you don't say it emphatically every second of every day?" She: "Chill, m'dear. But you're right about the weather. We can't go to the lighthouse tomorrow." Mr.: "You really do love me!" Mrs: *(rolls eyes)*.

Then we *zoom zoom* past as the Great War hits Europe, Mrs. Ramsay dies suddenly and without warning, their oldest son dies in battle, and a daughter dies in childbirth. Sad.

Ten years after the original dinner party, the family returns to the summer house again. Lily Briscoe goes there to paint, and Papa Ramsay finally decides to take James and a sibling to the lighthouse. When it takes longer than he wants to get going, he throws a tantrum then runs to Lily for comfort.

Lily: Dude, grow up.

Mr. Ramsay: Butbutbut my wife always coddled me.

Lily: Yeah, I'm not your wife. Deal with it like an adult.

Mr. Ramsay: (wallows in self-pity).

James: *Dad!* You're so *embarrassing*.

They eventually get going, and the kids actually have fun being with their dad. Even though James still hates him for never taking him to the lighthouse. Until now. While they're off on their little daytrip, Lily finally finishes a painting that she started the last time they were there. All done. As is this book. FINALLY.

Moral: Cave to your kid's demands, or he'll hate you forever.

Virginia Woolf tends to spend a lot of time in her characters' heads. Perhaps a bit too much. Couldn't get out of her own head, either. But the best writers are a few marbles short, I hear. Just don't get stuck in a writer's mind too long or you might go for a long swim in the River Ouse with lots of marbles in your pockets.

Tom Jones by Henry Fielding

Published: 1749
Category: novel (serialized)
Banned for: prostitution and promiscuity, not to mention rape and pseudo-incest. We keep those skeletons firmly in the closet where they belong, right next to Dorian's portrait (page 179) and Havisham's wedding cake (page 83).

> *"We are obliged to bring our Heroe on the Stage in a much more disadvantageous Manner than we could wish; and to declare . . . that it was the universal Opinion of all Mr. Allworthy's Family, that he was certainly born to be hanged."*

This is supposed to be a comedy? Execution. Hahaha!
You kill me . . . oh. I get it.

Can someone PLEASE fix the caps lock on Henry's keyboard? Spell check, too. I mean, this guy's writing is all over the place. It's like there weren't any spelling or grammar rules when he wrote this. Sheesh.

One day Mr. Allworthy—symbolism alert!—comes home from a long trip, tired and ready to crash. *Yawn.* When he goes to his bedroom, someone is already in his bed. OMG, creepy. Serial killer much? The guy in his bed could scream bloody murder, but commit it? Not so much. It's a baby. Who abandons a baby in someone else's bed? Church steps, yeah. Dumpsters, not cool but still done. But someone's bed? Weird.

Allworthy names the kid Thomas and after some digging figures out that the mother is Jenny Jones, though she won't say who the not-proud papa is. Allworthy boots her from ~~her daytime talk show~~ the county and makes his sister, Bridget, raise the kid.

Jones's street cred would be ruined by the whole unwed mother thing, but no one would know in another town. It works out in an odd sort of way.

Bridget ~~Jones~~ Allworthy falls in love with this guy named Blifil and they get married. For reasons beyond comprehension, they have a son and name him Blifil. Talk about cruel and unusual punishment. She raises Tommy and Blif together. Blif grows up to be a ginormous prick and is über-jealous of Tom. He does everything he can to ruin Tom's life. Lovely.

Since our dude ain't got no parents, he's pretty much SOL when it comes to prospects in life. Tom's a bit gaga over Sophia, but again, since dude ain't got no parents, he's pretty much SOL. So he takes up with Molly, the daughter of the gamekeeper. Molly gets knocked up, and everyone believes Tom is responsible—even Tom thinks it's his kid—but then they find out that Tom wasn't her first lover. Good news for Tom, who is now able to pursue Sophia. Except that he's still a bastard, and her dad would never go for it. Instead, Sophia's pops tries to force her to marry Blif. He doesn't really care about Sophia—except as a way to spite Tom. Sophia loves Tom, though, so when her daddy finds out, he locks her up and plans a wedding.

Bliffie figures out how to get Tom in trouble, so the bastard gets banished. He heads off for London and, like a good martyr, swears he'll never see Sophia again so as not to drag her down in ruin. But he manages to save some lady named Mrs. Waters from being raped. Her hubby's an officer in the army. She's so grateful to Tom for his help that they get it on.

He'll never have Sophia, so a guy can totally rebound, amirite? True—except Sophia escapes and stops at the inn where Tom is enjoying Mrs. Waters's, um, company. Awkward. She doesn't disturb them (good thinking) but leaves her muff on his bed as a calling card and heads for London. Totally understandable that not even days after leaving he's swinging from the chandeliers with some randy woman, right? But Tom still loves her, maybe? Tommy Boy flips out when he realizes that Sophia stopped by while he was *otherwise engaged*, so he takes off after her.

Sweet little Sophia goes to stay with her relative Lady Bellaston. When Tom tracks her down, he's so happy that he has an affair with Bellaston. What the—seriously? Dude, you need to stop thinking with your pants.

But secretly he's still pursuing Sophia, and she still loves him, even though he's boinking any woman with a pulse. Things take a turn for the overly dramatic when just about everyone shows up looking for someone. Sophia's dad shows up with Blif looking for her, only to interrupt an attempted rape that Bellaston engineered. Who does that? I mean, if you don't like your cousin, tattle to the grandparents. That's what mature people do.

Allsworthy heads to London to figure out what the blazes is going on. Plus, he wants to make sure Sophia isn't forced into marriage, which is pretty much what the other guys are trying to do. Then there's the husband of a lady who ran off to London with Sophia. He thinks Tom was doing the nasty with his wife and attacks our not-quite hero. Tom actually kept his pants zipped and wasn't banging the wife—hard to believe but true—but he goes to jail anyway when he stabs the hubby with a sword. No self-defense here, I guess, but he gets sprung from the pokey after they find out that Tom didn't strike first. Well, that and the guy survived, so there was no murder for a murder charge.

Then Tom finds out that Mrs. Waters is actually . . . ~~Oprah~~ Jenny Jones! What? He was boinking his own mom? Sick.

Except not really because the chaos finally resolves when everyone stops lying through their teeth. There's probably some kind of moral to this, but, eh, who cares? Now the dramatic conclusion: Tom is actually the son of Bridget Allworthy. *Gasp!* She raised him as not-her-son, even though she knew he actually was. Even better? Blif gets cut off and booted out, though Tom has yet another attack of compassion and gives his bro a yearly allowance. That might actually be an even better revenge because Blif will live the rest of his life on his brother's support, receiving money that would have been his had the old man kicked the bucket before everything came out. Which reminds me, Blif knew about his bro for a while but didn't tell anyone because he was McGreedypants. Bridget confessed it right before she croaked. Blif thought he was in the clear when the only person who knew the secret—or so he thought—was six feet under.

Who's the bastard now, eh Bliffie?

Henry Fielding was a bit of a playa himself. But then he fell hard for Charlotte Craddock, and they went off like fireworks. When Char died ten years later, Henry's passion for her remained steadfast. Methinks someone would do well to have a chat with Heathcliff (page 268). Obsessing over a first love for the rest of your life until you die sucks the big one.

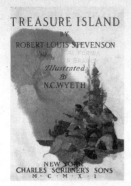

TREASURE ISLAND
BY
ROBERT LOUIS STEVENSON

Illustrated
By
N.C.WYETH

NEW YORK
CHARLES SCRIBNER'S SONS
M · C · M · X · I

Treasure Island
by Robert Louis Stevenson

Published: 1883
Category: novel (serialized, children's)
Banned for: not being to the Nazis' taste.

"Fifteen men on the dead man's chest—
Yo-ho-ho, and a bottle of rum!"

How sloshed was the guy who wrote your songs?
No drinking games necessary, I guess.

Life is boring for Jim Hawkins. It's workworkwork at his parents' inn in Bristol, called the Admiral Benbow. Geez, even the name of the inn sounds boring. That is, until mystery and death and buried treasure arrive. Well, it's actually a mysterious man, Billy Bones, who receives a paper with a BLACK SPOT on it. Not the *blot of ink* on a *piece of paper*!

Har, harrrr, Billy. Billy? Oh, he's dead. Check that off the list. Now how about that buried treasure? Well, when Jim and Mama Hawkins figure out that the dead sailor had something valuable, they return it to his family with their condolences. Just kidding. They totally ransack his trunk and take important-looking papers. Those are always valuable. (Even when they only offer 25 percent off at the Burger King. There's a crown on it, so it must be special.)

Right before the bad guys bust into the inn, they grab a log book and a map. Looks promising. Jim, naive young lad that he is, takes the map to some guys he knows. They've had themselves some edumacation, so they'll know about stuff like this. Because that's where you learn about seafaring—in a drafty old classroom. Obviously.

Dr. Livesey and Squire Trelwney realize what the kid has and dash off to charter a ship to look for buried treasure. Two stodgy old men and a prepubescent kid going off to sea in a ship filled with pirates pretending to be your everyday murderous-looking sailors?? We're gonna need more popcorn.

The treasure they're hunting is from the infamous pirate Captain Flint. He buried it on a deserted island, where our intrepid treasure hunters are headed. Jim and his buds are pretty much like men with anything that comes with instructions: They blunder around and mess it all up because they have no freaking clue what they're doing and they already threw out the instruction manual. Don't deny it, guys. We've seen too many tantrums. We know your M.O.

Anyway, Jim is doing something below deck, which probably involves mischief of some kind. (It's really all that boys know how to do, so they do it well.) That's when he overhears Long John Silver, creepy sailor with various body parts gone AWOL, plotting. Mutiny? Is that some kind of fish? Not so much, as Jim figures out. He scampers off to the ship's captain, who also happens to be the only good guy who knows anything about being at sea. Odds aren't in their favor, but don't worry your little head because the adults have a plan to ditch the pirates once they find the treasure. It's fail proof. Uh huh, right.

When they get to Treasure Island, the good captain gets most of the men off the ship on shore leave. Since he's so good at making mischief, Jim tags along with the pirates. Kid, you're just raring for a Darwin Award, aren't you? The pirates scare the pee out of him (figuratively), so he runs off and hides while Silver kills any of the crew who won't join their mutiny party. Is this adventure exciting enough for you yet, Jimbo?

With the crap scared out of him by now as well, he runs inland. Get lost on deserted island with bloodthirsty pirates on the loose. Good plan. Then who should he meet but Ben Gunn, a pirate marooned on the island by Captain Flint years before, and who's gone more than a little loony tunes over the years. He should have started a message-in-a-bottle correspondence with Robinson Crusoe (page 196). They could trade kelp recipes, delousing tips, and complain about the weather. "It's hot today. Again."

The good guys come ashore, and some not-really-negotiating takes place with the pirates, which means they're standing around and plotting how to murder each other, followed by minor skirmishes. You know, just another day at sea.

Since Jim is such an awesome spy now, he takes off and finds a boat that crazy Ben hid in the woods. When the kid finds it—yes, he actually finds it by himself—he decides to float out to sea and cut the ropes anchoring the ship so it'll drift off and the pirates will be stranded. Good plan . . . if you and your pals don't get stranded, too. Let's see how this goes, shall we?

The ship drifts off. Jim gets his little boat out to the big one and convinces the pirate guard to run it aground. Which the guard does—and then tries to kill Jim. So Jim shoots him. Wait, when did we start reading *Lord of the Flies*? (page 132) When Jim returns to the island to find his friends, they've disappeared, but guess who hasn't. The pirates! They take the kid hostage, but Jim and Silver team up when they realize the rest of the pirates are about to mutiny from the mutiny.

Finally they decide to search for the bloody treasure . . . and someone has already dug it up. Ha ha! Sucks to be you! All that way for . . . nothing? But then the stodgy good guys and one crazy man dash in and save the day by shooting at the pirates, who scatter.

Turns out that Ben had so much time on his hands that he already found the treasure and dug it up. He keeps his little dragon hoard in the cave where he lives ~~on the island of Monte Cristo~~. Good going, Ben. I think. It takes them three days to haul the loot to the ship, and then they're off. They ditch all the pirates except Silver, who disappears along with some of the treasure a few days later and eventually gets a gig cooking up lots of fried fish and hush puppies. Good luck with that one, Gimpy.

In the end, they return home, safe and rich. What does Jim get as a reward for all his epically awesome treasure hunting? Nightmares about pirates and gold for the rest of his life.

Robert Louis Stevenson's dad was a bit strict. You know the kind: plotting out his kid's life from birth to death, with an occasional potty break in between. Amazing, isn't it, that a kid who didn't want to do what daddy wanted would write about a kid escaping on an adventure to dig up lost treasure?

The Turn of the Screw
by Henry James

Published: 1898
Category: novella

"No, no—there are depths, depths! The more I go over it, the more I see in it, and the more I see in it, the more I fear. I don't know what I don't see—what I don't fear!"

Here, why don't we try on this nice white jacket with extra long arms? They're the cutting edge of style . . .

Here's a fun game: Let's screw with a nervous nanny to the point of breaking, then sit back and watch the fun. Though an especially neurotic nanny could hypothetically freak out the kids so bad that they die of fright. Nah, that would never happen. Except this one time with this one governess a few years ago. (Names have been changed to protect the identity of the woman who failed miserably at her job. Would you like to see her résumé?) Of course, she's written a memoir detailing the experience. Playing up the death of a kid you were responsible for is a great way to pad the retirement fund.

The book starts with a guy named Douglas telling a *spoooooky* story at a party. He *swears* this all really happened to his sister's governess. Question: Knowing that the story ends with one kid dead and the other cuckoo for Cocoa Puffs, WHY WOULD YOU LET HER WATCH YOUR SISTER? "Don't worry. She's a bit insane, but she's really great with children!"

So some super-sexy guy hires the governess to watch his orphaned niece and nephew. He's a great uncle. I mean, he pays her plenty—and is *hawt*—though he doesn't actually want to interact with the kids, like, ever. But he loves the kids, really. Just don't ever contact him about them. Miles and Flora are totes adorbs. Little Miles *did* just get kicked out of school, but it's because he's so much better than all the kids there. Obviously.

Things are going so well with the kids that she really wishes Uncle Hottie would stop by for a performance evaluation or something. Then the manure starts to fly. Governess keeps seeing some strange dude staring at the house. When she mentions it to the housekeeper . . .

Housekeeper: That's Peter Quint!

Governess: Oh. He some local weirdo?

Housekeeper: He's the groundskeeper—

Governess: So he—

Housekeeper: —who died a year ago.

Governess: Well, look at that. Isn't it time to take your medications?

The housekeeper is probably just some superstitious country bumpkin. No biggie. But then governess sees a woman off in the distance.

Governess: Who's the lady?

Housekeeper: Must be the previous governess, Miss Jessel, who died mysteriously a year ago.

Governess: So I'm being haunted by the help?

Seems Quint and Jessel were getting all kinds of jiggy in their free time.

Housekeeper: You have to promise not to tell anyone—but they got a bit too *personal* with the kids, if you know what I'm saying. It's all very mysterious. But no worries. Ghosts don't exist, do they? Heh heh. OK, gotta go.

The ghosts start showing up all the time, but only the governess can see them. Weird. She figures they're coming back to hang with the kids. They're just . . . attentive and dedicated former staff. That must be it. Even more fun, the kids have started acting all cray-cray, with

Miles wandering outside in his PJs after dark, and Flora staring out the window at *something* in the middle of the night. But neither will admit to anything. It's like *Children of the Corn* all over again.

Governess is properly freaked out by that point, so she decides to write a letter to Uncle Hottie, telling him he must come see the children *at once*. Oh, and bring a bouquet of long-stem roses when you come. No reason. Then the letter mysteriously vanishes. Weird.

Nanny McCrazy sees the ghosts pop up all the time now. They're so inconsiderate, never calling in advance, making a mess and never cleaning up after themselves (for rude). Plus, they're sending off these evil vibes, like they want to take the children off somewhere to suffer for eternity. *Bwahaha!* Someone needs to cut back on the cough syrup.

It's strange, though, that no one else sees them. But then little Flora starts swearing. There has to be an evil presence in her life because little girls just don't say bad words. Kindly ignore the fact that little Miles was booted from school for saying naughty words he learned from someone else . . . like maybe a guy who worked in the gardens.

When they find Flora talking to herself out in the woods, McCrazy completely flips and makes the housekeeper take the kid to the uncle.

Now Miles is alone with the governess, who talks to him about all the strange goings-on. "So weird, right? I mean, it's not like *I'm* imagining things. No way. Wh— SOMEONE'S AT THE WINDOW. DON'T YOU SEE THEM AT THE WINDOW?"

Miles: Um, is it the dead governess?

Governess: NO, IT'S THE OTHER GUY. WHY AREN'T YOU SCARED? THIS IS SCARY! I'LL PROTECT YOU. *(ghost disappears)* Whew! See, I saved you.

She turns around and—oops. The nanny literally freaked the kid to death. Then she went on to have a long and illustrious career . . . until someone invented the nanny cam.

So were there ghosts? Or was the governess just schizoid?

Henry James liked all that gothic scary ghost stuff, but not the boring teen slasher crap or the freaky wannabe vampire stuff. No, this guy knew how to tell *real* ghost stories, the kind that scare you in your dreams because it *could* be real or maybe not but you don't know—wait, what was that noise?

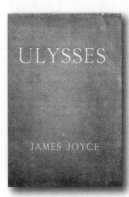

Ulysses by James Joyce

Published: 1922
Category: novel (serialized)
Banned for: pretty much everything. Perhaps it's good that *Ulysses* is such a thick book. With all the bonfires that people in America, Canada, Ireland, and England were making out of it, they kept warm all winter long.

"History is a nightmare from which I am trying to awake."

You have those dreams with Genghis Khan chasing you through the Pyramids on his pet T-rex while singing "The Marseillaise," too? No? That's weird. I could've sworn you were there.

Stephen Dedalus, nice to see you again. What's it been, a year since we saw you? How'd the whole trip abroad to find yourself go? (page 187.) Good, good. Don't really care.

Let's see. It's June 16, 1904, and the day's looking packed, so let's get going. Ready, Steve-o? Early in the morning, he's just trying to avoid his jerk of a friend Buck, and his English friend Haines. "Dude, leave your key here, and just meet us at the pub around noon-thirty."

10:00 a.m. Stephen heads to work where he teaches history at a boys' school. He waits after class to get his paycheck from Garrett Deasy, who runs the school, and who is an even bigger jerk than Buck. Cue narrow-minded man's lecture on what Steve should be doing with his life. Also, Deasy wrote a fascinating letter to the editor about diseased cows, which Steve says he'll drop off at the newspaper. Run, Steve! Run while you can! So he dashes out, walks down Sandymount Strand, and thinks about his life. Can we speed this up a bit, Steve? We already spent way too much time on moocows in the last book. While he's wandering, he writes a poem on a scrap of paper torn from Deasy's editorial. Hard to say which would be a more riveting read: bad poetry or sick cows. Tough call.

8:00 a.m. Let's rewind a bit and watch Leopold Bloom getting ready for his own day. Honestly, I can't think of anything more exciting. But Leo's a good husband, you know? He brings his wife, Molly, breakfast in bed and gets the mail for her. Oh look, she got a letter from her tour manager. She's an excellent musician. He'll be by at around 4 to meet with her. Leo's pretty sure they're doing the nasty. "On the agenda today we've got a nice chunk of time blocked out for sex. Let's get started."

Leo goes back downstairs and reads a letter from their daughter, Milly. Then he goes to the outhouse for his morning constitutional. Two words, Leo: indoor plumbing. It'll change your life. At least he didn't take his daughter's letter for bathroom reading.

10:00 a.m. Leo's running errands. He picks up a letter at the post office from Martha Clifford. She thinks she's writing love letters to some goober named Henry Flower, but it's really just Leo. And there goes the sympathy that your wife is cheating on you, as you're all creepazoid with the fake identity and pen pal.

11:00 a.m. Hey, look! A connection between Bloom and Stevie boy, though honestly it wouldn't be at all surprising for them never to meet during the entire novel. Jimmy and Virginia, what a pair, I tell you (page 157). Anyway, Bloomie's riding with Steve's dad, Simon, plus Martin Cunningham and Jack Power, on the way to a funeral. The other guys ignore Leo, so he contemplates the deaths of his son and his father. Well, that's certainly pleasant.

12:00 p.m. Bloom's at the Freeman newspaper office working on some deal for a local ad. Some guys are discussing politics when Steve shows up with Deasy's brilliant letter. Steve and the guys leave for the pub just as Bloom gets back. The editor rejects Leo's work on the ad while he's walking out. Good times.

1:00 p.m. LB runs into an old girlfriend, and they talk about another friend who's at the hospital having a baby. He stops for lunch and thinks about this one time when he and Molly had some fun times. Afterward, as he's walking down the street, he spots tour manager lover boy and dashes into the National Library to avoid him. Good call.

2:00 p.m. Wouldn't you know, but Steve is there informally presenting some theory about *Hamlet,* which a famous poet pooh-poohs and then leaves. Buck shows up and makes everything better by harassing Steve about not showing up at the pub. As they leave, they walk past Leo, who's on some work-related errand.

4:00 p.m. Steve's dad, some other guys, and the tour manager are at a hotel bar when Bloom spots the manager's car. Because he's a glutton for punishment, Leo watches his wife's lover take off for his meeting at the Bloom house. He stews while his wife is getting some and then responds to the love letter from the lady who thinks he's someone else.

5:00 p.m. Bloom gets to the pub for a meeting, but the other guy isn't there yet.

A drunk guy picks a fight with Bloom because he's Jewish. Leo responds by spouting off about love and peace. They fight anyway. A bit later, Leo is chilling on Sandymount Strand as the sun starts to set. A woman named Gerty sees him watching her on the beach, so she shows off her gams for Leo, who proceeds to get freaky with himself. On a public beach. She leaves, and he takes a nap. Typical.

10:00 p.m. Bloom wanders to the hospital to see how his friend is doing with giving birth. Oh, that. Right. I almost ~~cared~~ forgot. Steve and some of his med school friends are chilling at the hospital. They invite Leo to join them at the pub. So they all head over and have their drinkies until closing time. Then Stephen convinces his friend to go to a brothel with him. This is obviously a good plan, so Leo follows to make sure the boys don't do anything stupid.

Bloom finally locates Stephen and Lynch at the brothel. Steve's drunk and thinks he sees his mom's ghost, so he smashes a lamp. Totally normal. Then he staggers off, Bloom running to catch up. Stevie boy gets in a fight with a British soldier and loses, so Leo wakes him up and gets him some coffee to sober up a bit.

Wine o'clock in the morning. Steve's in no shape to wander off alone, so Bloom takes him back to his own house. They have hot chocolate and chat about themselves. Leo offers to let Steve crash at their place, but Steve leaves.

When Leo gets ready to head upstairs for bed, he notices evidence that Molly and her manager had a very, uh, productive meeting. Nice. But Leo's actually kind of cool about it, at peace with the world. When he gets into bed, he tells Molly about his day as she lays there groggy because it's who knows what time in the morning. Then he asks her to bring him breakfast in bed when he wakes up.

He falls asleep, but his weird request keeps Molly up. Isn't she the one who gets breakfast in bed every morning? What's going on? Then her mind starts with the wandering (here we go again) and meanders from her childhood living in Gibraltar to the sexytimes that afternoon with her manager. Which leads naturally to her musical career and thinking of the hubs sleeping beside her and the good times they had at Howth. *Zzzzzzzzzz.*

James Joyce went with an *Odyssey* theme for this book (page 162), with Stephen playing the part of Telemachus, Leopold Bloom as Odysseus, and Molly as Penelope. That little bit of info might give this book some actual meaning instead of being completely random. Yeah, not so much. Each of the book's eighteen "episodes" is patterned after a different adventure in the *Odyssey*. But the best part is that Joyce uses a totally different literary style for each episode. So not only is the book totally incomprehensible in a uniquely Joycean way, it's done in eighteen different styles on top of that. No thanks.

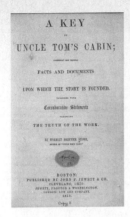

Uncle Tom's Cabin
by Harriet Beecher Stowe

Published: 1851
Category: novel (serialized)
Banned for: being anti-slavery and portraying equality. Obviously, southern slave-owners didn't like the book because it made them look bad. But why did Russia get all up in arms? Apparently, Tsar Nicholas I didn't want his serfs reading about the dangerous idea of equality.

> *"'I looks like gwine to heaven,' said the woman; 'an't thar where white folks is gwine? S'pose they'd have me thar? I'd rather go to torment, and get away from Mas'r and Missis.'"*

So . . . better to reign in hell than serve in heaven? You might want to check your math on that one again.

Decent guy Arthur Shelby owns Uncle Tom, but when the Kentucky farmer gets a pile o' bills too high to handle, he has to sell some of his property. Meaning slaves, specifically Uncle Tom ~~Dick~~ and Harry, to a slave trader named Haley. Harry's mom is a house slave serving Mrs. Shelby, so when she overhears talk of losing her kid, she warns Tom and his wife, then takes off with Harry. Haley chases after his runaway merchandise. They get across the Ohio River before he can get to them, so Haley sends a pair of slave catchers after them.

Tom, however, doesn't run ~~because he's an idiot~~. Instead, he finds himself floating downriver to New Orleans. Before they arrive, Haley buys up more "merchandise," and then they're off to the slave market. Along the way, Haley proves himself an even more upstanding fellow by selling one slave's baby without telling the young woman. Classy.

Meanwhile, the escaped slaves are making their way north to Canada. Did anyone mention how cold it gets up there? Let's hope they're wearing lots of layers. Eliza's husband, George, finds them on a Quaker farm. Nice people, those Quakers. Opposed to slavery—and they make a mean breakfast, too.

Still floating down the Mississippi on a riverboat, Tom meets an angel in the form of a girl. She's about to become a real angel—until Tom saves her from drowning. Evangeline St. Clare is pretty much perfect in every way, so she immediately likes Tom and makes her dad buy him.

Eva: Please, Daddy? I've always wanted a person of my own.

Papa St. Clare: Well, all right. Can't deny my daughter anything. You know how it is with kids.

Tom: Actually, I don't. I was just taken away from my wife and three children and sold as property to someone else.

Awkward.

But at least Tom's away from that Haley character and off to live in New Orleans with Eva's family, including her dad, cousin Ophelia, and . . . then he meets dear mother, a racist, spoiled brat. Tom gets along great with Eva, though, and they read from his Bible all the time. Eva learns about Christianity, and she even likes it. Mr. St. Clare kindly writes a letter for Tom to send back to his wife to let her know where he is.

Up north, George, Eliza, and Harry, plus a couple of other escaped slaves, are heading to the next stop on the Underground Railroad when slave hunters spot them. Time to haul some horse and buggy! George shoots one of the guys chasing them, then the rest of the posse takes off. Eliza convinces the others to bring the wounded man with them to be treated.

In New Orleans, Tom is in charge of grocery shopping for the household. *Zzzzz.* Then St. Clare buys Topsy, a little slave girl.

Mr. St. Clare: Look what I got for you, cousin Ophelia. It's your own living doll! You can dress her up and teach her things. Isn't that great?

Ophelia: Whatever. Come with me, whoever you are.

Eva goes on being angelic until she croaks. Tom even helps Mr. St. Clare see the light of Christianity and nearly converts him. St. Clare is planning to free Tom and make it so his slaves can't be sold if something ever happened to him. Wanna bet what's about to happen? Before the paperwork is finalized, he's stabbed to death, and the Mrs. sells most of the slaves. So close.

If Haley the slave trader was bad, Simon Legree is worse. He buys Tom, plus two women, one as a pleasure toy for Sambo, the black overseer, and the other one for himself. Hey, at least he's thinking of others' needs in addition to his own, right? OK, one other person's needs, and that's probably just because he doesn't want to share. He owns a decrepit plantation in the marshy swamps of the Louisiana bayou, where he has a bunch of cotton fields. So Tom gets to pick cotton every day for the rest of his life. Not. Fun. Working out in the beating sun makes Tom start to lose faith. Legree trying to break Tom or kill him might also have something to do with that.

Tom tries to help Legree's sex slave, Cassy, and the other girl, Emmeline, escape. Doesn't work, and Tom gets punished *hard*.

Meanwhile, Eliza and crew have made it all the way up to near Lake Erie, where they plan to make a break for the border. But slave catchers are waiting to nab them before they can cross. They wear clever disguises—your handlebar 'stashe is a bit crooked—and dash across the finish line. Safe!

Tom's not doing so hot, but then the sex slaves figure out a way to escape by hiding in Legree's room while he's out searching the swamp for them. Who gets blamed for their escape? Tom. So who gets beat to death? Tom. Harriet pulls out all the stops on this one as Tom whispers to his tormenters, "I forgive you."

Then it just so happens that George Shelby, son of Tom's previous previous owner, shows up and wants to buy Tom. Wouldn't you know, he arrives minutes too late, just in time to hear the poor slave's dying words. And wouldn't you know it, but runaways Cassy and Emmeline run into George Shelby as they reach the riverboat heading north.

Another woman comes forward and says she's George Harris's sister. Then Cassy realizes that George's wife, Eliza, is her daughter. Wow. So many amazing coincidences. How many degrees away from Kevin Bacon are they now?

All the runaway slaves float off together to Canada, where puppies and rainbows welcome them, and they meet up with their suddenly expanded family. George Shelby goes home to the farm with the tragic news of Tom's death, but he frees all the slaves, saying that they owe their freedom to Uncle Tom. They do indeed. *<gag>*

Harriet Beecher Stowe's enormously best-selling book came out a full decade before the Civil War started, but, so the story goes, even Abe Lincoln gave her credit for getting things rocking: "So you are the little woman who wrote the book that started this great war." Who's he calling *little*? Oh. He was six-four and she wasn't even five feet tall? I'll allow it.

TITLE PAGE OF "VANITY FAIR"

Vanity Fair by William Makepeace Thackeray

Published: 1848
Category: novel (serialized, satirical)

"All is vanity, nothing is fair."

So if the preacher sayeth that he rideth the bus—wait, that's not right . . .

Amelia Sedley is boring. No offense to Mary Sues of the world, because it is possible to be interesting while being a goody-two-shoes. But this girl? Wow. If you could bottle staid piety, it would look like this: l'eau de nun, with top notes of starch and mothballs and subtle hints of guilt.

Becky Sharp, though, is a hottie, and girl knows it. She grew up a penniless orphan, so her one ambition in life is to marry rich and spend money like crizazy as an honored guest at the most fashionable parties in town while sporting the absolute latest fashions. It's the simple things really. Men drool over her—figuratively speaking, of course, because man drool is disgusting and stains. So let's just say she has a plan for becoming the biggest thing in the Vanity Fair. No, not the magazine. (See page 182.)

Commence stage one: Snag rich husband. After graduating from Miss Pinkerton's Academy for Girls, Becky goes to stay with Amelia until she can find herself a suitable position as governess or the perfect man to be her ~~wallet~~ husband. She sets her eyes on Amelia's brother, Joseph Sedley. So he's not the ideal candidate—boorish, fat, and egotistical—but he has a cushy job in India as well as wealthy 'rents back home in England. Score (sort of).

Simple little Amelia doesn't care for the glamour and competition that makes the Vanity Fair so irresistible to Becky. The only thing Amelia wants is to be Mrs. George Osborne. *Sigh.* George is kind of a prick, which Becky notices immediately, so she's happy to let Amelia have him. But then the ass goes and ruins her plans to ~~trap~~ marry Sedley. All it takes is a few well-placed taunts about Becky's lack of heritage from Georgie boy, and Sedley loses his, um, infatuation with Becky.

With stage one in the crapper, Becky sets in motion stage two: Become a governess and marry someone wealthy from the family. When offered the governess position at Queen's Crawley, she finds several interesting prospects. First, she ingratiates herself into Sir Pit Crawley's favor so that she's nearly indispensable as his assistant. No one cares if the kids get educated; that's not the point. Becky's there to snag a man—the richest one she can land.

When Pitt's mega-rich spinster half-sister stops by for a visit, everyone's on edge—except our delightful Becky, who turns the charm up to eleven for Miss Crawley. Not too surprising, then, that Miss Crawley takes her back with her as her companion. Pitt's not happy with that at all, but he's technically still married. But wait! Pitt's second wife conveniently dies, so he rushes to London to propose—and learns that Becky's already married. To his second son, Rawdon. Did she forget to mention that? Oopsie.

Pitt isn't the only one erupting like Vesuvius, though. Miss Crawley can't believe that her favorite nephew—voted most likely to inherit gobs of cash—would debase himself enough to marry the *governess*. It's bad enough that his father planned on it, but him? Ugh. Cut out of the will. FOREVER.

Poor Becky came this><close to hitting the jackpot, and now nada. You should know by now that a pretty face only leads to poverty, having to work, or massive piles of debt to ditch somehow. Becky goes for option three and drags Rawdon along for the ride. Well, it's more like she can't get rid of him . . . tomato, tomahto.

Sweet little Amelia gets her heart's desire when she becomes engaged to George. Life is just so perfect . . . then the economy collapses, and her family loses everything. But it'll be OK, because George will stick by her during such a difficult time. Right, Georgie? Yeah, not so much. Even though Amelia and George's parents have been besties for, like, forever, the moment the Sedleys bottom out, Mr. Osborne says buh-bye to his dear friends. He can't let such leeches suck him dry, now can he? But that means George has to ditch Amelia if he wants to inherit from his dad. Decisions, decisions.

George's good friend William Dobbin, pretty much the only decent, intelligent, and wise person in the entire book, makes him keep his word to Amelia, even though that means Dobbin can't marry the girl he loves while his selfish friend gets someone he doesn't deserve. No one said life was fair, right? Anyway, George and Amelia marry, and he's promptly disinherited. They're poor but happy together, right honey? Honey? George isn't what you'd call an attentive spouse, but it doesn't matter much because war breaks out between England and Napoleon, and all the guys get called up for military service. They bring their wives along with them when the army parks for a bit in Brussels.

The night before the Battle of Waterloo, George flirts outrageously with Becky, who gives him all kinds of (not quite subtle) encouragement. George is tired of Amelia because she's kind of . . . well, boring. So when a fiery woman comes along, he's ready to get burned. He slips Becky a little note arranging a secret tryst. *Ooh la la!* But then they're called up to battle and George dies.

What? But Amelia loved him, and she can't live without him. Her dear, devoted, loyal George is dead. Except, oh dear, she's kind of pregnant, so she has to stay strong for mini-George, who will always remind her of her dearly departed ~~scumbag~~ husband.

Rawdon, Joe Sedley, and Dobbin all survive, though Sedley had a rough time after the first cannon blasted and he tucked tail and ran. But of course he was a great war hero, which he tells everyone he ever meets. He heads back to India. Dobbin sticks around to help out Amelia—anonymously, of course. Amelia *and* Becky squirt out little baby boys. Amelia develops an unhealthy obsession with her son, while Becky ignores her own. Hard to say which is worse.

Becky more or less prostitutes herself to pay her bills, hanging on various wealthy men, especially Lord Steyne. Rawdon of course knows nothing about all this *(wink wink)*, though he was probably just gullible (as usual) and thought Becky was only *pretending* to do whatever it is she does with the rich men. When he finds out otherwise, he takes off to a governorship that Steyne arranges for him on Coventry Island and dies not long after of yellow fever. Rawdon's older brother raises baby Rawdon because Becky couldn't care less . . . until her son becomes heir to the whole Queen's Crawley estate. Then suddenly she's the bestest mother *ever*. "Now, where did you put mummy's check, dear?"

Meanwhile, Amelia can't afford to ~~spoil George like she wants to~~ support her parents while taking care of little Georgy too, so Grampa Sedley takes him in and turns him into a worse brat than the kid's dad. Because that worked out so well the first time.

After many years in India, Dobbin returns and helps fix the mess between old Osborne and Amelia. The old man changes his will to leave Georgy half his fortune plus a little for her.

Becky becomes a washed-up, alcoholic, hanger-on to anyone who'll glance her way. Not looking so hot there, Becks. When she stumbles upon Joe Sedley years later, she makes him her boy toy again, which eventually leads to his death and her getting all his money. Eek. Before that, though, Becky does Amelia a single favor: She shows the grieving widow the note that George gave Becky the night before he died, asking her to run away with him. Amelia finally realizes what an ass her husband was, clearing the way for her to love the great guy who's been puppy-dog loyal from the moment he met and fell in love with her. Dobby even helps ~~Harry~~ li'l Georgie get over his brattiness and learn to appreciate his mama. Happy ending! . . . except for the part where Dobbin realizes that Amelia is shallow, and that he doesn't love her as much as he did before. Eh. *Details*—but that's another magazine for another time.

William Makepeace Thackeray based the character of Becky on . . . his grandmother? Um, wow. Aren't grandmas supposed to be cute little old ladies who bake cookies? Dobbin's near-obsessive devotion to Amelia possibly came from Thack's unrequited love for the wife of a friend. Ouch.

Waiting for Godot
by Samuel Beckett

Published: 1953
Category: play (drama)
Banned for: spite. Beckett didn't like that the Irish clergy kept banning his friends' work, so he preemptively banned Ireland from staging any of his plays.

"Let's go." "We can't." "Why not?" "We're waiting for Godot." "Ah!"

Lather, rinse, and repeat fifty-three million times.
Where did those boys leave that noose?

This one's short, but you're probably not going to like it.

Vladimir and Estragon meet at a tree and discuss how they're both waiting for a man named Godot. Then two other guys come along. Pozzo has his slave, (not so) Lucky, on a leash and plans to sell him at the fair. They chat. Lucky does a cute little dance and entertains them by ~~rambling psychotically~~ thinking aloud. Pozzo and Lucky leave.

Just you wait until we get to the exciting part. (Hint: there isn't one.)

Back at the tree, a kid trots up and says he has a message from Godot: Too busy to make it tonight, but I'll totes be there tomorrow. Laters! They quiz the kid about Godot, and then the kid takes off. V&E decide to scoot, but they don't move. Aaaaaaaaand scene!

The next day, V&E show up at the tree again to wait for Godot—who really should have called by now or at least texted to say that he was running late so they don't have to stand around all day waiting for him like a couple of rubes. Some people are so inconsiderate.

Pozzo and Lucky stop by for another chat. Well, Pozzo does. Lucky is dumb . . . as in can't talk, not dumb like this play. Not much better off, Pozzo's blind now. But neither of them remembers seeing the two dudes by the tree yesterday. So it's déjà vu all over again . . . except not? Pozzo and Lucky take off because there's really no point—*zzzzz* . . . oh sorry—to being there in the first place. V&E wait some more. There's a lot of taking boots off and putting them back on because really the climax of any successful play should be trying on footwear. And carrots. Don't forget the carrots.

Hey, look! It's messenger boy again. But, get this, he didn't talk to the two dudes yesterday either. Wanna guess what he has to say? You got it: Godot ain't comin' suckas, so you gots to wait some mo'. The kid leaves, so V&E decide to head off as well. They chitchat for a bit about hanging themselves, but wouldn't you know it, they don't have any rope. They remain where they are, and the curtain falls yet again.

This is a prime example of Theater of the Absurd, so let's play Guess This Mess and see if we can select whatever oddball significance others have applied to this monstrosity. Smart and sophisticated people say the play means:

A. Life is useless and has no meaning.

B. Everyone has amnesia.

C. Beckett's just messing with us.

D. The French are *totalement* weird.

E. Who the hell cares?

F. It's all symbiosis.

G. This is the dumbest play ever.

If you answered c, e, or g, you can be my friend. If you answered f, then bravo you for understanding whatever the hell Beckett was trying to say. Sadly, intellectuals have ~~wasted~~ taken a lot of ink interpreting *Waiting for Groundhog Day on Downers* through different kinds of glasses—theological, political, Freudian, etc. But really the only kind of glasses you need to make any sense out of it are shot glasses. Pop one back every time someone says "Godot." You're welcome. Cheers!

Samuel Beckett wrote *Godot* in French then later translated it to English. As a young man in Paris, he was James Joyce's assistant (see pages 187 and 243)—so no surprises on the weirdness front. Speaking of fronts: during World War II he joined the French Resistance. What he should have resisted was the urge to write this godawful play.

War and Peace by Leo Tolstoy

Published: 1869
Category: novel (serialized, historical)

*"We can know only that we know nothing.
And that is the highest degree of human wisdom."*

You're talking riddles, man. Say it plain in Nadsat (page 41).

Napoleon's throwing a huge party in Western Europe, and he wants to invite Russia. They're not as excited as Napoleon would like, but he's a generous host and is willing to bring the party to them. Road trip!

Oh, look, Anna Pavlovna's already got a party going in St. Petersburg for all the elite of Russian society. There's a monstrous cast of characters here, which you'd expect from a book that's *twelve hundred* freaking pages long. The next time an author wants to write a book more than a thousand pages long, they should be hit over the head with a hardbound copy of this brain buster. If they wake up—big if—maybe they'll rethink the decision. Brevity, people. BREVITY—and you can suck it, Leo.

Anyway, let's intro the gang:

Pierre Bezukhov is an awkward turtle of a man. People like him even though he's a bastard. His pops is a *très* rich count, and that's how counts roll. Andrew Bolkonsky is pretty smart and has ambitions with a capital AM. His pops is a retired army guy. Vasili Kuragin's family is sneaky and likes to stir up trouble, and he's rather wily himself. Anatole Kuragin is looking for a sugar mama. Helene Kuragin is hawt with a capital Sizzle. Which, if you haven't been paying attention, always leads to problems. Someone gave Natasha Rostov a bit too much sugar in the womb; girl is lively. *(boing boing)* She's also a bit of a romantic. Sonya Kuragin's the quiet one, an orphan, and engaged to Nicholas, who tends to be impulsive, which might explain his sudden desire to join the military. Well, that and Shorty Bonaparte crashing the party.

Both Nicholas and Andrew are sent to the front lines—always the best place to be when you want a good seat . . . except in war, where you just die first. Andrew gets wounded and survives, but everyone thinks he's dead. You should have some fun with that, Andy. No? Fine, suit yourself. Even though he's illegit, Pierre becomes sole heir to daddy's fortune and then gets hitched to Helene. She cheats on him while the ink on the marriage contract's still wet, so new hubby obviously has to challenge her lover to a duel. Pierre had figured marriage would be better than, well, *her*, so he ditches Helene and becomes a Freemason.

When Andrew gets back home, he's shocked to learn that he now has a son, and they're shocked to learn that he's still alive. Even more unexpected is his wife, Lise, dying in childbirth. Which means Andrew's sis Mary gets to raise his kid. "Andy, enough with the surprises. Seriously, stop it."

Nicholas comes home on leave from the army to find the family in financial ruin, helped by Nick's rather large gambling debts. Uh oh. The fam tries to convince him to marry an heiress who's rolling in the dough, but he's already engaged to Sonya, an orphan. Eh. Dump her! He goes back to the army where it's much safer (oy, family drama), and sees Napoleon and Tsar Alexander play nice.

Natasha's all growed up now and attends all the social events, falling in love with all the eligible men she sees until her sights fall on Andrew. But Andy's daddy says *nyet* and makes him wait a year before they can get married. Natasha's all whatever, and Andy travels the world. Way to watch out for your girl, bud. You'd better hope someone else doesn't come along and—

Too late. Now she has the hots for Anatole, so they elope. Except they don't, and Andrew comes back a tad grumpy. Dude, I warned you! He (understandably) dumps Natasha, who goes all sadface, so Pierre comforts her and then he starts to fall in love with her. Probably not a good idea, guy. But then Natasha gets sick.

Up until this point, France and Russia have been getting along ~~like a house on fire~~ great, but then Napoleon decides he doesn't want to play well with others and invades Russia. Sigh. OK, back to war, guys. Andrew goes back to the army. Pierre goes nuts and thinks he has a secret mission to assassinate Bonaparte. Good luck with that.

When the Frenchies get near the Bolkonski crib, people tell Mary and her pops to abandon ship. But dad dies right when the frog army arrives, and Mary is booted out. The peasants aren't terribly fond of her, but Nick rides up in the, uh, nick of time and saves her. They start to notice some sizzle between them. The Russians take on the French at Borodino and kick their derrieres, even though zee Fronch outnumber them. *Quoi?* Shorty is a tad confused—and upset.

Back in St. Petersburg, life among the rich continues pretty much as normal despite Moscow being occupied by the enemy. Eh, their problem. Helene decides to annul her marriage to Pierre so she can snatch a foreign prince. Pierre goes even more crazypants and wanders Moscow all by his lonesome. The Rostovs pack everything so they can evacuate, but then they get a case of conscience and take wounded soldiers instead, including Andrew. Pierre is still crazypants in Moscow and watches as the city goes batshit with fire, looting, and murder. All in a day's work. He still thinks he needs to off Bonaparte, but he ends up saving a girl from a fire before getting nabbed by the French police. In jail he gets a front row seat to watch some of his fellow prisoners get executed. Lovely.

Nick's aunt tries to make him marry, uh, Mary, but he says *nyet*, still engaged to Sonya. Mary visits Andrew as he nears death. Andrew forgives Natasha for falling in love with someone else after he kinda abandoned her for a while. Then he dies. Wait, that's not supposed to happen. They love each other, so they should get married and have babies and—oh, sorry. Forgot for a second that this is a Russian novel. Carry on with the misery and woe.

Meanwhile, the Russian army returns to Moscow, but the French have already hightailed it after losing so badly at Borodino. The frogs drag all their prisoners of war along with them, including Pierre. When the Ruskies catch up, there's some fighting, and Pierre goes free. But then he gets sick for three months. When he gets better, he realizes that he's in love with Natasha. With Andrew dead, she falls for Pierre and they get married. A little quick, wouldn't you say, Nat? She eventually becomes a frumpy Russian woman who'll box your ears for talking back, young man.

Nick and Mary marry (heh), which fixes his family's money problems. Yay, everyone's happy! But what about Sonya? Eh, who cares. She's an orphan.

If that all comes across a bit rushed and jumbled, maybe you should try your hand at condensing a complicated 1,200-page book into 1,200 *words* and see how much better you do. Get back with me when your sanity returns.

Despite writing an entire book about war, **Leo Tolstoy** was actually a big fan of nonviolence. Later in life he wrote a bunch of stuff about pacifism, which Gandhi read and used as the basis for his civil disobedience, which has inspired tons of other people. Way to pay it forward, Leo.

The Wind in the Willows by Kenneth Grahame

Published: 1908
Category: novel (children's)
Banned for: Some people didn't really like that satyr god Pan makes an appearance in the story, or that Toad and friends used knives and guns on occasion, like when kicking weasel trash out of Toad Hall, so they just LEFT OUT some of those sections and changed things up a tad so it would be super duper sanitized clean fun for kids. Perhaps that's why Disney took such a liking to the story.

"The Wild Wood is pretty well populated by now; with all the usual lot, good, bad, and indifferent—I name no names. It takes all sorts to make a world."

Plead the fifth? Good plan, Badger. Those coppers won't get nothin' out of you.

Boy, does Mole have a lot of spring cleaning to do, so he decides to visit the riverbank. Such a hard worker, Mole. There he meets Ratty the river rat, who shows him the ropes. First up: rowing a boat. Mole has some issues with that . . . like losing paddles and capsizing. Eventually, Mole learns not to dunk them every time they paddle about, and he and Ratty spend their lazy days floating on the river. Ain't that the life.

Down the riverbank at Toad Hall lives the super-rich and eccentric Toad. He likes stuff. Lots of stuff, because he gets bored fast. But he's got tons of cash, yo, so he can buy anything he wants. One day, Mole and Rat drop in to find Toad with his new caravan. Because toads obviously want to be gypsies. They all take off in Toad's fab house on wheels, where Mole and Rat end up doing all the work. (So *that's* how vacations work? Note to self: find gullible friends.) As they're plodding along, a car zips by and scares the horse pulling Toad and friends, which overturns and—

Waitwaitwait. Hold up. In the world of the Willows, small critters are like people, but a horse is still a pack animal? I call bull crap . . . pig puckey . . . horse apples? Whatever. It's all a bunch of baloney (that's not made from horses).

The moment Toad sees that shiny new car zoom by, he abandons the caravan and his friends and hightails it to London to buy himself one of those fandangled new contraptions. He returns with his very own sports car—ooh, shiny—which he uses to terrorize the neighborhood. *Meep meep!*

Meanwhile, Ratty tells Mole about his elusive friend Badger, who doesn't like company. Well, if that's not an invitation for a partay at Badger's crib, I don't know what is. Mole sneaks out while Ratty is taking a nap. So smart. Wander off on your own in the big scary woods in the middle of winter without a map or a clue . . . it's the perfect recipe for a molecicle. Dude, get some GPS or something. Ratty finds him and they oh so conveniently stumble on Badger's pad as a blizzard starts.

Badger harrumphs but lets them in, and they have a lovely time gossiping about Toad and his cars. Plural. Frogboy has already crashed *six* of them. Luckily he was only hospitalized after, like, three accidents, and he hasn't killed anyone yet, so it's all good.

Spring arrives, and Badger's had enough of Toad's vehicular she-nanigans, so he takes it upon himself to fix the sitch. Badger recruits Mole and Ratty to help him in his excellent plan to quell a reckless, obsessive-compulsive millionaire: They put him under house arrest. This can only end well.

When Toad escapes (surprise, surprise), he steals a car and takes off. Unfortunately, he speeds past a cop and gets arrested and sentenced to twenty years in prison for auto theft. Because it's never too early to teach your kids about grand larceny. But Toad is an amazeballs escape artist, so now he's on the run.

When he finally ends up at Ratty's house by way of floating down-river, he learns that weasels have overrun Toad Hall, and we have tele-ported to *The Odyssey* (page 162). With Badger's help, they devise a plan to invade and take back Toad's home. Because Badger's first plan worked so well. After an epic battle—without any violence or death, so *yawn*—~~Odysseus~~ Toad gets his house back. Then he throws a party, and they all live happily ever after as best buds forever.

The Wind in the Willows started out as bedtime stories that **Kenneth Grahame** told his son, Alistair, whom he called Mouse, and used as the basis for the character of Toad. Just to clarify, in the real world we're not all talking animals. Well, some of us aren't—but still.

The Woman in White
by Wilkie Collins

Published: 1859
Category: novel (epistolary, serialized)
Banned for: not being to Charles Dickens's taste? Really. The two were bestest buds,

and Wilk wrote for Dickie's magazine *All the Year Round*.
That meant Dickie had control over the editing and what made
it into print ~~like criticism of the middle class and sexytimes~~.
Some friend.

> *"The best men are not consistent in good—*
> *why should the worst men be consistent in evil?"*

You have a point there, but bad guys are so much
fun to hate.

Walter Hartwright, a young art teacher, is hired to teach a pair of
half-sisters. On the spooky, foggy night when Hartwright arrives at
Limmeridge House, a ghostly woman in white appears on the road he
is traveling. He's understandably nervous, but he talks to the freaky
woman for a bit. Gotta play nice with the neighbors, even if they are
dead. She rants about some of the people at Limmeridge, which makes
his new job even more exciting. I mean, who *doesn't* want to work for
crazy people?

Hartwright—which technically means "deer maker" *(ew)* but
probably is just a pun on an art teacher who has his *heart* in the *right*
place—meets the half-sisters, Marian and Laura, who actually like
each other. There's a first. When Walter tells Marian about his bizarre
encounter the night before, she wants to solve the mystery. Especially
once he mentions that Laura looks frighteningly similar to the Woman
in White.

Marian, as plainer sister, becomes the "good friend," while her gorgeous half-sibling becomes the object of Walter's affection. But, tragedy, she's already engaged to a mean baronet. Laura proceeds with the
arranged marriage, though, because it's what daddy wanted before he
died. Remember, kids: Dead parents always know what's best for their
children, especially when circumstances change and they're not around
to resolve unforeseen complications like the guy they set you up with
being a colossal jackass.

Marian advises Walter to skedaddle before the fiancé arrives. Ain't that always the way? Meet a nice girl, then have to deal with her ghostly doppelganger and jerk fiancé. Then Laura gets a mysterious letter telling her not to marry the baronet because he's a wicked, wicked man.

Walter: See, you shouldn't marry that guy. Marry me instead.

Laura: But I have to do what daddy told me, even though he's dead and won't ever know if I don't go through with it.

Walter: Fine, I'm leaving for South America.

Before Walter leaves, he meets the Woman in White, who is actually Anne Catherick and who was committed to the crazy house by our friend the baronet. She escaped to warn Laura, but disappears again before the fiancé arrives. At least she can take a hint.

Enter the ~~bastar~~—ahem, *baronet* Sir Percival Glyde, leading contestant for the prize of Worst Fiancé Ever. He marries Laura and they take off for an Italian honeymoon, but not before he arranges to get all of Laura's money if she dies. Only the best of intentions. Obviously.

Fast forward six months to Marian visiting her sister at her new house, Blackwater Park. (It is, in fact, mandatory that creepy old British houses have dark, foreboding names. See *Wuthering Heights*, page 268.) Turns out that Sir Percy brought his bestest bud Count Fosco on the honeymoon—because that's not a red flag—to act as Laura's unofficial creepy babysitter.

The sisters try to solve various mysteries with Anne Catherick until one day Marian gets sick. *Of course* your tea isn't poisoned, *my dear*. Laura is whisked away to London, where she soon dies.

Walter returns to learn that his beloved Laura—the pretty one!—is dead. He visits her grave where he meets Marian . . . and *Laura?* The evil baronet is evil and had Laura committed to the asylum in Anne Catherick's place, then dragged Anne off to London where she died looking very much like Laura. Bad man wants to grub pretty lady's money.

Marian helped her sister escape, and now the Bobsey twins go back to unearthing secrets. Before her death, Anne mentioned something about a *big bad secret* the baronet had. After some digging, they discover that Sir Percival's parents never got married. He really *is* a bastard! Which means he also can't be baronet.

When Glyde tries to destroy incriminating documents at the parish church, he sets the whole thing ablaze and dies in the fire. Laura gets her money back and marries Walter. Don't you just love happy endings? Especially when the bad guys die. Much more satisfying that way.

You're never going to believe this, but **Wilkie Collins** lived a highly duplicitous life. In addition to his "housekeeper" and not-technically-wife Caroline Graves and their daughter, he kept another house for his *other* other family, where he used the name William Dawson. No wonder he crafted such excellent mysteries. He was living one.

The Wonderful Wizard of Oz by L. Frank Baum

Published: 1900
Category: novel (children's)
Banned for: promoting witchcraft. Plus it makes kids cowardly and teaches that women are equal to men. No such equalizing propaganda allowed here.

"'Come along, Toto,' she said. 'We will go to the Emerald City and ask the great Oz how to get back to Kansas.'"

You could do that, or, since the "good" witch is withholding crucial information, I could just tell you to click those snazzy Louboutins and whiz on home. But why would I want to ruin the fun? Run along now.

Little orphan Dorothy Gale (read: tornado) lives in Kansas with her Aunt Em and Uncle ~~En~~ Henry in a one-room cabin. In the center of the house lies a small cyclone cellar hidden by a trap door. This is the frontier, people. One day, Dorothy stares at the wide-open landscape—yup, still black and white—when . . . *Tornado!* Aunt Em scrambles down the ~~rabbit~~ cyclone hole before helping others. Doesn't matter, though, because the tornado picks the whole house right up and carries it gently away. Right.

Dorothy falls asleep only to wake at the tiny bump of a landing. That's one considerate tornado. She opens the door and . . . this isn't drab old Kansas anymore. Up marches some really old lady with several grown men almost as tall as Dorothy.

Old Lady: Thanks for killing the Wicked Witch of the East.

Dorothy: What? I didn't kill anybody. I'm just a kid.

Old Lady: Your house killed her, same diff. Anyway, it's all good because that b—*witch* is dead. She had enslaved the Munchkins, but now they're free. Yippee skippee.

Old Lady is actually the Good Witch of the North. Because it's important to acquaint young kids with death early on, Northie shows Dot the dead witch's feet sticking out from under the house before they shrivel in the sun. Hey, Eastie had style; those ~~ruby~~ silver slippers are fab. Northie gives the shoes to Dorothy, making sure to shake out the witch dust first. Gee, thanks.

Dorothy: So how do I get home to Kansas?

Munchkins: Dunno. Ask the Wizard.

Dorothy: OK, so who's the Wizard and how do I find him?

Northie: Follow the Yellow Brick Road to the Emerald City. Duh.

Dorothy: So I, a young child, am supposed to follow a strange road through dangerous places all on my own until I reach a magic city and talk to some creepy old man?

Northie: Yup. Now scram.

So Dorothy and Toto set out for a nice long walk, where they meet a Scarecrow who needs a brain, a Tin Woodman who needs a heart, and a Cowardly Lion who needs courage. Yadda yadda, you know that part. Fast forward to the Emerald City. Special effects courtesy of the special green-tinted glasses everyone has to wear inside the city. The oddball group meets with the awe-inspiring and powerful wizard, but before he gives them what they want, he hires them as ninjassassins to take out the Wicked Witch of the West. Yes, all-powerful Oz, send a little girl to commit the second murder of her short life. Does anyone know the number for Child Protective Services?

Off they trot, a hodgepodge of killers-for-hire. Westie sees them coming and sends out animal defenders. This is a nonviolent children's book, so the Tin Woodman hacks up forty wolves and the Scarecrow breaks the necks of forty crows, plus other poor creatures that Westie had enslaved. Then she sends flying monkeys (from her butt), which tear the Scarecrow and Tin Woodman apart and carry Dorothy and the Lion off to the Witch (and her Wardrobe) to be her slaves.

This new arrangement sucks big-time for Dorothy, who has to clean the kitchen for days on end. But then Westie steals one of the silver shoes, which makes Dorothy so angry that she drenches the witch with a bucket of water. Westie melts.

Yes the witch is dead. Go ahead, sing the song; lemme know when you're done.

OK, so the freed Winkies ask the Tin Woodman to be their king. But first, back to see the wizard for payment on the contract killing. The blustery Oz tries to blow them off, but smart little Toto knocks over the screen hiding some normal guy from Omaha who landed in Oz by accident and just pretends to be a powerful wizard. Awkward.

Oz isn't a complete liar, though, because he stuffs some bran into the Scarecrow's head for some "bran-new brains" (har har). Then he gives the Woodman a silk heart stuffed with sawdust and the Lion a courage potion. Yeah, he gave them all placebos. What a quack. For Dorothy, he pulls out his hot air balloon, the one that dropped him in Oz in the first place. He wants to go back to the circus, so he's happy to bring Dorothy along with him. Uh, sure, why not. But then Toto bolts and Dorothy misses her flight.

Someone tells her to go see Glinda, the Good Witch of the South, so they're off again. What, you thought the story was over? No such luck. Now they're traveling the rest of the country to see some other stupid b—witch. Meanwhile, they have to escape through a forest of Fighting Trees, go through China Country without stepping on anyone's toes *(ba-dum-ching!)*, and dodge freaky Hammer-Head creatures. Then Lion has to eat a large spider that has been tormenting the creatures there. They're so happy, they want to make him king.

They *finally* get to Glinda's place, and guess what. Dorothy had the key to getting home the whole time. Yep, three clicks of the heels, and the shoes will take you where you want to go in three steps. Thanks, Glinda. You couldn't have mentioned this, I don't know, *earlier*? So Dorothy goes home to Kansas and her drab gray world and is never prosecuted for murder.

Coming up with names for characters and places is hard stuff. I mean, Tin Woodman must have taken forever to conjure up. For some real naming inspiration, **L. Frank Baum** turned to his trusty filing cabinet. Literally. The land of OZ gets its name not from Australia but a filing cabinet drawer labeled O–Z. Talk about A-C (anti-climactic).

Wuthering Heights
by Emily Brontë

Published: 1847
Category: novel
Banned for: so much *passion*. Whew. Is it getting hot in here? Instead of banning it outright, however, they just ignored it and didn't buy copies. Which is why God invented e-readers, so no one can tell that you're reading erotica on the bus.

"He's more myself than I am. Whatever our souls are made of, his and mine are the same."

Sounds like someone should talk to a nice psychiatrist . . .
or perhaps an exorcist.

What do you get when you put a spoiled brat together with a gorgeous wild boy with whom she can fight and make up ad nauseum? I don't know, either. Let's find out!

Papa Earnshaw comes home from a business trip with a present for his kids: a gypsy boy! *WTF?* Yeah, that's Hindley and Cathy's first reaction, too. Cathy grows to love her gypsy, but Hindley hates him. Daddy's preference for the adopted over the biological son might have something to do with it. Maybe.

Cathy and Heathcliff spend most of their time playing on the moors. Hindley spends most of his time tormenting Heath. It gets so bad that papa sends the biological off to college, because that'll make peace between them. But don't worry; they say distance makes the heart grow fonder . . .

After a few years, Daddy Earnshaw croaks. Too bad, so sad doesn't begin to cover it when Hindley comes back with a wife and *really* tortures Heath, who goes from golden child to filthy servant. While Heath and Cathy are out one night to torment the prissy neighbors, a dog attacks her. The neighbors keep her there for five weeks. Perhaps the son, Edgar, had something to do with it. Nah. It's not like he has a crush on Cathy and wants her for himself.

Cathy goes back a changed girl. She has manners, which means that she's infatuated with Edgar, his status, and his money. Heathcliff sees fifty shades of green. When Hindley's wife dies giving birth to a son, Hareton, papa takes to the bottle, ignoring his kid and taking his rage out on Heath. Doesn't alcohol always make things better? Cheers to that!

Cathy loves Heathcliff, but she loves social climbing more, so she marries Edgar. Upset, Cliffy takes off for three years. Later alligator! Anger and vengeance solve everything, so Heath takes up both. He comes back stinking rich and marries Edgar's sister, Isabella, so he can emotionally abuse her. That's what I call a love-hate relationship. Cathy and Heathcliff are so in love with each other that they marry other people and make the lives of everyone around them absolutely miserable.

Cathy has a baby girl named . . . Cathy. Which won't make anything confusing. It doesn't matter, though, because Cathy I dies. The end. Er, not quite yet.

If you thought Heath was bitter before, just wait. He plays up his gypsy heritage and begs Cathy I's spirit to stay, even if just to haunt him. What could possibly go wrong?

Pregnant Isabella flees to London, where she has a sickly boy named Linton. Fast forward thirteen years. Cathy II takes after her mom—*uh oh*—but her gentle papa keeps her from going completely wild. Too bad. She could've been a whole lot of fun. She knows nothing of Wuthering Heights until she stumbles upon it one day while playing on the moors—because no one knows how to throw a decent indoor party in this place. She finds a new playmate in Hareton, the current recipient of Heathcliff's cruelty.

Isabella dies (single tear), so Heath gets stuck with his whiney kid Linton. Heath is even meaner to his kid than to his now-dead wife, if that's possible. Fast forward three years.

Cathy II is out playing on the moors again when she meets Heathcliff. Dark brooding neighbor? Eh. Not so much. She prefers his angry nephew. Heath plays nice—let's see how long that lasts—and takes her to meet his own kid, Linton. She starts a super-secret, um, *romance* with Linton by passing notes across the moor. Too complicated. Just send coded texts instead.

Cathy II's nanny destroys the letters, so Cathy takes to sneaking out at night because she's in *luuurve* . . . until she finds out that Linton is only dating her because Heath is making him. That isn't weird or gross. At all. Then Edgar gets sick to death, literally, so Heathcliff lures Cathy II over to Wuthering Heights where he holds her hostage and forces her to marry Linton. Then her papa, Edgar, dies, followed by the heartbreaker Linton.

Heathcliff now controls ALL THE PEOPLE and makes Cathy II work at Wuthering Heights as a servant. Even worse, he takes away her books. Having a visual reminder of Cathy I makes Cliffy a tad neurotic, though it doesn't disincline him to complete his revenge. Talk about maniacal devotion to a cause. He grows even more obsessed with Cathy I—*how is that even possible?*—so much so that he talks to her ghost and chases her across the moors.

Heathcliff dies and is buried next to Cathy I, becoming the second slice of her Manwich that has Edgar on the other side. After plenty of bickering—she *is* Cathy II, after all—she falls in love with Hareton, and they get married. Let's hope the second generation realizes how crazypants the first was and, you know, doesn't do that.

Emily Brontë died really young but crafted what some people call one of the best works of literature in the history of ever. Unfortunately, many of her contemporaries, including sister Charlotte (page 108), didn't share that admiration of the volatile Heathcliff. Sisters can be so cruel.

ACKNOWLEDGMENTS

To the ladies Brontë, thank you for showing me how to appreciate the sexiness of a brooding man. *Rawr*. Anne, please don't be upset that I couldn't include you in this book. I'll get you next time. Promise. I'm also grateful to Jane and all the late nights filled with girl talk. That woman is a genius at setting up girls with their soulmates. You're looking for another Darcy for me, right?

Oscar, thank you for being a friend. You always know how to make me feel better with your witty quips. Call me next time you're in town. We'll go shopping and do some people watching. I'll introduce you to my bestie, Amethyst Greye, and my agent, Jean Sagendorph, and we'll have a fabulous night out filled with catty gossip and snarkasm. Remember to bring your ID, though. You know what happened last time.

Mon cher Victor, vous savez que je vous aime autant que Paris, mais je ne peux pas vous visiter tout le temps. Si vous vous décideriez à m'acheter un appartement, je vous promet de mettre votre nom plus haut sur ma liste de remerciements dans mon prochain livre. Bises!

Dickie, you are such a great virtual friend. We'll totally meet up IRL, hopefully soon. Your tweets are hilair, and those pics on FB? Wow. You so crazy. But I really didn't need to know what an Oliver Twist is. Cannot unsee!

To all the Russians, that's the last time I invite you to book club. I specifically said no vodka or lamenting about your horrible love lives. You got Thom Hardy riled up about divorce and cousins, and then Sophocles started ranting about how marrying your mom is not a good idea. Like we didn't already know. I'm just glad Johnny Steinbeck and Jackie London were there to put the smack down on all y'all. You can thank my editor, James Jayo, for making me include you three in this book because I was so very tempted to leave your butts out. Seriously, guys, lighten up. Life isn't always a tragedy.

We'll always have Verona, Will.

AUTHOR INDEX